UNIVERSITY OF
WOLVERHAMPTON
KNOWLEDGE • INNOVATION • ENTERPRISE

Feminist cultural theory
process and production

EDITED BY BEVERLEY SKEGGS

MANCHESTER UNIVERSITY PRESS
Manchester and New York

distributed exclusively in the USA and Canada by St. Martin's Press

Published by Manchester University Press
Oxford Road, Manchester M13 9NR, UK
and Room 400, 175 Fifth Avenue,
New York, NY 10010, USA

Distributed exclusively in the USA and Canada
by St. Martin's Press, Inc.,
175 Fifth Avenue, New York, NY 10010, USA

British Library Cataloguing-in-Publication Data
A catalogue record for this book is available from the British Library

Library of Congress Cataloging-in-Publication Data
Feminist cultural theory : process and production / edited by Beverley Skeggs.
        p.   cm.
    ISBN 0-7190-4470-7. — ISBN 0-7190-4471-5 (pbk.)
    1. Feminist theory – Methodology.   2. Feminist criticism.
I. Skeggs, Beverley.
HQ1190.F445   1995
305.42'01 – dc20   95-3502 CIP

ISBN 0 7190 4470 7 *hardback*
ISBN 0 7190 4471 5 *paperback*

First published in 1995

99 98 97 96 95   10 9 8 7 6 5 4 3 2 1

Printed in Great Britain
by Biddles Ltd, Guildford and King's Lynn

Contents

Contributors   *page* vii
Acknowledgements   ix

Introduction
BEVERLEY SKEGGS   1

PART ONE: TEXTS AND RESPONSES

1 The rights and wrongs of culture: issues of theory and
  methodology
  CELIA LURY   33

2 Studying *Roseanne*
  KATHLEEN ROWE   46

3 Common knowledge: the 'nature' of historical evidence
  JANET THUMIM   62

4 Finding a place from which to write: the methodology
  of feminist textual practice
  LYNNE PEARCE   81

5 The lost audience: methodology, cinema history and
  feminist film criticism
  JACKIE STACEY   97

6 Writing *Femininity in Dissent*
  ALISON YOUNG   119

PART TWO: RESPONSES AND TEXTS

7 Mothers watching children watching television
ELLEN SEITER   137

8 I want to tell you a story: the narratives of *Video Playtime*
ANN GRAY   153

9 Questioning the 'ordinary' woman: *Oranges are not
the Only Fruit*, text and viewer
JULIA HALLAM AND MARGARET MARSHMENT   169

10 Theorising, ethics and representation in feminist
ethnography
BEVERLEY SKEGGS   190

11 The personal, the professional and the partner(ship):
the husband/wife collaboration of Charles and Ray Eames
PAT KIRKHAM   207

Index   227

Contributors

Ann Gray lectures in the Department of Cultural Studies at the University of Birmingham. She is currently working in areas around consumption and everyday life, and writing a book on research methods. She is the author of *Video Playtime* (Routledge, 1992).

Julia Hallam lectures in Film and Communication Studies at Liverpool University. She has published articles on femininity and feminist methodology and is currently completing her doctorate on representation and recruitment in the nursing profession.

Pat Kirkham is Professor of Design History and Cultural Studies at De Montfort University, Leicester. She has written widely on design, gender and film. Her books on design include *A View From The Interior: Feminism, Women and Design*, edited with Judy Attfield (The Women's Press, 1989), her study of Charles and Ray Eames (MIT Press, 1995) and *The Gendered Object* (edited anthology, MUP, 1996).

Celia Lury is Co-Director of the Centre for Women's Studies (with Beverley Skeggs). She also teaches Women's Studies and Cultural Studies in the Sociology Department, Lancaster University. Her research interests are popular culture, identity and consumer culture. She is the author of *Cultural Rights* (Routledge, 1993).

Margaret Marshment lectures in Media and Cultural Studies at Liverpool John Moores University. She is co-editor of *The Female Gaze* (The Women's Press, 1988) and has published articles on feminism and representation.

Lynne Pearce teaches English and Women's Studies at Lancaster University. She is co-author of *Feminist Readings/Feminists Reading* (1989) and author of *Women, Image, Text* (1991) and *Reading Dialogics* (1994). Her next project, *Feminism and the Politics of Reading*, will combine a selection of her published essays on reader-positioning.

Kathleen Rowe is an Assistant Professor of Film Studies in the Department of English at the University of Oregon. She has published articles in *Screen*, *The Journal of Film and Video*, and other feminist criticism on film and television. She is the author of *The Unruly Woman: Gender and the Genres of Laughter* (University of Texas Press, 1995).

Ellen Seiter teaches Media Studies in the Department of Telecommunications at Indiana University, where she also serves as graduate director. She is the author of *Sold Separately: Children and Parents in Consumer Culture* (Rutgers University Press, 1993) and co-editor of *Remote Control: Television, Audiences and Cultural Power* (Routledge, 1989). Her articles on film and television have appeared in *Cultural Studies, Screen, Feminist Review, Journal of Communication,* and many other scholarly journals.

Beverley Skeggs is Co-Director (with Celia Lury) of the Centre for Women's Studies, University of Lancaster where she teaches courses on Feminist Methodology and Theory. She is the author of *The Media* (Nelson, 1992), numerous articles on ethnography, music and culture, and of the forthcoming books on *Becoming Respectable* and *Black Symbol/White Distinctions.*

Jackie Stacey produced this chapter from *Star Gazing: Hollywood Cinema and Female Spectatorship* (Routledge, 1994). She taught in the Department of Sociology at Lancaster University from 1988–1994. In October 1994 she started working in the Centre for the Study of Women and Gender at the University of Warwick, returning to Lancaster in 1995. She is co-editor of *Off-Centre: Feminism and Cultural Studies,* with Sarah Franklin and Celia Lury (Routledge, 1991); *Working Out: New Directions for Women's Studies,* with Hilary Hinds and Ann Phoenix (Falmer Press, 1992); *Romance Revisited,* with Lynne Pearce (Lawrence and Wishart, 1995). She is presently working on a new book entitled: *Teratologies: Gender, Cancer and Health Cultures.* She is also an editor of the journal *Screen.*

Janet Thumin teaches Film and Television Studies at the University of Bristol Department of Drama, Theatre, Film, Television. She is the author of *Celluloid Sisters: Women and Popular Cinema* (Macmillan, 1992) and editor, with Pat Kirkham, of two collections of essays about the construction of masculinity in the cinema, *You Tarzan: Masculinity, Movies and Men* (Lawrence and Wishart, 1993) and *Me Jane: Masculinity, Movies and Women* (Lawrence and Wishart, 1995, forthcoming). She is currently researching the relation between women and broadcast television in the UK in the 1950s and 1960s.

Acknowledgements

I would firstly like to thank all the women who gave me access to their lives to make my research possible. I will remain grateful always to Mary Mullaney, Karen Smith, Angela Shatwell, Jane Capewell, Sarah Hart, Sue Cliffe, Jane McDowell, Alison Jane Scholtze, Jo Harrop, Michelle Murphy, Julie Dodd, Sue Callary, Marie Allen, Janet Winton, Caroline Brammeld, Michelle Powell, Catherine Tilley, Beverley Vaughn, Diane Gilbert, Michelle Davies, Michelle Kidson, Lynette Hughes, Alicia Drinkwater, Debbie Snell, Pam Clarke, Jackie Hargrove, Carol James, Amanda Jefferies, Babs Naylor, Wendy Owen, Yvonne Worrall, Sharon Worrall, Rachel Cooke, Sue Cottrell, Darren Eyes, Darren Fowles, Ann-Marie Egerton, Kerry Gandy, Kate Evans, Lynne Astles, Andrea Berry, Julie Preen, Louise Potts, Diane Ratcliffe, Andrea Read, Julie Shallcross, Kate Townsend, Shirley Tracey, Elizabeth Wilson, Catherine Tilley, Janice Worrall, Louise Williams, Karen Welch, Sheila Bailey.

So many friends have contributed to my thinking and my sustenance. Val Atkinson, Jean Grugel, Nickie Whitham and Pat Kirkham have continued to debate with me through good and bad times. I owe them lots. Alex Callinicos, Denis Gleeson, T. V. Sathyamurthy and Mary Maynard were formative influences. Chris Griffin has also been an inspiration right from the start. My first colleagues, Erica Stratta, Kate Berry and Catherine Neale remain inspiring. Mairtin Mac an Ghaill and Joe Bristow are excellent examples of what can be done. At the Centre for Women's Studies, Lancaster, I have the best colleagues I could ever wish for; they are intellectually stimulating, rigorous, generous, enjoyable and good friends, especially: Celia Lury, Rosemary Deem, Lynne Pearce, Alison Young and Jackie Stacey and my WS201, MA and PhD students have helped me to clarify my thoughts and Janet Hartley and Cathie Holt's stalwart efforts continually provide excellent support. Thanks.

I'd like to thank the contributors who struggled to meet deadlines and Katharine Reeve (from MUP) who initiated this project. Amos Zamorski provided love and music. My wonderful parents provided support, love (and food, when desperate).

To my mother and father

There have been long-running debates in feminism over methodology and debates *within* theory; there is excellent abstract writing on epistemology (the theory of knowledge)[1] but there is little that relates these debates to each other. And there is a serious lack of work which interrogates its own theoretical production.[2] This paucity of enquiry into knowledge production is a cultural problem, a form of cultural reproduction, which colludes in the idea that knowledge comes from nowhere; but all knowledge comes from somewhere. It also makes invisible the mechanisms by which we *learn* to critique, theorise and construct feminist explanations.[3] This book should equip the reader with the requisite skills to interrogate the methodological underpinnings of any academic work. It should also enable them to evaluate theories in relation to their conditions of production, for as Haraway (1991) shows, all knowledge is situated knowledge. To make it absolutely clear from the start, a methodology is a theory of methods which informs decisions about such things as what to study, how to analyse, which theories to use, how to interpret, how to write. These methodological decisions enable the production of the more abstract theories, such as theories of identification, organisation, desire and distinctions which we often see as the end product.[4]

If we have done research we all know that it is a difficult, messy, fraught, emotional, tiring and yet rewarding process; we know about all the elements involved, but how does anyone else get to know? All they usually see is the clean, crisp, neatly presented finished product. Intellectuals may excel in describing other people's implicit assumptions, but they are as implicit as anyone else when it comes to their own (Johnson, 1986). As Probyn (1993b) notes, as theorists we don't know what to do with ourselves.[5] How are disciplinary boundaries, so often the bastions of abstract male knowledge, to be traversed if methods and techniques of analysis remain a closely guarded secret? And how do we make evaluations of the knowledge we receive if we do not understand how it was produced? All knowledge is produced from social and cultural relations, underpinned by economic and institutional organisation, but from reading published research we might begin to doubt that this is the case.

Knowledge is a process, a product, a resource and increasingly a commodity; so by examining how knowledge products – the already published books and journal articles of the contributors – were produced and how knowledge resources were deployed in

Introduction

BEVERLEY SKEGGS

By asking a group of feminist cultural theorists who have produced exemplary interdisciplinary scholarship in the 1990s to reflect upon their approaches, this book explores how feminist theorising is done. The contributors show that behind what comes to be known as feminist cultural theory lies particular use of methods: that there is method to all theorising. They show how questions of methodology cut across all disciplines, inform all theory and underpin all analysis, including textual, visual and empirical. Literary and film critics, for instance, may believe that they do not employ methodologies, but they do, they just don't recognise them as such. Most of the academic work we see and read is the end product of a long process, but we rarely have any understanding of this process. The representations of knowledge as a final product mask the conditions of its production. The lack of methodological insight and the focus on the end product became apparent when I was compiling accounts of how feminists have researched soap operas. Here was an area overloaded with ungrounded speculations: women were said to respond like Pavlovian dogs to textual positions, being positioned as: convinced, troubled, creative, divisive, delighted, distracted etc. These responses were due, we were told, to a variety of psychic longings which, it appeared, all women experienced. I went through one book writing 'for example?' all over it and pondered over how such wild universalistic speculations (do women have the same psychic make-up regardless of differences of nation, of class?) had gained space and validity. And, more importantly, why should we take this work seriously? It made me ask, are feminist cultural theories just a matter of speculation? Can anybody do it? What is the process by which we come to theorise? It seemed there was a gap in our feminist understanding of how what we take to be knowledge comes to be produced this process, we can investigate not only how and why we get the final product but also enhance our understandings of how to produce feminist theory. It seemed a good idea to ask those who were engaged in feminist cultural criticism and theory exactly what it is they do. The authors were picked because I admired their work and had been inspired by it; I felt it had broken new ground.[6] They have all made important contributions to debates in and outside of their areas of study. I also knew that they were reflexive and sensitive analysts, who could interrogate their own work.

The contributors analyse the different forms of production processes involved in feminist knowledge. They explore the actual labour involved in doing research and their locations in wider social relations of production (such as institutional positioning and lack of it). They examine the methods they use and the conceptual decisions made. They also analyse the political and ethical elements of production, which involve an understanding of power relations, such as: what to do with intimate information, how to disseminate research, who to speak to, which texts to choose, how to write the narrative of the research. They explore the use and production of specific methodologies such as textual analysis, ethnography, audience responses and memory work. In each case combinations of these elements influence the end product. Each chapter shows how this occurs.

I realise that by using the term feminist cultural theory I am involved in a naming process; the contributors may also want to be known as literary theorists, film scholars, sociologists, design historians. But even though there are differences in their approaches, what designates their work as cultural is the emphasis on representation, cultural practices and cultural (re)productions. The chapters each discuss a specific area of research including female film spectators; 1950s female film representations, writing design history, literary research, cultural reproduction, ethnography, VCR usage, responses to TV drama, mothers and TV viewing, representations of women at 'Greenham Common' and *Roseanne*.

My own location as a feminist ethnographer forced me to confront methodological issues. Issues of power relationships, representations and method have dominated recent debates in this area (see Skeggs, 1994). It was from my experience of these that I generated a series of questions to enable the contributors to focus on their methodologies:

– why was the area of study chosen, what institutional, economic and socio-political factors underpinned the choice?
– which frameworks of established knowledge were used, referred to, challenged, ignored and why?
– which methods were chosen for study and why? Why were other approaches not used?
– how did the initial questions and research relate to the final product?
– how did the process of writing influence the final product?

I felt it was important to draw authors from a range of areas to demonstrate the interdisciplinarity of feminist cultural theory and critical practice and to show how methods are used across disciplines in a variety of ways. By exploring the multitude of ways of doing feminist theorising and research and by putting on the agenda and making explicit the methodologies of textual analysis, the best academic secrets can be revealed. Through the process of doing research the contributors have mapped out new approaches and new ways of thinking about and doing feminist research.

Their research has led them to question previously (academic and lay) 'taken for granted' categories used in much cultural analysis. For instance Celia Lury (Chapter One) provides a caution about the slippage which often goes unnoticed between the terms cultural and social. This understanding was generated through her interrogation of the processes of cultural reproduction which showed how culture or the cultural itself is constituted in relation to gender, and social and political categories. Julia Hallam and Margaret Marshment (Chapter Nine) also warn about using the term 'ordinary' to describe any woman; in the course of their research they could not find any women who could fit this description. Their empirical research supports Charlotte Brunsdon's (1991) analysis of how the identity 'feminist' has historically been constructed partly in contrast with 'ordinary women'.

The interdisciplinarity of the contributions to this book points to the breakdown of the dichotomies, generated through political struggles between and within disciplines, which are used to categorise research, such as those between: textual/empirical; theory/practice; literary/sociological. The crucial difference between the dichotomies is the focus and the methods used to investigate the focus: some will have a text (such as a literary or theoretical text) as the object of their theoretical conceptualisations, others will have economic systems or people's lives as their focus. The notion of a text depends on the methodology, on how it is put to use; texts will be used and analysed in different ways.[7] Texts are social products just as people and systems are all social products and thereby impact upon each other (although, once produced, they may have autonomy from their production). Even when the concentration is on the text, as the first six chapters in this book demonstrate, the understanding of the text is produced through a reader, through a reader's response, and that reader is socially positioned. Similarly, most of the authors who were studying women's responses, and what is often defined as 'lived culture', were doing so in relation to particular textual representations. Those who were looking at general rather than specific textual responses were conscious that responses were always mediated through wider discourses. For instance, Ann Gray's analysis of women's use of the VCR (in Chapter Eight) clearly showed how women always evaluated their responses in accordance with wider discourses of popular culture. So they would always preface their comments with 'I know this is bad for you' and such like. Kathleen Rowe (Chapter Two) notes how responses to *Roseanne* constantly referred to the discourse of vulgarity. My own research examined how women constructed their subjectivities through discourses of caring, femininity and heterosexuality. Ellen Seiter's participants were so very conscious of the morality of how they *should* use television that it influenced their assessments of their own self-worth (see Chapter Seven). The women who responded to Jackie Stacey's (Chapter Five) requests for memories of film stars often utilised the same discourses of stardom and nationalism provided by representations of the 1950s. Jackie Stacey was analysing stars through textual responses. Those who were doing what looks like pure textual research, such as Lynne Pearce (Chapter Four) and Janet Thumim (Chapter Three), were doing it on the basis of their own situated responses: their history and motivations. The texts generated responses and responses were mediated through texts. This shows how foci and method are two central elements in the production of feminist theory.

This introductory chapter is divided into five sections. The first section explores the locations and context for the production of the researcher and the research; mapping the context and conditions from where, how, why and for whom we do research and theorising. The second section briefly investigates the link between feminist epistemology and ontology to prepare the ground for the third section which interrogates how the concept of experience is used in feminist research. The discussion of experience focuses attention on how subjectivities are produced through the research process, made particularly acute in the book by authors who are continually trying to define their positionings through their research. Ann Gray (Chapter Eight), for instance, addresses how research is strongly influenced by a sense of self-worth, something which is often difficult for feminists to maintain in academia. The processes of evaluation which we apply to ourselves, the research we produce and the readings we make of other research, are examined in the fourth section, which asks: why should you take this book seriously? The final section provides brief overviews of the chapters contained herein.

The emphasis on cultural forms in this book should not detract from the social, historical, political and economic significance of these forms: All representations occur within a political economy which is social and cultural but to which they cannot be reduced (Angus and Jhally, 1989). Moreover, lived culture is different from representations of it; as Johnson (1986) argues, culture can be studied systematically, precisely because it is understood as a social product with its own forms of existence and its own shapes.

Locations

As researchers we are located and positioned in many different ways. We also locate and position ourselves, but this is always circumscribed. For instance, we are positioned through locations such as history, nation, gender, sexuality, class, 'race', age. These positionings will have influenced our access to locations such as those of education and employment and, more indirectly, the media. They may also circumscribe the discourses such as femininity, high culture, the popular, to which we have access. Two themes have emerged, independently, from these chapters. The first is that of access: who has access to cultural forms? Who has the requisite skills to understand and use culture in particular ways? The second is, what positions are available for people to occupy? Representations may circumscribe the 'subject positions' available for us to inhabit, for example: 'the good mother'; 'the grotesque woman'; 'the Greenham Common woman'; 'the genius'; 'the artist'. We recognise the configurations attached to these categories, they all provide discursive structures for understanding the positioning of ourselves and others. In our institutional locations we will be positioned in hierarchies of knowledge, some disciplines grant greater material reward and status than others. In our disciplinary locations we will be positioned through theoretical traditions and genre styles of writing. All these locations and positionings impact upon whether we do research, consider ourselves to be researchers and the research we actually do.

For instance, in the first place our research is produced from the position of the female-embodied social subject (de Lauretis, 1990). We are part of the social relations we study (see Stanley, 1990). Our modes of existence, our being and doing, our thinking, are produced through social-political-cultural-economic locations and processes. Feminist knowledge is produced from female-embodied, situated subjects who are part of a specific, emergent, conflictual history, and this is made clear by the contributors to the book. Ann Gray, Lynne Pearce, Ellen Seiter, Julia Hallam and Margaret Marshment, and myself all address our contradic-tory locations as woman inside and outside of academia. It is these contradictions which have led so many female academics to feel that they do not belong, that they should not be there and that they will be exposed as fraudulent (see also Walkerdine, 1989).

Secondly, we all occupy institutional positions; this impacts upon how, where and why we do research. Some of the con-tributors were doctoral students at the time of their research, others worked from established positions, others received little support and funding. The procedures by which research projects become accepted and funded is still very traditional. There are clear economic, social and cultural constraints on who gets into the academy, where there are still far fewer female than male staff in British and US universities, and who gets to theorise. This is more acute now that one of the central criteria for appoint-ment is productivity measured through publications; it is those who have been able to take time to write (rather than working part-time to feed their family, for instance) who have the right credentials. We may have deconstructed the category 'woman', but women make up only 5 per cent of professors in British universities[8] and women are disproportionately positioned at the lower end of the wage scales, and also predominantly on temporary and/or part-time contracts. Publishers' criteria are also central to which research we see, as are our locations in support networks outside of our institutions. I still remember Janet Finch's (1983) descriptions of all the unpaid, unnoticed female labour that goes into enabling male academic work.

Our social and cultural location may inform what we say and how we say it, and who gets to hear and respond. It is what Braidotti (1991) defines as a 'politics of enunciation'. For instance, feminism has been used as a space for white women to speak from whilst simultaneously remaining alienating for the majority of Black women (Carby, 1982; Amos and Parmar, 1984; Bryan *et al.*, 1985; Ngcobo, 1988; hooks, 1989). Black women have found alternative ways of being heard, and in so doing have challenged the (limited) institutional privileges of white women. Yet, as Spivak (1990) notes this is a continual form of resistance for she is always being positioned by others: the expectation is always placed on her to speak *as* woman, *as* colonised subject.

The contributors are positioned through (US and UK) nationality, although national boundaries can be crossed as the recent developments in diasporic theory suggest (Gilroy, 1993a, 1993b). Our dialogue with others displays our positioning. They speak to other Anglo-American feminists and indirectly with French, Italian and German theory. We choose who we want to argue with or admire. The language we use positions us within specific traditions: the terms hegemony, determinism and collusion refer to Marxist debates; the language of subject positioning, difference, and representation display a post-structuralist affiliation.[9] My language use is a product of wanting to hold on to notions of limitation, of being circumscribed by economic and social locations, whilst also trying to speak of contingency, movement and agency. We are also located in the contemporary, and we forget many of the important theorists who in the past may have enabled our learning. Our access to the feminist work which is being produced elsewhere restricts that which we can know and speak. And we may not record our access to the conversations with friends, who may be as significant to our understanding as our reading of theorists, but who are not cited in the texts because we write as part of an academic mode.

This academic mode with its rhetorical and linguistic strategies enables the production of the formal, neat and tidy representations here in this book. This is very different from the often traumatic, sometimes exhilarating way in which we come to understand and to know. Most of the authors draw attention to this, but writing the messiness of research and writing is far harder than actually dealing with it. Nava (1992) argues for the centrality of the psyche in the processes by which we come to research, write and speak. The sentence 'I was blocked for six months' cannot convey the emotions, insights and pain generated through that period. It is impossible to document the minutiae of everyday life that contributes to our theorising, but what we can do is to draw attention to the more general processes involved. This points to the complexity of how we understand the impact and influence of all these different locations and positionings. This is why I want to avoid the idea of a simple correspondence between our circumstances and how we think. Rather, I want to suggest that we, the theorist, the researcher, are positioned in historical, economic, socio-political and discursive locations but they do not determine us.

It is impossible to know how these locations work to inform our subjectivity for, as Gramsci (1971) argues, 'knowing thyself' is a product of the historical process to date which has deposited in us an infinity of traces without leaving an inventory. Our memories of our locations are, the Popular Memory Group (1982) note, like all common-sense forms, strangely composite constructions, resembling a kind of geology, the selective sedimentation of past traces. Resonances from past and present locations may predispose us towards certain theories. Theories of inequality, usually a variant on Marxism, and based on feminist analyses, gave the contributors who felt marginal in their universities a way to speak. Janet Thumim speaks of her rage being channelled through the 'personal is political' slogan of feminism, Lynne Pearce discusses finding a place from which she feels she can speak and be heard and Ann Gray notes how difficult it is to establish confidence and the authority from which to speak. However, Probyn (1993b) warns us not just to concentrate on ourselves, but to think how our resonances resonate with those of others.

The contributors show how as feminist theorists they have to navigate their way through the dominant paradigms of their disciplines. When we begin research we always enter into and are positioned by already established debates; to gain credibility and legitimacy we may feel we have to enter into these debates. We are recruited by the dominant discourses, which we may adapt, transform and/or resist. This need not be seen to be a waste of time, but rather as a way of acquiring theoretical skills and of passing through different formations of knowledge in an attempt to develop our own. Some of the contributors use traditional male theorists for their explanatory power. Their reappearance in different contributors' chapters signals particular historical locations and political affiliations. It also suggests that some theories are better for explaining certain phenomena over others (see Craib, 1992). Ann Gray, Janet Thumim and myself were all engaged in critiques through responses to Althusser and Gramsci in which Bourdieu and Williams make brief appearances. These document positions in a historical debate in which new attempts were made to understand the political nature and value of culture, which until this time had been dismissed as something people did (high/low culture) which was outside of political struggle. Pat Kirkham was engaged in similar debates within working-class history and had to find her way through the discourses of modernism. Lynne Pearce and Kathleen Rowe, coming from widely different texts (the poet John Clare, and *Roseanne*) found Bakhtin's theories of dialogics impelling. Jackie Stacey and Kathleen Rowe both worked with and against the dominant paradigm of psychoanalysis and Freud. Foucault is ubiquitous, having been plundered for the usefulness of his methods and analysis of power[10] and Benjamin informed Celia Lury's theoretical framework. Alison Young is in dialogue with Derrida and Irigiray.

In some cases we locate ourselves by drawing from a wide variety of sources which we weave together into a feminist framework. The appropriation of theories from areas which are epistemologically incompatible may disturb some theorists, especially when the psychoanalytic and the social, which are defined against each other, combine. Psychoanalysis is based on an exploration of the unconscious developed against the empirical belief that it is possible to capture, understand and write the real (Clough, 1992). The unconscious, Foucault (1972) argues, demarcates the limit of what can be known about the social; it is necessary to the construction of the boundary about what we *cannot* study if we want to say anything about social reality. Moreover, Heath (1986) argues that psychoanalysis fixes things into static, given, oppressive identities which have no connection to socio-historical relations. Yet Jackie Stacey and Kathleen Rowe have effectively put together these two supposed-ly incompatible areas to generate understandings of femininity

and gender (and nation and class) positioning. I used psychoanalytic concepts in a sociological way. It is this refusal to be
contained by knowledge categories which leads to the breaking
down of the myth of epistemological and methodological purity
so essential to the maintenance of disciplinary boundaries which
have for so long restricted feminist scholarship. This translation
of concepts from one discipline to another can transform them
in the process (Gates, 1987).

All the authors in this collection take their feminism for
granted, and have a feminist orientation to their work. They do
not make any justifications for using feminist analysis or concentrating on women. This again is a product of historical circumstances. Many of the battles to have feminism taken seriously
and to generate a public/publishing space were fought by an
earlier generation. In Britain Helen Roberts (1981), Angela
McRobbie (1982) and Liz Stanley and Sue Wise (1983) argued for
the specificity of feminist methods and feminist research. In 1980
Diane Leonard was arguing for autobiographical justifications
research to expose the underlying interests of knowledge. These
feminists followed an earlier generation such as Juliet Mitchell
(1971) and Sheila Rowbotham (1973) who had pointed out the
absences of women from academic discourses. Numerous
feminists, across the disciplines, generated space for feminism
through international journals and conferences. The hard fought
battles to create Women's Studies courses made it easier for a
later generation to take up these spaces (I, for one, am very
grateful). Whereas feminism used to bang its head against the
bastions of male knowledge, it now constructs its own. The
theory, research and audience are designated as feminist.
Feminist research is now so firmly established that it has become
diversified and (positively) fragmented. There may be fashions
but there are no longer any hegemonies. As this book clearly
demonstrates we all no longer believe we should write, do and
think in unified ways.

This means the chapters also suggest a different motivation
to research than one which just sees it as a job to be done, work
to be accomplished, a publication achieved. The research, in most
cases, impinges upon the subjectivity of the researcher. Many
of the contributors define who they are through their research.
Their emotional and political investments in their research are
high. Their research is deeply located in their lives; for example
even after just giving birth, Ellen Seiter felt compelled to turn

the experience into a research opportunity. Fonow and Cook (1991) identify this 'use of the situation at hand' as typical of feminist research. As feminists we are involved in continually theorising the situations and locations of ourselves and others, we are already implicated before we begin research.

The research we do is not just a matter of where we come from and where we are located but also where we look to. Our work is motivated by our political aspirations. Behind each contribution stands a clear desire for change. It ranges through my idealistic desire to change the world, to challenge categories of 'common knowledge', to deconstructing the representations which damagingly position women, to change theory. Because the research occurs in the academy does not mean it is not political. Alison Young (in Chapter Six) is at pains to point out, a rarely acknowledged fact, that the academy is actually part of the real world and that research can hold transformation potential in and outside. If we do not challenge the knowledge categories by which we navigate our way through the world, we may reproduce oppressive ways of thinking and knowing: the universalism associated with the term 'woman' is a case in point. It is too easy to construct a knowledge/politics-theoretical/practical divide. All knowledge is political because of its intentions, effects and the fact that it is produced in the interests of particular groups; although some knowledge may have more direct political implications. But the more feminist knowledge we have, at the widely diverse levels and sites, the greater the potential for understanding and change.[11]

Our ability to theorise is circumscribed by the conceptual resources to which we have access. These may be academic and they may not. Barbara Christian (1987), for instance, argues that people of color have always theorised, often in narrative forms, riddles and proverbs, and through play with language which unmasked the power relations of the world. The process of feminist theorising involves continually putting under scrutiny the concepts we come to take for granted, as the next section shows.

Linking processes

Some feminist concepts have become so deeply entrenched in previous theorising that when we come into contact with them we may take their meaning for granted. Recently fundamental concepts such as culture, identity, woman, gender, sexuality, class and experience have been carefully deconstructed. Crosby (1992) shows how the concept 'difference' and differences such as sexuality, gender, class, race and identity have become substantive, something in themselves, which has actually blocked theorists from thinking through what these terms mean. Scott (1992) notes how feminist theory often sees the concept of identity realised in the facts of history and takes the historical facticity of identity as already established (as an a priori fact) so that theorising is but the recognition of what one has already become: 'woman'. The abstract interrogation of concepts is very important to feminist politics for it challenges the very categories of knowledge that are available to us, an activity which has enabled feminist work to present new ways of thinking, which should also impact on ways of doing.

For instance, the deconstruction of the term 'woman' (see Riley, 1988; Alcoff, 1988) had led some feminist theorists into an impasse, wondering where to go if the central and certain object of their attentions has disintegrated. But the deconstruction of the term was designed to be productive, to make feminists think through their assumptions and their universalisms. It was designed, Denise Riley (1992) argues, as a polemical argument to make us question our assumptions.[12] It was not designed as a methodological prescription to make us abandon the category completely. On the contrary, Butler (1992) argues, if feminism presupposes that 'women' designates an undesignatable field of differences, one that cannot be totalised or summarised by a descriptive identity category, then the very term becomes a site of openness and re-signification. Similar arguments have been made about the terms 'race' and 'class'. Omi and Winant (1986) draw attention to the way the sign 'race' has been historically produced. By studying the use of the concept in different historical periods they show how, whilst the category 'race' remains the same, the meanings have significantly changed. The term 'class' has been so heavily criticised for its universalising pretences, reductionism and inapplicability to the complexity of differences that it has almost disappeared from feminist theory.

Yet for those who are still made conscious of their class, gender and race positioning on a daily basis this abandonment may have dire consequences: it may once again serve to silence marginalised groups. We need to learn to think about what these terms actually mean. A significant number of authors in this collection refer to their gender and class-based experiences as a motivation to particular research and theorising and they show how their class and gender locations inform their choice of methods and theory, thereby producing knowledge which is indirectly informed by their positioning. The ontological recognitions of our raced, gendered and classed existence are linked to wider debates about epistemology, about what knowledge actually is. These recognitions are important springboards into wider, and more systematic understandings of process. As Probyn (1993b) in her excavations of 'the self' notes:

> I want to emphasise the importance of ontological moments of recognition – moments when I realise my gendered (*sexed, classed, raced, aged, etc.*) being. Consequently I argue that the ontological must be met with an epistemological analysis. In putting these ontological moments of being to work within the elaboration of an epistemological analysis, I want to extend the reach of these momentary flashes of gendered (*sexed, classed, raced, aged, etc.*) selves. I want to stretch my experience beyond the merely personal, not as a way of transcendence but as a way of reaching her experiences, the experiences of selves and women. In other words, I want to put forward a mode of theorising that encourages lines of analysis that move from her experience to mine, and mine to hers. (p. 4) (my italics)[13]

By asking contributors to articulate the processes of research I wanted them to make links between these ontological moments, where our differences speak to us, and how we use them to speak out, into wider epistemological questions about knowledge, about how it is produced, in order to speak to others. Feminist epistemology is here used as defined by Lennon and Whitford (1994) to be:

> neither the specification of a female way of knowing (there is no such thing) nor simply the articulation of female subjectivity which reveals itself to be diverse, contradictory and at least partially discursively constructed through patriarchal oppositions. Feminist epistemology consists rather in attention to epistemological concern arising out of feminist projects, which prompt reflection on the nature of knowledge and our methods of obtaining it. (p. 13)

This book hopes to make linking processes, whereby the ontologies of researchers are linked to the production of their knowledge, which links to epistemological understandings of how knowledge is produced, which links into wider feminist understandings. However, in some feminist theorising, rather than being linked, epistemology and ontology are collapsed on to one another, so that theorising is locked into descriptions of experience. I will now direct attention to the concept of experience which is so central to feminist understandings.

Positioning experience

Experience, de Lauretis (1988) maintains, is the *basis* of feminism in the sense that feminism began the moment women started talking to each other about their experiences in a very simple way.[14] And it was the perceived disjunction between individual women's experiences and the (few) representations offered by traditional disciplines that provided the spark for feminist research (Fildes, 1983). This perception certainly motivated many of the contributors. Yet even though representations of women's experience have been central to correcting male representations of women, we do not have an adequate conceptual framework for understanding what experience really is. Experience can mean anything. Experience, Lazreg (1994) shows, is rarely defined in a systematic way. It is usually taken as a given, a self-explanatory concept that each feminist specifies in her own way. This is used to refer to feelings, emotions, the personal, personality, subjectivity and such like. Or experience is represented as unmediated: spoken words are placed directly on a page with no account given of how and where they came from, the power relations involved, the publishing deals signed, the editing and selection processes. Or researchers take as self-evident the identities of those whose experience is being documented. Often experience is set against thinking and theorising, yet as the contributors to this book show, thinking is as much an experience of research as doing. Our experience is part of a social, historical, cultural, economic, political process. Indeed, as Scott (1992) notes, it is not individuals who have experience, but subjects who are *constituted* through experience. We need to know what makes experiences possible and what makes us represent them in the way we do.

The contributors draw on their experiences to show how these can in fact be systematically understood by linking their 'personal' insights on to analysis of the contexts, positionings and representations involved in the research process. They show how their researcher subjectivities and the experiences of others were produced through the research. The experiences of the researcher are partially constitutive of the reality to be known, the final product. For instance, narrative representations are problematised by Ann Gray and Jackie Stacey; the reader's experience of the text is explored by Lynne Pearce; categories of experience are interrogated by Julia Hallam and Margaret Marshment and I explore the framing of experience through representations of respectability. The use of the visual metaphor of transparency which is often deployed to describe experience is problematised. Our ability to see things is very much embedded in social locations and seeing always involves interpretation (Scott, 1992). How do we know what we see if we do not invoke social language? What one sees during research is a product of positioning and different accounts of the world involve political struggle over how to see and how to interpret (Braidotti, 1991) and, importantly, of access to vision.

One of the earliest principles of feminist research was to validate the experience of women[15] and a great deal of feminist theory was (and still is) generated from the idea that women have a particular way of knowing and seeing the world. These principles, however, centre on the empirical argument (and those associated with this position are often called empiricist feminists[16]) that all knowledge springs from experience and that women's experience carries with it special knowledge and that this knowledge is necessary to challenge oppression.[17] For some standpoint theorists, such as Harstock (1983) and Hill Collins (1990), these positions of oppression generate epistemic privilege;[18] only those who have the appropriate experience of oppression are able to speak about it. This reduces knowledge to a formula of being = knowing, a formula which has dogged philosophers since Kant. It also grants an authority and hierarchy to certain groups and silences others (Bar On, 1993), leading to confrontations over identities in which differences are collapsed into a 'listen to me', 'hear my difference' power play (Probyn, 1990). This has led to a form of identity politics based on the idea of 'authentic subjective experience' which restricts politics to the personal.[19] Parmar (1989) argues that 'identity politics may be enough to get started but not enough to get finished' (p. 61). (See Adams, 1989; Parmar, 1989 and Fuss, 1989 for extensive debates.)

If we take experience as a category of knowledge we need to 'know': how do we generate knowledge from experience; is generating knowledge an experience; do we have to have an

experience in order to know about it?[20] How do we understand
that which we have not experienced? How do we move beyond
our own experiences? Can we ever talk about the experiences of
others, of systems of oppression? How do we make links to other
forms of oppression? How do different experiences fit together?
Using categories of experience as the basis for knowledge is very
much dependent on how experience is used to theorise. For
instance, Scott (1992) shows how the statement 'I am a working-
class (substitute any other category) woman' when used to gain
authority simply reflects on the facts of historical location. It is
to assume that ontology is the ground of epistemology, that what
I am determines what and how I know. But how do I know who
I am? (or who she is?) In historicism the answer is easy: I am my
differences, which have been given to me by history.[21] We are
thus left with a constant defining descriptor and all that changes
are the descriptions which are sometimes squeezed to fit. Motherhood and femininity, for instance, are defined by the experience
of it. We understand it from the categories which have emerged
from the experience of it. But if we explore how these categories
came to be produced, how we are constituted through our
experiences, how we come to be gendered, raced and classed
through experience, we may open up space for systematic understanding of process.

Moreover, we cannot be reduced to our experience. As Grimshaw (1986) notes, we cannot analyse women's exploitation
solely on the basis of women's experience; the unconscious
and/or the organisations of international capital, for instance,
may also need to be understood. We can, however, explore the
processes by which we are positioned, and hence come to see
how our experiences and understandings of who we (and others)
are are always known and interpreted through the discourses and
representations available to us. Our positioning means that we
are likely to have different access to the discursive resources
(such as critical insights) available for understanding 'our
selves'.

Therefore, if feminist theory is a means by which 'woman' is
known, we need to understand the processes involved in her (our)
representation. Experience is at once always already an interpretation and in need of interpretation (Scott, 1992). We need to
know how these representations and interpretations come to be
produced because they always embody power relations. Each
contributor to this book makes explicit her part in this process.

They all add to our knowledge of the production of the category woman, to feminist understandings, and they all do so from their positioning as women (and ... their other locations).

The contributors map out their different locations and situations, speaking from the critical and multiple positions taken up in response to domination (Haraway, 1991). Alcoff (1988) argues that positionalities are part of a constantly shifting context in a nexus of overlapping conditions such as economic, institutional, discursive, cultural. This does not mean, I'd argue, that we can take up any positioning. There are obvious structural (such as 'race' and class positioning) and institutional limits and we may have critical distance on some positions but not on others. But our experience is contextualised and processed from these positionings. Our experience of ourselves in our various subject positions (such as feminist researcher) is always located. Our experiences are constitutive of what is to be known (as feminist research) whilst we are also constituting ourselves. Opening this process out to scrutiny should advance our understanding of feminist knowledge production.

So whilst the researchers in this book draw on their experiences of research (and the experiences of the researched in some cases) they do so from a *politics of positionality*. Lynne Pearce, Ann Gray, Pat Kirkham and myself chart our movements between knowledge, institutional and social positions, exploring how we have been positioned and how we position ourselves. In this sense we make strategic use of our experience, as Spivak (1985) suggests. Experience is an important start for politicising the flashes of recognition which enable us to identify systems of differentiation and their consequences: from ontology into epistemology.

I do not want to abandon the concept of experience or deconstruct it until all the explanatory power and political potential disappears. Rather, I want to advocate that we explore the experience of the researcher (and researched) as discursively understood and located in a nexus of positionalities. Positionalities can be explored because the research experience always brings with it an account of context. Knowledge of how experience is produced, interpreted, mediated and represented enables an acknowledgement and transcendence of that context. In this sense, the book is an exercise in reflexivity, a collection of self-critical accounts of the experience of feminist research by analysing the process and production of feminist cultural theory and theorists.

Evaluations

So why should you take this book seriously? Why is it so different from the speculations cited at the beginning of this introduction? How do you evaluate it? Whether we like it or not we are always involved in evaluation, for as scholars critical evaluation is our purpose, and most of us are aware that when we write or speak we are opening ourselves to the scrutiny of others. The evaluative responses given to this book will be contextualised and contingent. Responses depend upon a whole range of locations and positionings, informed by prior knowledge and prior understandings. Responses are also fuelled by the way we learn to interpret. I'll now move into the dialogic mode to address you, the reader, because I hope that you are already beginning to formulate your evaluations. You may find things in chapters that the authors did not know were there (reminding you that a text cannot be reduced to authorial intention and its conditions of production). Resistances to feminism may, for instance, have been generated before you began. This book may (or may not) speak to where you are and who you think you are and you will evaluate it on this basis. If you are prepared to move, it may provide conceptual resources for you to assess and understand things differently. It may not. Your evaluations will also depend on what you want to use this book for: tips on methods, understanding feminist cultural theory or frameworks for political action.

I'd hope that you would see that the grounded investigations of the contributors are more than just speculations (although speculations can be an important starting-point). They are engagements in persistently critical practice. By making explicit the *processes* of production the contributors locate and situate their knowledge and themselves. They make apparent the combinations of different elements involved in the production of knowledge. They display their privileges (and lack of them). The knowledge produced is located, political interrogations of our positions are made explicit: who we speak about and for and to whom and the processes of interpreting and representing. Attempts are made to explore ethical understandings of power relations and their embodiment has been put into practice. The contributors are all vigilant about their own practice. To recognise how the subject is implicated in the knowledge produced is to make the context of discovery relevant to the context of justification (Lennon and Whitford, 1994). The contributors make their accounts accountable and show how they are located in wider debates. They show that knowledge comes from somewhere and all knowledge is in someone's interest: in this case feminist interests which are also being redefined in the process of research. Their reflexivity makes apparent their partialities and their attempts to avoid universalisms. It enables their political intent to be put under scrutiny. By exposing the mystery of intellectual production they contextualise the process of knowing.

Their research displays movement: between the particular and the general; between theories; between positionalities; between locations. It shows that knowing about things is an ongoing, communicative, interpretative process which can never be fixed or complete (Code, 1991). Each chapter provides an indication of how time (to read, to think, to plan, to talk to people) is crucial to the production of knowledge and how time is dependent upon positionality (such as access to grants, institutional time, etc.). This book was produced in the gaps between teaching and administrating.

By knowing about the epistemology makers we may learn more about how epistemology is made and how knowledge is an institutional, historical and inter-subjective product (Code, 1991). By showing how feminist cultural criticism and theory is done the links built between ontology and epistemology are made and displayed. This display should provide tools for how to read and evaluate feminist theory in general. Fraser (1989) asks of Foucault: what were the sources of his engagement? What was his practical intent, his political commitment? She evaluates Foucault for feminist understandings on the exigencies of political practice. I hope you will now do the same with this book, remembering that research and knowledge production is always a political practice.

Sketches

The first part of the book represents those authors whose primary focus is textual representation. They construct frameworks for understanding how texts operate, how they position us and chart specific responses to them. Celia Lury begins with a critical reflection, produced after the completion of her book *Cultural Rights* (1993), on how feminists need to pay particular attention to the term 'culture'. She notes how culture is often taken as an ungendered given but how her research shows that gender is implicated in the very constitution of cultural categories. She illustrates the problems she faced coming to this theoretical understanding.

Kathleen Rowe explores how her interest in the controversies of *Roseanne* led her from a straightforward analysis of the media into early modern histories of the unruly woman. She charts her non-linear journey through different resources and methodologies, coming to construct theories about the potential transformations women can make through comedy. She reflects on her interview with Roseanne and celebrates the pleasure involved in her research, published as *The Unruly Woman: Gender and Genres of Laughter* (1995). Lynne Pearce charts a similar journey. She gives us her biography as a feminist reader (documenting the production of *Woman/Image/Text* (1991) and *Reading Dialogics* (1994)) by exploring how she was recruited by particular texts and theoretical discourse. She shows that textual analysis entails responsibility and that the text is anything but a passive object of study. The political implications of this are spelled out when she notes how the theories of de-essentialising de-essentialised her.

Janet Thumim and Jackie Stacey, whilst working on similar areas – women and film in the 1950s – have different foci and use different methods. Janet, motivated by her personal positioning, and located in Marxist debates about common knowledge and hegemony, conducted a detailed systematic historical analysis of representation, which was published as *Celluloid Sisters* (1992). She notes how she needed a methodology which would question the status of knowledge whilst simultaneously producing it. Jackie discusses the processes of doing her research which was written up as *Star Gazing* (1994). She explores the ideas and methods which did and did not come to fruition. In her discussion she analyses the theoretical implications of the different sources of audience research in the history of 1940s and 1950s cinema. Her method involved examining texts through narratives from letters and questionnaires.

Another form of reading representations was developed by Alison Young in her study of Greenham Common women published as *Femininity in Dissent* (1990). Using analysis of media discourse, legal categorisations, representations and commentary from the women at Greenham, Alison shows how she pulled all the different theories and methodologies together to produce an analysis that looked very different to the disciplinary methods of law. Her subjective relationship to ideas (her possession and excitement) show just how interested we can become in our work.

The next part pulls together authors whose focus is on 'lived culture'. They speak to other women to understand textual and cultural responses. Their own responses are, however, part of this process. Ellen Seiter, after her dissatisfaction with the single ethnographic interview, used her support group to investigate how mothers and children use television, published as *Sold Separately* (1993). Here, she maps out the discursive limits to the talk she was able to engage in, showing how value judgements are always implicated when mothers speak about television. She is particularly reflexive about the different positionings held between the researched and her role in their reproduction. Ann Gray also investigates women's responses to media, through their use of the VCR, published as *Video Playtime* (1992). Using narratives to analyse narratives whilst deconstructing narratives she places her research as a product of a specific personal/ intellectual/institutional conjecture. She notes how important beliefs in self-worth are to feminist researchers who feel marginalised in the academy.

Jeanette Winterson's *Oranges are Not the Only Fruit*, a story of lesbian passion and rabid fundamentalism was a surprising success on British television. Julia Hallam and Margaret Marshment set out to find out why and I set out, by interviewing them, to find out how they went about it.[22] The analytical and cultural resources of two researchers brought together an unusual combination of textual and aesthetic understandings which enabled them to interrogate the centrality of the visual in viewer memories. In the process of their research they also came to challenge many of the taken-for-granted categories of feminist cultural theory.

The final two articles do not directly explore textual responses although they are informed by textual readings. My research, soon to be published as *Becoming Respectable: an Ethnography*, centres on how a group of young women construct their gendered and classed subjectivities.[23] The focus of my chapter is on the relationship between theory and practice in ethnography, on the ethical dilemmas raised for a feminist doing ethnography and on the problems posed when representing the researched. It shows how my own subject positions informed my responses to these issues. Pat Kirkham deals with a different set of dilemmas. Her research explored the relationship between two famous designers, examined in detail in the forthcoming *Charles and Ray Eames: Designers of the Century*. Charting an autobiographical journey, Pat documents how her history and social background motivated her interests. She shows how theoretical debates in the 1980s informed her readings of the 1960s. Pat discusses understanding the relationships of her research through her personal life and grapples with the limited categories available to her to understand exemplary talent and aesthetics.

Conclusion

You may notice that many of the chapters raise questions which were generated from the dilemmas of doing the research or from thinking through different theoretical explanations. This is a good sign. Good research should traverse the frameworks it uses so it can interrogate its own production and also look out towards new ways of thinking, doing and knowing. The arguments put forward in this introductory chapter advocate paying close attention to the methods used and the methodological assumptions which hide behind theoretical constructs. I have argued for an understanding of how a politics of positionality informs our understandings and readings of texts and theory. Even the most abstract of theorising is indirectly tied to this positioning because the methodological choices over how to do and think about research are socially located. The end product is produced through a complex methodological process informed by contexts, locations and positionings. To understand this it is important to see the experience of research as a means of linking the epistemological to the ontological; the process of doing research, of producing theory, constantly moves between the two. Hence, the experience of doing research is not divorced from our social locations: it is the means by which we are produced as gendered, classed and raced subjects. Research is one of the processes through which our subjectivity is produced.

I realise that the book speaks to different audiences at different stages of their research, or to different interests in feminist cultural theory debates. Because the particular practicalities of doing research are linked to more general theoretical debates on methodology, it is hoped that not only are different levels of analysis addressed but the boundaries between them are traversed. I hope the reflexivity of the contributors provides resources for learning both how we do and how we know. By setting out the many different elements involved in production, the processes of doing research and becoming researchers is made explicit. The scaffolding on which theoretical constructs are built is exposed. In total this is a book about processes: feminist processes of being, becoming, doing, experiencing and knowing.

With enormous thanks to Rosemary Deem, Celia Lury, Lynne Pearce and Jackie Stacey for being such insightful readers and rigorous feminist critics, and to Andrew Sayer for the philosophical debates.

Notes

1 Epistemology is the study of knowledge *in general*. Different philosophies shape the approaches to epistemology, hence feminist epistemology. Or as Alcoff and Potter (1993) would argue we have many different feminist epistemolog*ies* because knowledge is always context dependent. Different philosophies also inform our methodologies, that is, how we combine methods to study the objects of our enquiry. This does not mean that there is one feminist methodology, rather that feminists use methods to answer, explore and construct theories and explanations of issues pertinent to feminism.

2 Debates over writing style and representation in anthropology such as Clifford and Marcus (1986) and Wolf (1990), and the sociology of science: Mulkay (1985); Woolgar (1988) have been useful, but have rarely addressed the specificities of feminist theorising. *Reading into Cultural Studies* by Barker and Beezer (1992) valiantly locates classical cultural texts into historical formations with less emphasis on the specifically feminist interests in the processes of knowledge production. The introduction to Nava (1992) is helpful.

3 Theory, as Butler and Scott (1992) note, is a highly contested term in feminist discourse. I am using theory to mean a conceptualisation, in which to theorise means to prescribe a particular way of conceptualising something (Sayer, 1992). To conceptualise is to make an abstract understanding or analysis of a phenomenon such as a text or social interaction. A theoretical framework is a means to connect different phenomena together for the purposes of explanation.

4 Even though all researchers use a theory of methods this does not mean that all researchers are theorists. The significant difference is that theorists construct abstract explanations from the phenomena they study.

5 This became particularly problematic when the debates in literary theory declared 'the death of the author', and all authorial intention, motivation and agency were lost. In de-centring authorial privilege the balance of power between author, text and reader has been radically revised (see Lynne Pearce, Chapter Four).

6 There are far more authors than those present in this book who fit this category so choice was often a matter of logistics (my placement and knowing people could write to deadlines) and availability.

7 There have been attempts by deconstruction theorists such as Derrida (1981) to define everything (cultural processes, people's lives, social relations) as texts in order to highlight the centrality of non-literary representations. This, however, Franklin *et al.* (1991) argue, obscures the specificity and significance of different kinds of practices: the analysis of the female body, for instance, becomes objectified if it is reduced solely to a text.

8 The figure for female professors in Britain increased with the creation of the 'new universities' from polytechnics and colleges of higher education. There are more women in positions of power in US universities, but not in the Ivy League universities.

9 It is also worth noting that the ability to use language is a form of cultural capital, a cultural resource, related to our location in social and economic relations.

10 The attractions of Foucault are wide and varied as Fraser (1989), McNay (1992) and Ramazanoglu (1993) demonstrate.

11 The dangers of not thinking through the theoretical dimensions to feminist actions were made apparent at events such as 'Reclaim the Night' marches in Britain which failed to explore the racist consequences for feminist action.

12 Although, sadly, as Spivak (1990) notes, there are feminist deconstructionists who refuse to take responsibility for the political implications of their work.

13 For the purposes of this book I want to continue with Probyn's (1993b) use of ontology. She uses it to signify the context of being. This is different from the more traditional use of ontology as a theory of what exists (e.g. things, forces, relations, etc.)

14 From an interview with Teresa de Lauretis edited by Anu Koivunen (1988).

15 At the Women's Studies Network Conference, July 1994, Portsmouth, UK, Celia Kitzinger raised the question of how do we validate women's experiences when they are anti-feminist. Validation presupposes that theory must operate in the interests of experience and does not take into account the discursive structuring of experience. The idea of validation is based on the assumption that permanently locates experience as an origin or foundation of knowledge that is more immediate and trustworthy than any other form of knowledge.

16 Oddly the concept of experience belongs to a classical empiricist tradition, the very source of positivist science which feminism was at odds to challenge.

17 These arguments do not just apply to empirical research but to any research whose foundation is that women are different because of their experiences. Gynocentric textual analysis was developed on this basis (see Probyn, 1993a).

18 The use of the term standpoint has become closely associated with ossified positions in feminism. Its use in labour history had a completely different meaning. It meant taking a standpoint – anyone could do it – and making a connection. It was not tied into experience but to political commitment (see Popular Memory Group, 1982).

19 See Chapter Seven in Fuss (1989) and Brunsdon (1991) for the implications of these arguments for feminist pedagogy.

20 A great amount of recent research on masculinity suggests that the experience of being male does not necessarily lead to any critical understanding of it.

21 This short explanation does not do justice to the complexity of the arguments presented by Joan Scott (1992). For anyone thinking about theorising from experience or using experiences of others in their research, her chapter is an absolute must. It is a fine example of abstract feminist theorising.

22 See Marshment and Hallam (1994) and Hallam and Marshment (forthcoming).

23 See also Skeggs (1989; 1991; 1994) for reports of the research.

Bibliography

Adams, M. L. (1989), There's no Place Like Home: On the Place of Identity in Feminist Politics, *Feminist Review*, 31, 22–34.

Alcoff, L. (1988), Cultural Feminism versus Post-structuralism: The Identity Crisis in Feminist Theory, *Signs*, 13:3, 405–36.

Alcoff, L. and E. Potter (1993), *Feminist Epistemologies*, London, Routledge.

Amos, V. and P. Parmar (1984), Challenging Imperialist Feminism, *Feminist Review*, 17, 3–19.

Angus, A. and S. Jhally (eds) (1989), Introduction, *Cultural Politics in Contemporary America*, London, Routledge.

Barker, M. and A. Beezer (1992), *Reading into Cultural Studies*, London, Routledge.

Bar On, B.-A. (1993), Marginality and Epistemic Privilege, in L. Alcoff and E. Potter (eds), *Feminist Epistemologies*, London, Routledge.

Braidotti, R. (1991), *Patterns of Dissonance*, Cambridge, Polity.

Brunsdon, C. (1991), Pedagogies of the Feminine: Feminist Teaching and Women's Genres, *Screen*, 32:4, 364–82.

Bryan, B., S. Dadzie and S. Scafe (1985), *The Heart of the Race: Black Women's Lives in Britain*, London, Virago Press.

Butler, J. (1992), Contingent Foundations: Feminism and the Question of Post-modernism, in J. Butler and J. Scott (eds), *Feminists Theorise the Political*, London, Routledge.

Butler, J. and J. Scott (eds) (1992), *Feminists Theorise the Political*, London, Routledge.

Carby, H. (1982), White Woman Listen! Black Feminism and the Boundaries of Sisterhood, in CCCS (eds), *The Empire Strikes Back*, London, Hutchinson.

Christian, B. (1987), The Race for Theory, *Cultural Critique*, Spring, 51–63.

Clifford, J. and G. Marcus (eds) (1986), *Writing Culture: the Poetics and Politics of Ethnography*, Berkeley, University of California Press.

Clough, P. (1992), *The End(s) of Ethnography: From Social Realism to Social Criticism*, London, Sage.

Code, L. (1991), *What Can She Know: Feminist Theory and the Construction of Knowledge*, Ithaca and London, Routledge.

Craib, I. (1992), *Modern Social Theory: From Parsons to Habermas*, London, Harvester.

Crosby, C. (1992), Dealing with Differences, in J. Butler and J. Scott (eds), *Feminists Theorise the Political*, London, Routledge.

de Lauretis, T. (1990), Upping the Anti (sic) in Feminist Theory, in M. Hirsch and E. Fox Keller (eds), *Conflicts in Feminism*, London, Routledge.

Derrida, J. (1981), *Writing and Difference*, London, Routledge and Kegan Paul.

Fildes, S. (1983), The Inevitability of Theory, *Feminist Review*, 14, 62–70.

Finch, J. (1983), *Married to the Job: Women's Incorporation into Men's Work*, London, George Allen and Unwin.

Fonow, M. M. and J. A. Cook (1991), *Beyond Methodology: Feminist Scholarship as Lived Research*, Bloomington, Indiana University Press.

Foucault, M. (1972), *The Archaeology of Knowledge*, London, Tavistock.

Franklin, S., C. Lury and J. Stacey (eds) (1991), *Off-Centre: Feminism and Cultural Studies*, London, Hutchinson.

Fraser, N. (1989), *Unruly Practices: Power, Discourse and Gender in Contemporary Social Theory*, Cambridge, Polity.

Fuss, D. (1989), *Essentially Speaking: Feminism, Nature and Difference*, London, Routledge.

Gates, H. L. Jr (1987), What's Love Got To Do With It: Critical Theory, Integrity and the Black Idiom, *New Literary History*, 18:2, 345–62.

Gilroy, P. (1993a), *The Black Atlantic: Modernity and Double Consciousness*, London, Verso.

Gilroy, P. (1993b), *Small Acts: Thoughts on the Politics of Black Cultures*, London, Serpent's Tail.

Gramsci, A. (1971), *Selections from the Prison Notebooks of Antonio Gramsci*, ed. Q. Hoare and G. Nowell-Smith, London, Lawrence and Wishart.

Gray, A. (1992), *Video Playtime: The Gendering of a Leisure Technology*, London, Routledge.

Grimshaw, J. (1986), *Philosophy and Feminist Thinking*, Brighton, Wheatsheaf.

Hallam, J. and M. Marshment (forthcoming), Case studies in reception of *Oranges are not the Only Fruit*, *Screen*, 1995.

Haraway, D. (1991), *Simians, Cyborgs and Women: The Reinvention of Nature*, London, Free Association Books.

Harstock, N. (1983), The Feminist Standpoint: Developing the Ground for a Specifically Feminist Historical Materialism, in S. Harding and M. B. Hintikka (eds), *Discovering Reality: Feminist Perspectives on Epistemology, Metaphysics, Methodology and Philosophy of Science*, Dordrecht, Reidel.

Heath, S. (1986), Joan Riviere and the Masquerade, in V. Burgin *et al.* (eds), *Formations of Fantasy*, London, Methuen.

Hill Collins, P. (1990), *Black Feminist Thought: Knowledge, Consciousness, and the Politics of Empowerment*, London, Routledge.

Hooks, B. (1989), *Talking Back: Thinking Feminist, Thinking Black*, Boston, South End Press.

Johnson, R. (1986), The Story so Far: and Further Transformations?, in D. Punter (ed.), *Introduction to Contemporary Cultural Studies*, London, Longman.

Kirkham, P. (forthcoming), *Charles and Ray Eames: Designers of the Century*, Cambridge, Mass., MIT Press.

Koivunen, A. (ed.) (1988), Are You Experienced – An Interview with Teresa de Lauretis, *Lahikuva*, 4, 33–4.

Lazreg, M. (1994), Women's Experience and Feminist Epistemology, in K. Lennon and M. Whitford (eds), *Knowing the Difference: Feminist Perspectives in Epistemology*, London, Routledge.

Lennon, K. and M. Whitford (eds) (1994), Introduction to *Knowing the Difference: Feminist Perspectives in Epistemology*, London, Routledge.

Leonard, D. (1980), *Sex and Generation: A Study of Courtship and Weddings*, London, Tavistock.

Lury, C. (1993), *Cultural Rights: Technology, Legality and Personality*, London, Routledge.

Marshment, M. and J. Hallam (1994), *Oranges are not the Only Fruit*, *Jump Cut*, 39, 40–50.

McNay, L. (1992), *Foucault and Feminism*, Cambridge, Polity.

McRobbie, A. (1982), The Politics of Feminist Research: Between Talk, Text and Action, *Feminist Review*, 12, 46–59.

Mitchell, J. (1971), *Woman's Estate*, Harmondsworth, Penguin.

Mulkay, M. (1985), *The Word and the World: Explorations in the Form of Sociological Analysis*, London, Allen and Unwin.

Nava, M. (1992), Introduction: Intellectual Work in Context and Process, in M. Nava (ed.), *Changing Cultures: Feminism, Youth and Consumerism*, London, Sage.

Ngcobo, L. (ed.) (1988), *Let It Be Told: Essays by Black Women in Britain*, London, Virago.

Omi, M. and H. Winant (1986), *Racial Formation in the United States*, London, Routledge and Kegan Paul.

Parmar, P. (1989), Other Kinds of Dreams, *Feminist Review*, 31, 55–66.

Pearce, L. (1991), *Woman/Image/Text: Readings in Pre-Raphaelite Art and Literature*, Hemel Hempstead, Harvester Wheatsheaf.

Pearce, L. (1994), *Reading Dialogics*, London, Edward Arnold.

Popular Memory Group (1982), Popular Memory, Theory, Politics, Method, in R. Johnson *et al.* (eds), *Making Histories: Studies in History-Writing and Politics*, London, Hutchinson.

Probyn, E. (1990), Travels in the Post-modern: Making Sense of the Local, in L. Nicholson (ed.), *Feminism/Postmodernism*, London, Routledge.

Probyn, E. (1993a), True Voices and Real People: The 'Problem' of the Autobiographical in Cultural Studies, in V. Blundel *et al.* (eds), *Relocating Cultural Studies: Developments in Theory and Research*, London, Routledge.

Probyn, E. (1993b), *Sexing the Self: Gendered Positions in Cultural Studies*, London, Routledge.

Ramazanoglu, C. (1993), *Up Against Foucault: Explorations of Some Tensions Between Foucault and Feminism*, London, Routledge.

Riley, D. (1988), *Am I That Name*, London, Macmillan.

Riley, D. (1992), A Short History of Some Preoccupations, in J. Butler and J. Scott (eds), *Feminists Theorise the Political*, London, Routledge.

Roberts, H. (ed.) (1981), *Doing Feminist Research*, London, Routledge and Kegan Paul.

Rowbotham, S. (1973), *Hidden from History: 300 Years of Women's Oppression and the Fight Against It*, London, Pluto Press.

Rowe, K. (1995), *The Unruly Woman: Gender and Genres of Laughter*, Austin, University of Texas Press.

Sayer, A. (1992), *Method in Social Science: A Realist Approach*, London, Routledge.

Scott, J. (1992), Experience, in J. Butler and J. Scott (eds), *Feminists Theorise the Political*, London, Routledge.

Seiter, E. (1993), *Sold Separately: Children and Parents in Consumer Culture*, New Brunswick, New Jersey, Rutgers University Press.

Skeggs, B. (1989), Gender Reproduction and Further Education: Domestic Apprenticeships, *British Journal of Sociology of Education*, 10:4, 131–51.

Skeggs, B. (1991), Challenging Masculinity and Using Sexuality, *British Journal of Sociology of Education*, 12:2, 127–39.

Skeggs, B. (1994), Situating the Production of Feminist Ethnography, in M. Maynard and J. Purvis (eds), *Researching Women's Lives from a Feminist Perspective*, London, Taylor and Francis.

Skeggs, B. (forthcoming), *Becoming Respectable: an Ethnography*, London, Sage.

Spivak, G. C. (1985), Strategies of Vigilance, *Block*, 5, 5–9.

Spivak, G. C. (1990), *The Post-Colonial Critic: Interviews, Strategies, Dialogues*, ed. S. Harasym, London, Routledge.

Stacey, J. (1994), *Star Gazing: Hollywood Cinema and Female Spectatorship*, London, Routledge.

Stanley, L. and S. Wise (1983), *Breaking Out: Feminist Consciousness and Feminist Research*, London, Routledge.

Stanley, L. (ed.) (1990), *Feminist Praxis: Research, Theory and Epistemology in Feminist Sociology*, London, Routledge.

Thumim, J. (1992), *Celluloid Sisters: Women and Popular Cinema*, London, Macmillan.

Walkerdine, V. (1989), *Schoolgirl Fictions*, London, Verso.

Wolf, M. (1990), *A Thrice Told Tale*, Stanford, Stanford University Press.

Woolgar, S. (ed.) (1988), *Knowledge and Reflexivity*, London, Sage.

Young, A. (1990), *Femininity in Dissent*, London, Routledge.

PART ONE

texts and responses

1

The rights and wrongs of culture: issues of theory and methodology

CELIA LURY

The relationship between feminism and the study of culture has been the subject of much debate. It has never acquired (or sought) the public legitimacy of a marriage, unhappy or otherwise, but has, rather, been described in terms of an affinity, or an 'overlap' of interests (Franklin *et al.*, 1991). However, while this relationship continues to lurch onwards, it remains beset by doubts. In this chapter, I will present a commentary on the arguments put forward in *Cultural Rights* (Lury, 1993) to reflect on some of the dynamics of this relationship. At one level, these are the problems of bringing together cultural theory and feminism, when the former is still, in the main, not essentially concerned with issues of gender. While not wishing to downplay the importance of feminist work in the study of culture, it is my impression that current feminist cultural studies are repeatedly held back by the continued dominance of ungendered understandings of culture, both in its general uses, as a shared set of meaning resources, and in relation to particular cultural processes, as in definitions of signification, parody, performance and so on. The dominant presumption that culture itself is gender-neutral, that it is only specific *uses* of culture which are problematic from a feminist point of view, obscures the ways in which culture itself is constituted in relation to gender and other social and political categories.

At another level, however, this commentary investigates how conceptual and methodological issues are inextricably intertwined, through an exploration of the place of theorising in feminist work. In many early discussions of 'doing feminist research' the question of theory was posed as a problem, and was set in a fixed and somewhat simplified opposition to the category of 'experience'. Since then, however, the nature of the relationship between experience and theory has been opened up, and a variety of different ways of making that relationship productive have begun to be identified, ranging from so-called standpoint epistemologies (Stanley, 1993; Hill Collins, 1990) to poststructuralist interrogations and reworkings of lived experience (de Lauretis, 1987; Probyn, 1993). At the same time, however, the usefulness of the grand narratives of theory, and the social and political categories constructed in those theories, such as 'class', 'race' and 'gender', and especially 'woman' or 'women', have been challenged for their implicit claims to universality.

So, for example, a number of feminist writers (hooks, 1981; Scott, 1986; Riley, 1988) have recently argued that the historical emergence of the social as a category of political life was dependent upon particular understandings of 'women', and, vice versa, that the category 'women' has been defined in and by its relation to the social. The acceptance of this historical definition of women as a universal category, it is argued, has had the effect of excluding large numbers of women whose experiences are not made visible in this understanding of the social, including, for example, Black women. The wish to avoid such exclusionary effects has fed into the ongoing debate about the relationship between theoretical and methodological concerns in feminist research, complicated by debates about the scope and scale of the interpretations proposed by feminist scholars. The questions which face feminists now include: should feminists avoid not only grand but also so-called middle-range theory? Is it possible to talk to 'women' as a social and political category without implying a false universalism? What kind of authority should feminist knowledges have? How are those knowledges to be situated? What kinds of implications can be drawn from focused research in the development of feminist theory?

In what follows, I want to suggest that what is sometimes described as 'the turn to the cultural', that is, the increasing importance attached to cultural practices in analyses of gender, give these questions a new twist. What are the differences between social and cultural theory in relation to the questions above? In any case, can social and cultural theory be brought together? In many respects, it seems as if the turn to the cultural has sidestepped many of the problems which have arisen in feminist studies. So, for example, addressing the issue of cultural representation has given the methodological issue of representativeness a new dimension, encouraging feminists (and others) to move beyond a critique of positivist techniques and reductive interpretations of women's experiences to open up hermeneutic and post-structuralist enquiry. An understanding of the workings of narrative has opened up the study of biography and life history. However, I will argue that if culture, or the cultural, is not reflected upon as an analytic category, and its historical interdependence with the category 'women' is not made an integral part of any investigation, then questions of gender can only be 'added in' to cultural studies. I will suggest that this does not mean that we should abandon attempts to theorise the cultural. (Although, in my view, this might best be attempted in terms of middle-range, historically sensitive, theories, rather than as a grand theory.) This, I believe, will allow an exploration of not only the historical constitution of the cultural, but also its changing relationship with the social, and with categories such as 'women', 'race' and 'class'.

Many of my problems in *Cultural Rights* arose from my unhappiness with what has been called additive feminism, that is, with a feminism which added in women to the study of, for example, publishing or television, and my concern to think through the issue of how to show the ways in which the cultural has come to be gendered historically. One of the central arguments in *Cultural Rights* was that the social organisation of cultural reproduction in modern Western societies has implications not only for how men and women unequally participate in cultural reproduction, but also provides a way of conceptualising how gender is implicated in the constitution of the very categories high and popular culture, and with the (historically changing) differentiation of the cultural from other fields of reproduction, such as the social. But this was very hard to substantiate, because of the ways in which the sociology of culture and, to some extent, cultural studies, have tended to adopt ungendered understandings of culture itself. So one of the most frustrating problems I faced in trying to consider how the cultural field has been drawn was that there were very few studies available which considered how gender had been integral to the formation of the cultural field. The most relevant conceptual terms, including modernism, understandings of authorship and the distinction between high and popular culture were, with a few notable exceptions (Huyssen, 1986; Nead, 1988; Lovell, 1987; Tuchman with Fortin, 1989), largely developed at an abstract level without reference to gender, only adding in 'women' as a matter of historical description.

In addition, there is very little historical empirical research which is sensitive to gender *and* race, so that even what I was able to find was extremely problematic because of its assumption of a white subject.

More generally, one of the main drawbacks of the additive approach is that it tends to exclude any consideration of the way in which categories are not only interrelated, but internally linked. This means, for example, that while much feminist cultural studies has been concerned to explore the interrelationship between gender and culture, it has done so without explicitly problematising what is meant by the cultural itself. There are some exceptions to this tendency, though, perhaps the most well known of which emerged from the criticisms that have come to be made of what is known as the 'images of women' approach (Pollock, 1987).

In the influential article which crystallised many of these criticisms, 'What's wrong with images of women?', Griselda Pollock challenged the separation of 'women as a gender or social group versus representations of women' (1987: 41). In doing so, she not only problematised the conception that images of women are a reflection of reality, but also advocated the study of the meanings that 'are attached to woman in different images and how the meanings are constructed in relation to other signifiers in that discourse' (Pollock, 1987). She advocated the use of a particular methodological technique – the reversal of male and female figures in imagery – to uncover what she describes as 'a basic asymmetry written into the language of visual representation' (p. 46). It was through this kind of structuralist study, Pollock suggested, that it would be possible to identify the 'roles of the signifier woman within ideological representations' (p. 48).

In a later article in 1990, reflecting on the earlier piece, Pollock reiterates her critique of the 'images of women' approach, but formulates the alternative in slightly different terms. She describes the alternative as the

> careful analysis of the specific constructions of the feminine body as specific modes and the sites of representation and discussion of address and the imagined spectator. Here, woman/women cease to be the topic of representation. Instead, it becomes possible to perceive that the function of representation is the production of sexual differentiation for which a certain body image is the signifier. (Pollock, 1990: 206)

Indeed, she goes on to suggest that not only are 'we ... not looking at an image of woman, but also that we are hardly looking at a body at all' (1990: 214). In moving away from looking at the (structuralist) 'language of visual representation', she foregrounds the viewer, and thus moves away from her former position, which she now retrospectively defines as that of a 'star-struck structuralist'. In a post-structuralist move, she introduces the viewer as 'the point at which all the traces and currents activated by the signifying elements in the text ... converge' (1990: 214), but simultaneously fixes the viewer as the 'split subject of semiotics ... and of psychoanalysis' (1990: 214).

In doing so, she makes use of what has come to be one of the few understandings of the cultural in feminist research in which the cultural is explicitly gendered. This is the approach that has been developed in conjunction with psychoanalysis. Psychoanalytically informed feminist cultural studies has been enormously influential in a multitude of areas – the study of visual culture, mothering, sexual and gender identities. However, this (internally diverse) theorisation of the relationship between the cultural and gender has been much criticised (often, reflexively, by its advocates), for its tendency to universalise its claims and ignore social and historical context, as well as its neglect of 'race' and 'class' as key dynamics. This critique has been especially strong in relation to the study of relations of looking (Stacey, 1987; de Lauretis, 1987; Gaines, 1988), but it sometimes seems as if the appeal to a radical and ineradicable sexual difference translates, and ratifies, the difference between self and other which, in turn, becomes the equivalent of any difference (masculine and feminine, black and white, heterosexual and homosexual, etc.). In contrast, once again in relation to debates in the study of visual culture, Gaines (1988) has suggested that it is necessary to rethink ideas about looking 'along more materialist lines, considering, for instance, how some groups have historically had the license to "look" openly while other groups have "looked" illicitly' (pp. 24–5).

However, despite this critique, and the later emergence of research on the relationship between specific media and audiences which seeks to overcome these problems (Ang, 1993; Stacey, 1994), much feminist cultural studies has either tended to work within psychoanalytically informed theories of language and culture or avoid the larger question of how an awareness of the interrelationship of culture and gender might alter our understandings of both culture and the category 'women'. Indeed, in many ways, this question has been ruled out of court, since it is deemed to be a question which necessarily results in reductive and essentialist accounts of gender. As Gaines (1988) points out, those who have used psychoanalytic theory claim to treat looking positions (such as viewer/viewed) distinct from actual social groups (men/women) even while they are identified with gender, and in so doing 'keep the levels of the social ensemble [social life, representation, and so on] hopelessly separate' (Gaines, 1988). It is as if the complexities of trying to hold apart the specificity of the cultural and the social (that is, not understand images of women as merely a reflection of the social) have been so great that feminists have given up on seeing how they have come to be historically related in changing ways.

To orient my own work, then, I was dependent on the understanding of women as a sign that had emerged in feminist cultural criticism to locate the specificity of the relationship between gender and culture. However, as I suggested earlier, this understanding of woman as a sign is pitched at a very high level of generality; indeed, some would say that it is both dependent upon and contributes to a universalisation of the category 'woman', both when it is used in a psychoanalytically informed way (Mulvey, 1989; Pollock, 1989) to inform discussions of the subject or when it is used weakly as a historical abstraction in relation to women as a social group (Berger, 1973). In an attempt to contextualise historically the representation of woman as sign, I sought to show that by the mid-twentieth century at least, woman was not only the sign or the object for popular cultural reproduction, but also its audience or market.

This tendency is evident in, for example, the growth of popular cultural forms aimed primarily at women, such as women's magazines (Winship, 1987), popular romantic fiction (Radway, 1987; Modleski, 1982), the targeting of women for specific genres of film in the cinema (LaPlace, 1987), and the importance attached to women in the organisation and development of broadcasting as a domestic medium (Spigel, 1990). This is not to deny that many popular cultural forms are defined by the related processes of the objectification of women in the text and an attempted masculinisation of the viewing or reading audience. Rather, it is to suggest that there are contradictory tendencies at work in the address to the audience: the targeting of women as a key market for popular cultural production is cross-cut by an attempted masculinisation of the viewing or reading subject. I suggested that this organisation, in which different levels of what Gaines (1988) calls the social ensemble are contradictorily related, has had uneven consequences for those belonging to the category 'women'.

I further suggested that the unevenness of the incorporation of women into the process of cultural reproduction is complicated by the relationship between not only cultural reproduction and the social organisation of sexuality, but also between cultural reproduction and the work of domesticity. These are, necessarily, complex, historically changing relationships, sometimes working together, sometimes against each other. On the one hand, the display of commodities as spectacles offering the female shopper pleasure in looking, contemplation and the fantasy transformation of the self and her surroundings directly prefigured the pleasures which were to be offered to the female spectator in the cinema. On the other hand, the cinema screen can be seen to reproduce a 'display window ... occupied by marvellous mannequins' (Eckert, 1978: 4). In other ways, too, consumer culture and popular culture reinforced each other: the women making up an audience were available for commodification as a market to the consumer industries while, at the same time, the market of female consumers was addressed in ways which prepared them to act as an audience for the forms of popular culture associated with the new cultural technologies of the emerging mass media.

However, I also pointed out that despite the importance of the links between cultural and sexual and domestic technologies, the process of reinforcement did not result in complete overlap. I suggested that this was in part due to the elaboration of the practices of imitation amongst viewers and readers. I put forward the view that this process of imitation could be understood as a process of becoming, or doubling of representation, involving a blurring of the opposition between production and reception. In conclusion, I suggested that, although such practices of imitation were not new, as a consequence of the increasing commercial importance of the practices of the audience for cultural reproduction, the relationship between gender and culture might be seen to have undergone a significant change. I formulated this shift in terms of a move from 'woman as sign' to femininity as (dis)simulation, a mask for a non-identity, a bodily resubmission to 'ideas about herself' (Irigaray, 1985: 76).

As such, femininity (or the process of 'becoming woman') has come to figure contemporary anxiety about the relationship between the subject and representation, and the fear that, through the failure to mark a distance with respect to representation, identification is replacing identity.

From this perspective, I suggested, femininity as simulation is currently a pervasive manifestation of the (historically changing) ways in which the representational construct of 'woman' and the experience of women (variously identified and subject to multiple determinations) may come together to create 'gender'. The more general point was that they are not always related in the same way; that is, there is a historically changing relationship between gender, the cultural and the social.

While, in retrospect, I am choosing to identify my aims in this way, at the time of writing I was much less clear about how to formulate the conceptual implications of my argument. In part, this anxiety was related to the lack of relevant grounds with which to develop such an argument, and this, I think, contributed to the still falsely universalising nature of my explanations, but it was also related to what I perceived as the unfashionability of theoretical analysis which made use of the category of 'women' as a cultural *and* social group. This was related to the increasingly common move of 'destabilising' the social, because of what are seen as its reductive, reifying and universalising consequences. My feeling, then and now, however, is that the replacement (as opposed to the destabilisation) of the social by the cultural, and in relation to the category of analysis, of the replacement of women by the subject or the individual, does not avoid these problems; they cannot simply be sidestepped by focusing on the cultural in place of the social.

I have since come to feel even more strongly that there is a need to theorise the relationship between the social and the cultural as a result of the increased importance attributed to the cultural in both academic and lay accounts of everyday life. Commonplace examples such as the displacement of class by taste in many popular discussions of status and inequality, the political significance of popular cultural attitudes to nature in environmental politics, the role ascribed to architecture, heritage and tradition in the creation and maintenance of national identities, and the suggestion that ethnicity is a newly culturalised form of 'race'-making, imply that 'culture' is becoming explicit in people's understandings of themselves. As it becomes more explicit, it becomes available as a site of political contestation. At the same time, however, culture is attributed a totalising characteristic in many academic accounts[1] in ways which, it seems to me, may foreclose this political opportunity.

This is evident in the take-up of the ideas of performance in the constitution of personal identity. Much recent feminist philosophy and political theory has been particularly concerned with the issue of performativity, and with the need to redefine it in such a way as to avoid a voluntaristic interpretation of the term, that is, to avoid the assumption that performance is the natural capacity of a self-transforming subject. So, for example, Judith Butler stresses that performativity should be understood 'not as the act by which a subject brings into being what she/he names, but, rather, ... that reiterative power of discourse to produce the phenomena that it regulates and constrains' (1993: 2). She further argues that it is necessary to link the process of 'assuming' a sex with the question of 'identification', and with 'the discursive means by which the heterosexual imperative enables certain sexed identifications and forecloses and/or disavows other identifications' (p. 3). She thus points to the importance of locating what she calls the 'conditions of intelligibility' within which individuals come to assume a sex and seeks to relate them to what she calls the heterosexual hegemony or imperative. In this way, she points to the importance of recognising that culture, or what she calls the conditions of intelligibility, is not a gender-neutral resource for self-transformation.

But in other uses of the idea of performance – in academic, policy and everyday milieux – this critical recognition is downplayed or absent, and the question of the gendered access to and ownership of identity is not even posed. It is assumed that identities are universally available as resources, that identities are constituted as the cultural property of the individual which all individuals are equally free to exchange. This assumption fails to consider how an individual comes to possess an identity, whether women can possess an identity in the same way as men, of whether their identities are constituted differently in relation to the self. There is a failure to historicise the cultural, and an unwillingness to consider its relationship with the social; heterosexuality, for example, is universalised as an imperative. Culture tends to assume a totalising explanatory force which is both all-powerful and elusive; in these uses, the cultural itself becomes the source of a new essentialism, what might be called a cultural essentialism of the individual (see Lury, forthcoming, for more on this term,[2] and see Balibar, 1991, for a discussion of cultural naturalism in racism). As Gaytri Chakravorty Spivak has argued, if

> culture is taken as an agent, as in 'cultural construction of race,' [and, she later adds, gender] then what we tend to lose sight of is that culture is also something that is the effect of the production of cultural explanations, and cultural explanations are produced also because a certain culture needs to be fabricated, a monolithic explanation of a group needs to be fabricated. (1990: 123)

With Lisa Adkins, I have argued elsewhere (Adkins and Lury, forthcoming) that one of the things that makes possible this essentialism is the belief that the individualisation thesis put forward by some theorists of modernity (Beck, 1992; Giddens, 1993) is universal. This thesis proposes that a key transformation in modern societies is the identification of 'the individual' as the source of value, judgement and selfhood. However, a number of feminist theorists, including Pateman (1988), Riley (1988) and Acker (1990) have argued that individualisation is an intrinsically gendered process, dependent as it is on the prior existence of the sexual contract, a gendered division of labour and a separation between the private and public spheres. (And in this way, these writers provide an alternative intellectual tradition to the Foucauldian paradigm which has become increasingly dominant in feminist cultural theory, despite the recognition that his account does not directly consider issues of gender.) The ability to be an individual, including the ability to own an identity as a resource, to display it as a performance, is thus necessarily gendered. But how it is gendered, and how this process of gendering is also raced and classed, can only be determined through investigation. And this is where this theoretical digression returns to methodology.

The new emphasis on the individual and the cultural has not led to an abandonment of previous methods of interpretation and analysis in feminist research: discourse analysis has been added to textual interpretation, life histories, interviews, questionnaires and ethnography, which together comprise the most prevalent techniques in feminist cultural studies. However, what has changed are the ways in which theoretical implications are drawn from the use of such techniques. Across a wide range of analyses in feminist research, there appears to be a newly emerging orthodoxy in which the identification of 'the feminine', 'feminine identity' and 'femininity' is coming to replace (rather than supplement) the investigation of the category 'woman'.[3] In this process, the relationship between the individual and a gendered identity is either assumed, neutralised as an inevitably 'contradictory' process which cannot be clearly specified because of its complexity, or, through the use of psychoanalytically-derived theories of sexual difference, universalised. In all cases, the result is the same; as Eve Sedgwick (1994) has noted, there is, commonly, a collapse of the ontogenetic and the phylogenetic levels of analysis,[4] of the acquisition of an individual identity and membership of the social and political category 'women'.

This, then, is a plea for the development of historically specific understandings of the cultural, which neither assume that it is gendered through a universal process of sexual difference, nor assume that it is a gender-neutral field. As such it is also an argument for feminists to develop ways in which to interpret the findings of research which do not take for granted the individual or 'women' as pre-given categories. This will require a renewed sensitivity to the traditional concerns of methodology, such as those of validity, generalisability and representativeness. In even raising these questions, I fear that I will be seen to be advocating a return to 'mechanical' understandings of gender. Certainly, there were and are problems with what has been called social essentialism; but although cultural processes of representation intervene in, for example, how representativeness can be understood, they should not be taken to make it redundant.

The recognition that the category 'women' is not exclusively determined at the social level, but also at the cultural, and, vice versa, that what it is to be an individual in possession of a gender identity is not simply negotiated in the cultural domain, suggests that there is a need for a feminist methodology that is sensitive to both social *and* cultural specificity. Such a methodology would allow a consideration of how subjectivity and membership of collective categories such as those of gender are simultaneously, but never simply analogously or uniformly, achieved. It would allow us to look at the social effectivity of fantasy, of desire and processes of identification, and the subject effects of social changes. The development of such methods may help to prevent what may well otherwise be a slide from social to cultural essentialism, and from a falsely universalistic 'woman' to a falsely individualised 'feminine identity', in feminist theory and research.

Notes

1 For example, Judith Butler suggests that 'for the sake of argument [I] will let "social" and "cultural" stand in an uneasy interchangeability' (1993: 5).

2 I have deliberately chosen to use the term essentialism, despite the weariness which descends upon me when I hear it employed unthinkingly as a term of abuse. This is because I think its use here highlights the extent to which there are parallel problems in the use of totalising, ahistorical social and cultural interpretations of gender.

3 There is also a parallel tendency in men's studies to discuss 'the masculine', 'masculine identities' and 'masculinities' which, in my view, suffers from some of the same problems.

4 Sedgwick writes,

> Briefly, as regards gender and sexual identities, we fear a conflation of the question of what might be called phylogeny with that of individual ontogeny. The origin of this conflation probably has something to do with the double disciplinary genealogy of constructivism itself: on the one hand, through a Foucauldian historicism designed to take the centuries vertiginously in stride; on the other, through an interactional communications theory whose outermost temporal horizon is, in practice, the individual life span. The *phylogenic* question, which asks about the centuries-long processes – linguistic, institutional, intergenerational – by which such identities are or are not invented, manipulated, and altered, gets asked under the rubric of 'constructivism' as if it were identical to the *ontogenic* question: the question 'how did *such-and-such a person* come to be,' shall we say, gay rather than straight. (1994: 226)

Bibliography

Acker, J. (1990), Hierarchies, Jobs and Bodies: A Theory of Gendered Organizations, *Gender and Society*, 4:2, 139–58.

Adkins, L. and C. Lury (forthcoming), The Cultural, the Sexual and the Gendering of the Labour Market, in L. Adkins and V. Merchant (eds), *Power and the Organisation of Sexuality*, London, Macmillan.

Ang, I. (1993), *Desperately Seeking the Audience*, London and New York, Routledge.

Balibar, E. (1991), Is There a 'Neo-Racism'?, in E. Balibar and I. Wallerstein (eds), *Race, Nation, Class: Ambiguous Identities*, London, Verso.

Beck, U. (1992), *Risk Society*, London, Sage.

Berger, J. (1973), *Ways of Seeing*, London, BBC Books.

Butler, J. (1993), *Bodies That Matter. On the Discursive Limits of 'Sex'*, London and New York, Routledge.

de Lauretis, T. (1987), *Technologies of Gender: Essays on Theory, Film and Fiction*, Basingstoke, Macmillan.

Eckert, C. (1978), The Carole Lombard in Macy's Window, *Quarterly Review of Film Studies*, 3:1, 1–21.

Franklin, S., C. Lury and J. Stacey (eds) (1991), *Off-Centre: Feminism and Cultural Studies*, London, HarperCollins.

Gaines, J. (1988), White Privilege and Looking Relations: Race and Gender in Feminist Film Theory, *Screen*, 29:4, 12–27.

Giddens, A. (1993), *Modernity and Self-Identity*, Cambridge, Polity.

Hill Collins, P. (1990), *Black Feminist Thought. Knowledge, Consciousness and the Politics of Empowerment*, Boston, Unwin Hyman.

hooks, b. (1981), *Ain't I A Woman?: Black Women and Feminism*, Boston, South End Press.

Huyssen, A. (1986), *After the Great Divide. Modernism, Mass Culture and Post-modernism*, London, Macmillan.

Irigaray, L. (1985), *This Sex Which Is Not One*, trans. C. Porter and C. Burke, Ithaca, Cornell University Press.

LaPlace, M. (1987), Producing and Consuming the Woman's Film: Discursive Struggle in *Now Voyager*, in C. Gledhill (ed.), *Home is Where the Heart Is: Studies in Melodrama and the Woman's Film*, London, British Film Institute.

Lovell, T. (1987), *Consuming Fiction*, London, Verso.

Lury, C. (1993), *Cultural Rights: Technology, Legality and Personality*, London, Routledge.

Lury, C. (forthcoming), *Possessing the Self*, London, Routledge.

Modleski, T. (1982), *Loving with a Vengeance: Mass-produced Fantasies for Women*, London and New York, Routledge.

Mulvey, L. (1989), *Visual and Other Pleasures*, London, Macmillan.

Nead, L. (1988), *Myths of Sexuality: Representations of Women in Victorian Britain*, Oxford, Basil Blackwell.

Pateman, C. (1988), *The Sexual Contract*, Cambridge: Polity.

Pollock, G. (1987), What's Wrong With 'Images of Women'?, in R. Betterton (ed.), *Looking On* (1st ed. 1977), London, Pandora, 40–8.

Pollock, G. (1989), *Vision and Difference: Femininity, Feminism and Histories of Art*, London, Routledge.

Pollock, G. (1990), Missing Women. Rethinking Early Thoughts on Images of Women, in C. Squiers (ed.), *The Critical Image. Essays on Contemporary Photograph*, Seattle, Bay Press.

Probyn, E. (1993), *Sexing the Self. Gendered Positions in Cultural Studies*, London, Routledge.

Radway, J. (1987), Reading the Romance: Women, Patriarchy and Popular Literature, London, Verso.

Riley, D. (1988), *'Am I That Name?' Feminism and the Category of 'Women' in History*, London, Macmillan.

Scott, J. (1986), Gender: A Useful Category of Historical Review, 91, 1053–75.

Sedgwick, E. (1994), *Tendencies*, New York, Routledge.

Spigel, L. (1990), Television in the Family Circle: The Popular Reception of a New Medium, in P. Mellencamp (ed.), *Logics of Television: Essays in Cultural Criticism*, London, British Film Institute.

Spivak, G. C. (1990), *The Post-Colonial Critic. Interviews, Strategies, Dialogues*, ed. S. Harasym, London, Routledge.

Stacey, J. (1987), Desperately Seeking Difference, *Screen*, 28:1, 48–62.

Stacey, J. (1994), *Stargazing*, London, Routledge.

Stanley, L. (ed.) (1993), *Feminist Praxis*, London, Routledge.

Tuchman, G. with N. E. Fortin (1989), *Edging Women Out: Victorian Novelists, Publishers and Social Change*, London and New York, Routledge.

Winship, J. (1987), *Inside Women's Magazines*, London, Pandora.

2

Studying *Roseanne*

KATHLEEN ROWE

In 1988, the sitcom *Roseanne* made its debut on ABC TV and promptly dislodged *The Cosby Show* from its number one slot in the ratings.[1] For some media critics, the new show did not appear to be all that different from *The Cosby Show* and other sitcoms popular at the time. After all, its use of comedy based on everyday situations, its cast of characters and events from everyday family life, its combination of plots wrapped up each week with others that evolve more loosely – all located the show in the tradition of the domestic sitcom. However, *Roseanne* struck me as anything but familiar. For one thing, its orientation was more strongly working class than any successful US sitcom since *All in the Family* (CBS, 1971–79). For another, the presence that dominated the show – both in front of and behind the camera – was a woman's. And finally, that woman – like the show itself – seemed to elicit responses from critics and viewers alike that struck me as unusually intense and contradictory. Commentators and critics were outraged and appalled by Roseanne's 'tastelessness' and 'vulgarity', and criticized the show for poor acting and writing. Yet people *were* watching the show, faithfully and in large numbers. This apparent ambivalence triggered my curiosity about Roseanne and in large part motivated my research on her.[2]

I too felt some of that ambivalence and was often shocked by Roseanne's disregard for convention and her expressions of vulgarity. But, even more, I was intrigued by her irreverence, her 'attitude'. I loved her ill-humor and the anger which seemed barely concealed by her wit – and which was and remains so difficult for women to express (especially 'well-brought-up' women). I loved her unapologetic fatness. As a woman approaching my middle years, I loved her critique of a youth culture.

And as a woman immersed in the turmoil of marriage and family life, with three children of my own, I loved how she unmasked our culture's impossible ideals of femininity and motherhood. Most of all, I was compelled by how she embodied contradictions that I had rarely seen represented in mainstream media: how she relentlessly acknowledged and exposed her oppression as a working-class wife and mother, while at the same time finding dignity and fulfillment in those roles.

My own background is middle class, and my own work is professional. Yet those contradictions, especially the ones concerning gender, were not unfamiliar to me. While my class background has spared me the hardships of the pink collar ghetto chronicled in *Roseanne*, like most women I have felt the weight of balancing work and family. I also felt a connection to Roseanne because of my generational identity. I came to the women's movement after I had already set my life on a domestic course similar to Roseanne's, and as a result my own work history or 'career path' has been anything but linear.

My decision to return to graduate school in 1986 to earn a doctorate in film and television coincided with Roseanne's appearance on the national scene, and the feminist film and TV theory I was beginning to study seemed a likely source for the tools to begin my research. What I found, however, was a theoretical model that seemed somewhat at odds both with what I was observing with Roseanne and in part with my own experience.[3] While feminists have historically used a range of theoretical approaches to study film and TV, perhaps the most influential of these has been psychoanalysis, and much of the most powerful analysis I read early in my graduate career – the early work of Laura Mulvey, Mary Ann Doane, Tania Modleski, for example – was informed by it. From a psychoanalytic perspective, cultural forms such as film and television offer women little opportunity for agency, resistance or non-masochistic pleasure because these forms are enmeshed in symbolic systems structured according to a patriarchal unconscious. One might argue that because psychoanalysis was first used mainly in relation to film, its application to a figure primarily associated with the very different medium of television might already be suspect. Yet feminist scholars had long been producing influential and successful psychoanalytic readings of TV.[4]

Feminists have challenged and critiqued the psychoanalytic model from the outset for its determinism, ahistoricism and heterosexism, and in the late 1980s, when I was studying for my degree, feminist film theory was undergoing another period of intense self-reflection. In 1990, more than sixty feminist scholars contributed to a double issue of *Camera Obscura* addressing what Doane and Janet Bergstrom described as an 'impasse' in current feminist film theory arising from its failure to explain the nature of female spectatorship, or how the visual processes of consuming media produce subjectivity. One question that did not receive the attention it might have, however, concerned the impact of the choices feminists have made not only about their theoretical models but about the relation between those models and the kinds of *texts* or *genres* to which they apply them. I am referring here to the long-standing hold of melodrama on the female, and feminist, imagination. Melodrama – the woman's weepy film, the Gothic novel, the made-for-TV-movie, the TV soap opera – had provided an ideal ground for feminist film theory in its early stages because it so clearly and movingly exposes the plight of women under patriarchy. But it also appeared to be exhausted as a field of study.

I began to wonder what other consequences might have resulted from this apparent privileging of melodrama at the expense of other genres. What had resulted from the neglect of *comedy*, for example, the genre in which Roseanne had chosen to define herself? [5] How had this neglect influenced the shape of feminist media theory? What had been the relation between the study of melodrama and the influence of psychoanalysis as a feminist theoretical model, since both take as their given women's identification with suffering, victimization and loss? How might the study of comedy – or even better, a dialectical study of comedy in relation to melodrama – complicate these theories of spectacle, spectatorship and subjectivity?

Thus my study of Roseanne became an investigation not only of 'the Roseanne phenomenon' but of the relation between comedy and feminist theory, a consideration of how the study of comedy itself might open up new ways of thinking about feminist media theory. Above all what I wished to accomplish was an understanding of what we might learn from Roseanne about comedy both as a means of feminist resistance and female pleasure and as a source of less deterministic theories of female spectatorship. Like much enquiry in feminist cultural studies, this research took me across the boundaries of a number of academic disciplines. It also required me to integrate a range of methodologies and resources, among them social history, feminist theories of narrative, histories of the TV sitcom, formalist studies of Hollywood narrative films, and an interview with my primary subject, Roseanne. This research led first to an article 'Roseanne: Unruly Woman as Domestic Goddess' (1990), then to a dissertation, and finally to a book on television and film comedy, *The Unruly Woman: Gender and the Genres of Laughter* (1995).[6] In the remainder of this essay, I will attempt to re-create and reflect on my thinking as I conducted this research.

What is 'Roseanne'?

The answer to the question 'Why study Roseanne?' was not a difficult one to answer in the context of feminist and media studies: she is a powerful woman and an influential presence in the media. The next question to resolve was what exactly I meant by 'Roseanne', or how I chose to define her as an object of study. Because of my interest in the responses she elicited, I wished to examine her in the framework of cultural studies, which would allow me to define her as a text embedded in – producing and produced by – her culture. While I was not trained to pursue a sociological analysis of Roseanne's audiences, I did wish to consider the importance of popular responses in constructing her identity. Richard Dyer's work on stars (1979, 1986), in particular, provided the basis for my understanding of her as a star persona comprising her actual identity, her formal performances, and the popular discourse about her. I began to record not only her sitcom but her appearances on talk shows and other programs, and to accumulate references to her wherever I could find them – in the tabloids, women's magazines and so on. And I continued to talk about Roseanne in casual conversations with family, friends, neighbors, and strangers in checkout lines at grocery stores looking over the tabloids. Dyer's argument that stars become powerful because they mediate ideological contradictions provided an important foundation for my investigation of the ambivalence I found associated with Roseanne. Ultimately I came to understand her as an expression of ideological contradictions about gender that might be considered both as old as patriarchy and as new as the post-modern (but hardly 'post-feminist') age in which she gained national prominence.[7]

What kind of text is Roseanne?

Next, I wanted to study her significance not only in her contemporary cultural context but also in the context of form and its own traditions and histories. In other words, what *kind* of text was she? What set of semiotic and narrative conventions might help me understand her? As star of a situation comedy and as a comedian, she had clearly chosen a comedic voice with which to define herself. In keeping with the cultural orientation I wished to pursue, however, I wanted to avoid a primarily formalist conception of comedy, such as Northrop Frye's (1948, 1957, 1965), which I admire and which I used later in my study – in favor of one that was more grounded in material culture. By this time I had also encountered three articles that provided me with invaluable insights and bibliographies to guide my research. None of these was widely used in feminist media studies but each was a key factor in helping me explore the connections between comedy and feminist theory.

Mary Russo's (1986) 'Female Grotesques: Carnival and Theory' was the first and most important of these articles because more than anything I had as yet read, it made sense out of my responses to Roseanne and, I might add, to a group of classical Hollywood romantic comedies I had been watching and thinking about, as well. (I found the article by chance in *Feminist Studies/Critical Studies*, an anthology I had picked up while browsing in the university bookstore.) Russo begins with the suggestive observation that while women are constructed as spectacle in our culture, they are forbidden from 'making a spectacle' of themselves. She then raises a series of strikingly original questions about the uses women might make of that spectacle, especially through the mode of the grotesque. This perspective, which takes up a position Doane (1982, 1987, 1988–89) had tentatively considered but apparently abandoned, opened up a way out of the impasse Doane herself had acknowledged and explored. It also opened up for me a way of thinking about comedy and Roseanne.

Laura Mulvey's 'Changes: Thoughts on Myth, Narrative and Historical Experience' was the second of these articles. Here Mulvey moves past the determinism of her earlier and highly influential 'Visual Pleasure and Narrative Cinema', which repudiated the pleasures of narrative, to argue for the liberating potential of narratives and practices associated with 'the genres of laughter' – an argument I drew on as I later extended my own research to the Hollywood narrative film. Interestingly, while 'Visual Pleasure' continues to be widely anthologized, this more subtle essay is not, to my knowledge, as widely read. Finally social historian Natalie Zemon Davis, in 'Women on Top', defined a tradition and mapped out a method of study that bore directly on my analysis of Roseanne. Drawing on social practices, literature and popular forms of culture from early modern Europe, she identified the topos of the unruly woman and the structure of sexual inversion (or as I prefer, gender inversion). All three articles, but Davis's in particular, led me to the work of Russian linguist and semiotician Mikhail Bakhtin, which became the theoretical foundation for my understanding of comedy.

Bakhtin's work was first translated in the West in the 1960s but was slow to be absorbed into Western Marxism, and in literary and cultural studies his theories of language and semiotics (including such concepts as dialogism and intertextuality) have had a wider impact than his theories of the carnivalesque[8] (see Pearce, this volume, for example). What I found most valuable about Bakhtin was the case he makes for the social and political meanings of popular culture, especially those comedic practices and forms which, in *Rabelais and His World*, he associates with 'the carnivalesque'. According to Bakhtin's theory of signification, all signs are dynamic, charged with social meaning and 'dialogic' struggle. They are also intertextual, bearing traces of earlier uses, earlier struggles, and they cannot be understood apart from these historical elements. And so Bakhtin allowed me to examine Roseanne's use of comic conventions diachronically, to locate her in the *history* of a form, genre or topos as part of an ongoing working and re-working of comedic conventions that continue in Roseanne's television sitcom, her standup routine, and the very persona she has constructed. More specifically, Bakhtin's application of this theory to the aesthetics and semiotics of the *grotesque* enabled me to read that persona – her fatness, her style of speech, her body language, her vulgarity and 'offensiveness' – not as casual or unmotivated but as full of social meaning deriving from the formal tradition of the grotesque.

There are limits to and problems with this theoretical framework, of course, beginning with Bakhtin's tendency to romanticize 'the people'. However, he provided a counter to deterministic readings of popular culture common among critics influenced by the Frankfurt School, who have tended to see popular culture primarily as an instrument of oppression in capitalist society. For these critics – often suspicious of popular pleasures – comedy in particular has seemed to hold little interest or value.[9] Bakhtin also provided a basis to counter the determinism that troubled me about certain strains of feminist film and TV theory. His vision seemed more in tune with the excesses of Roseanne and the challenges she appeared to mount to these theories, suggested in fact by her own allusion to herself in her autobiography as 'Rabelaisian'.

One of the most serious problems I encountered in my research was the objection raised about Bakhtin's work (and my own) concerning the relation between earlier historical periods and our own. Much contemporary theory has rightly warned of the dangers of totalizing thinking, or of making facile connections among widely differing cultures and historical periods. This kind of thinking has too often reinforced the authority of a single, universal subject. However, I believed it was also misguided to avoid seeking continuities where they might exist between our historical period and those distant from us, or to accept too uncritically a critique that sees 'fragmentation', or the fragmentation of contemporary culture, as necessarily liberating. As I had learned earlier, from the work of Northrop Frye, comedy is among the most highly conventionalized of forms, with character types, plots, and gags that have remained remarkably unchanged over centuries. Bakhtin's perspective enabled me to see those conventions – reworked in and by Roseanne – not merely as literary tropes but as signs bearing the traces of social struggles.

For Bakhtin, of course, these struggles primarily concern class, but it was not difficult to extend that analysis – following Davis – to gender, and to see Roseanne's use of comedic conventions in the context of women's ongoing struggles against their oppressions. Davis provided me with an inventory of examples and a basis for gathering more from literary studies. As I accumulated these through reading and conversations with faculty, other students and friends, I developed a richer understanding of the semiotics of unruliness, drawing on theories from anthropology and sociology. Victor Turner's notion of liminality enabled me to place Bakhtin's analysis of carnival, based on studies of medieval and early modern culture, into capitalist society and contemporary media. With Peter Stallybrass and Allon White's (1986) study of the pig, I was able to show connections between Roseanne and Miss Piggy, another contemporary figure of female excess. Mary Douglas's (1988) work on marginality and dirt provided a theory to explain the ambivalence Roseanne elicited: Roseanne's 'grotesqueness' locates her near our culture's margins, giving her a source of power to destabilize conceptual and social frameworks.

Two other aspects of Roseanne demanded special attention: her fatness and her anger. In *Literary Fat Ladies*, Renaissance literary critic Patricia Parker (1987) provided me with wide-ranging examples of female fatness from literature and a provocative explanation for them, while Nancy Henley's (1977) *Body Politics* enabled me to understand in explicitly feminist terms what Bakhtin had identified as the 'grotesque' body. Feminist sociologists Marcia Millman (1980) and Susie Orbach (1982) gave me an analysis of female fatness rooted specifically in US culture since the 1960s and tied to the coincidence of the women's movement and the rise of anorexia among young women.

The anger I found crucial to Roseanne's appeal brought me back to Freud, despite my reservations about the extent to which psychoanalysis had been absorbed into feminist film theory. My use of Freud, like that of Bakhtin, typifies, I believe, a common feminist strategy in regard to the work of male theorists who have provided explanatory models that are powerful in many ways but that fall short in terms of gender: I took what was relevant to my own interests but did not feel obliged to accept his entire theoretical apparatus. Freud's study of the relation between laughter and aggression was extremely helpful to me in explaining the connections between joke-making and aggression, the misogyny evident in much comedy, and the cultural prejudice against women making jokes. Where I departed from him was in the limited role he assigned to women as passive object of the jokes. In effect, Roseanne both confirmed his theory but also extended it. The cultural resistance to her could be explained by the fact that she usurped the male prerogative of making jokes and expressing aggression. Yet she also demonstrated that women in contemporary popular culture can indeed become active *subjects* of joke-making.

Into narrative

Roseanne's freedom to construct her unruly persona arose in part from the fact that by working in standup comedy and the TV sitcom, she had managed to avoid the restrictions that more conventional *narrative* forms, like the Hollywood film, impose on representations of femininity. And yet I was also curious about what happened when narratives were built around the figure of the unruly woman. I wondered how the structure of gender inversion I had observed in Roseanne might enter into – or illuminate – narratives, especially comedic narratives. I felt it was important to pursue this because of the powerful and enduring appeal of narrative.[10] I also knew that a large body of films – the screwball or romantic comedies of the 1930s and 1940s – remained largely unstudied by feminists, despite the prominence of strong female roles and charismatic actresses in them. And so I decided to integrate my research on Roseanne with a study of film comedy; I hoped to link the distinctive media of television and film (and, in passing, some others as well) by means of a 'topos' that crossed both, the figure of the unruly woman. I eventually organized my book by first establishing that topos primarily through a semiotic study of the television figure of Roseanne, then moving toward an historical study of the relation between that topos and the narrative film genre of romantic comedy.

In researching this second part of my project, I attempted again to work synchronically and diachronically, focusing now on a *genre* rather than a collection of signifiers or 'tropes of unruliness'. Here I faced the problem of limiting the scope of my research. After noting briefly the structural similarities between the romantic comedy in Hollywood and its dramatic antecedents, I began to study films from romantic film comedy's 'Golden Age' during the 1930s and 1940s, noting how each depended on inversions of power according to gender and how the strength of this pattern declined in films after the Second World War.

What I eventually wrote was a kind of genre history – or history of the romantic comedy of gender inversion – based on a series of close readings of about ten films and briefer readings of others. I did not wish to attempt an exhaustive survey because I did not want to sacrifice the kind of close readings I felt were necessary to enable readers to see these familiar films in a new light. I also did not want to make claims I could not support about *all* romantic comedy. So I confined my study to the evolution of a structure evident in a limited historical period and a limited number of films. Several factors influenced my choice of films. They were generally known well by film scholars and readily available for teaching and study on videotape. They also raised the issue of gender inversion in provocative ways. I argued that the changes I was tracking were influenced by factors from social and industrial history – post-war paranoia, for example, and later the post-1960s threats to the authority of white males – but I dealt with those factors only briefly because they were generally not in dispute. Although I had originally planned to end this survey with what I saw as the end of the comedy of gender inversion in the 1950s, I was urged to bring my study to the present by the university press that subsequently published it.[11] This advice pushed me to think about my claims more deeply and to interweave my arguments about film with what I wanted to say about TV more closely.

Earlier in this essay I mentioned how feminist film theory had not sufficiently considered the impact of the genres or kinds of texts that had shaped it. There were important texts that I too decided not to study, and those omissions surely influenced my findings as well. Originally I had planned to write about independently produced feminist film and video, where much of the most outrageous feminist work in comedy can be found. With low production expenses and few sponsors or large audiences to please, these productions offer rich opportunities for experimenting with excess, taboo and transgression and for the kinds of comedy that could not find their way into a primetime sitcom or nationally distributed film. Most important, here is where the voices of women excluded from mainstream media – lesbians, women of color, mestizas, old women – can be heard.

Yet I decided to limit my study to mainstream US media, with the single exception of the Dutch film *A Question of Silence*, which is well known among feminist film scholars and which contains one of the most arresting instances of women's laughter on film or TV. One reason was purely pragmatic. I live in Oregon, a great distance from the few US cities (Chicago, New York City, Los Angeles) where alternative film and video are readily available. Because I was largely supporting my own research, I did not have the funds for extensive travel or film rentals. Another reason was my fundamental interest in *popular* culture, or media that reach wide audiences. At a certain point in her career, Roseanne had made the choice to aim for a mass television audience rather than to continue performing primarily before small audiences in off-beat comedy clubs. I was interested in the consequences of that choice and in determining what kinds of comedy or representations of female unruliness were possible in truly popular culture. The rest – the outrageous and often hilarious work in independent and experimental feminist film and video – remains for another study.

To the source

One product of my non-linear career path was a period of several years during which I worked as a newspaper reporter and editor, and I incorporated this experience into my scholarship by inter-viewing the primary subject of my research. In many cases, film and TV scholars have a unique opportunity to go 'straight to the source' of their studies, and yet do not avail themselves of that opportunity as often as they might. One reason may be the difficulty in gaining access to celebrities and other people who work in media industries. Another may be that we simply don't think of it. In academic fields related to the humanities, the kind of knowledge acquired through interviews and first-hand observation is often not as highly valued as that acquired through more standard academic means, by way of libraries, archives and so on. Knowlege gained from interviews may be considered im-pressionistic, 'journalistic', perhaps lacking in theoretical rigor – some of the same objections that have been leveled at ethno-graphic audience studies. Such knowledge is also subject to con-cerns about the interviewer's influence in shaping interview outcomes and about how the comments of a performer, producer or a media consumer are themselves in need of interpretation.

Nonetheless, I believed an interview with Roseanne would help satisfy my own curiosity about her as well as enriching my research. I spent close to a year telephoning, writing and faxing her TV network, production company, publicists, agents, and others associated with her, identifying myself and requesting a brief interview. I encountered friendliness and mild interest but no results until, in the spring of 1991, I posed my request in terms not of what I had to gain from her but of what I had to offer: a chance for exposure in a different realm from the popular, an opportunity to influence how she might be understood by people studying and teaching media in universities. By this point, I was communicating with her personal assistant. I had already accompanied many of my requests with copies of the article I had published on Roseanne, and when that article finally found its way to her and she read it, she agreed to speak with me. (To my frequent enquiries about material I had sent addressed to Roseanne, I was usually told that it was probably buried some-where among the thousands of pieces of mail she regularly received.) Initially Roseanne invited me to conduct the interview in her home, but then decided on a telephone interview because of last minute preparations for her second wedding ceremony with Tom Arnold, which was only days away. Her assistant set up the time.

I prepared for the interview by mapping out questions or areas I wished to cover, although I did not necessarily intend to use these questions when I actually spoke with her. From my news-paper experience, I had learned that I got more interesting results from listening attentively than from attempting to move through a series of prepared questions. Next I reduced this material into a short list of brief topics, some straightforward and others more open-ended, potentially leading to more complex and difficult material. These topics included her favorite and least favorite episodes of her show; the new ground she was covering in stand-up comedy; her reflections on the Star Spangled Banner con-troversy that had happened a year earlier;[12] how she saw her place in media history and who had most influenced her; how she saw her impact on the culture – what it was and what she would like it to be; other people she'd recommend that I'd speak with. I then sent this list to Roseanne, so that she would have an idea of the kind of information I was interested in and the interview could move as comfortably and efficiently as possible. I had hoped, I told her, that I would need no more than fifteen minutes. The actual interview lasted close to fifty minutes. I let her know from the outset (as I was required to by law) that I was taping the phone conversation and got her consent to do so. (Later, I had the tape transcribed.) Before the call came, I put my telephone line through a tape recorder with an inexpensive jack designed for that purpose. During the interview, I kept my notes before me to jog my memory if the conversation lagged and to remind myself to request her permission to use the material from the interview in my book.

My biggest surprise was the gap I found between Roseanne's public persona and the one she presented to me. I had expected to interview the wise-cracking, smart-mouthed jokester I had been studying with such interest for the past three years. The woman I spoke with was serious, reflective, articulate about her project and respectful of my own. This gap forced me to examine why I was so surprised. When she had said in magazine interviews and elsewhere that her 'act' is 'who she is', had I too readily assumed that there was not another side, or sides, to her as well? More disturbingly, had I assumed that the lack of formal education that was part of Roseanne's working-class act meant that she – as performer or character – might not also be sophisticated about her artistic goals? Or well-informed and knowledgeable about feminist theory? When I asked her how she wished her work to be understood, she answered it was not her responsibility as an artist to explain what she does. In effect, she was telling me that that was *my* job. But she also told me how some people see her as crude and others as spiritual, providing me with an example in her own words of that very ambivalence that had first drawn me to her.

Most of the material from the interview found its way into my book, in some cases to clarify factual errors but mostly to give substance and weight to the argument I was building about her. While my argument did not depend on her *knowingly* manipulating comic conventions toward a feminist end, it was supported, I believe, by fact that she did. Most of all, I valued the chance to let her speak for herself in my book, with the immediacy and flavor of her own language. My only major disappointment with the experience was my difficulty in sustaining an ongoing professional connection with her, primarily, I believe, because of the high rate of turnover in her staff.

Finally, the interview left me with only one major concern: the greater warmth I felt toward Roseanne as a subject. It was hard to avoid feeling somewhat starstruck after the interview, especially since she had shown such graciousness and interest in my own work. I worried about the effect my increased enthusiasm for her as a fan would have on my supposed disinterest as a scholar. Yet more important, the experience served as a reminder of the fact that *no* research is disinterested, and that scholars as well as journalists need to be vigilant about their responsibilities, whenever they write, whatever or whoever their subject.

Notes

With thanks to Beverley Skeggs for her skillful editing and overall support.

1 For most of its six-year run, it has remained at or near the top of the ratings. Its chief rival was *The Cosby Show*, and often the two alternated first and second spots. By the fifth and sixth seasons, newer shows began to displace it on occasion as number one, but it has remained securely near the top in both primetime and syndication.

2 For the remainder of this paper, I will be using 'Roseanne' to refer to the star persona of Roseanne Arnold, who was known as Roseanne Barr until 1991 when she married Tom Arnold and became Roseanne Arnold. In the summer of 1994, she initiated divorce proceedings against Tom Arnold and changed her name simply to Roseanne.

3 I also had the good fortune of finding mentors in graduate school who encouraged this project from the outset. When I first spoke with Ellen Seiter about my interests in film and television comedy, she urged me to keep watching the new sitcom *Roseanne*, even though at that point the show's future was still uncertain. When I learned that Julia Lesage shared my response to the scene of women's laughter in Marleen Gorris's film *A Question of Silence*, I was encouraged to pursue my interests in a feminist study of comedy. Bill Cadbury directed me to an abundance of classical film comedies.

4 See Sandy Flitterman-Lewis (1992) on the relation between television studies and psychoanalysis. Her essay includes an extensive bibliography.

5 There have always been exceptions, of course, most notably Patricia Mellencamp (1986) who has been producing psychoanalytic readings of film and television comedy (and the culture at large) since the early 1980s.

6 The book's publisher is the University of Texas Press. As I presented my research at conferences on film and TV (the Society for Cinema Studies, Console-ing Passions), I also discovered that I was in good company and that other feminist scholars – most of them early in their careers – were also turning toward comedy. See, for example, Shari Roberts (1993), Pamela Robertson (1993), and Candice Mirza (1990).

7 The term 'post-feminist' has circulated in the 1990s media to describe an apparent completion of the feminist project and fruition of its goals. If the term bore a closer relation to reality, its use would probably not elicit the frustrated responses from feminists it so often has.

8 Initially, in literary studies, Bakhtin's (1984) theories of the carnivalesque were most influential among scholars interested in medieval and early modern Europe. In film studies, Robert Stam (1987, 1989) was the first to make extended use of these ideas. Earlier, Horace Newcomb (1984) applied the concept of dialogism to television.

9 I found *Rabelais and His World* to be a wonderful 'read' which often made me laugh out loud, and I have since wondered about the meaning and value of humor in oppositional intellectual work.

10 Mulvey was not alone among feminist scholars who, after an earlier critique of narrative, were now acknowledging the inevitability of its appeal and the need to work around and within it. These include Teresa de Lauretis and Susan Suleiman.

11 Thomas Schatz, editor of the University of Texas Press Film Series, provided that sage advice and more. Patricia Erens also gave many helpful suggestions on revising the manuscript for publication.

12 This episode generated the most intense and hostile storm of publicity in Roseanne's career. In July 1990, Roseanne was invited to sing the national anthem before an audience of 30,000 on Working Women's Night at a baseball game between the San Diego Padres and the Cincinnati Reds. She sang with a screeching voice and then, parodying the gestures of baseball players, spit on the ground and grabbed her crotch. Before leaving the field, she made an obscene gesture to the audience, many of whom were booing

loudly. While many celebrities have been criticized for performances of the national anthem deemed 'disrespectful', none to my knowledge has elicited such outrage. Some people spoke up in her defence, seeing her performance as consistent with her identity as a comedian rather than a singer. But more typically, commentators – including President George Bush – reacted with indignation and disgust. Major newspapers printed the story on Page One, sponsors threatened to withdraw from her show, and she received threats on her life. She was seriously shaken by the ordeal, explaining that she sang as she did because of feedback from the sound system and that the baseball players had suggested the parody.

Bibliography

Bakhtin, M. (1984), *Rabelais and His World*, trans. H. Iswolsky, Bloomington, Indiana University Press.

Bergstrom, J. and M. A. Doane (1989), The Female Spectator: Contexts and Directions, in J. Bergstrom and M. A. Doane (eds), *The Spectatrix*, special issue of *Camera Obscura*, 20–1, 5–27.

Davis, N. Z. (1975), Women on Top, *Society and Culture in Early Modern France*, Stanford, Stanford University Press, 124–51.

de Lauretis, T. (1987), Strategies of Coherence: Narrative Cinema, Feminist Poetics, and Yvonne Rainer, in de Lauretis (ed.), *Technologies of Gender*, Bloomington, Indiana University Press.

Doane, M. A. (1982), Film and Masquerade: Theorising the Female Spectator, *Screen*, 23:3–4, 74–88.

Doane, M. A. (1987), *The Desire to Desire: The Woman's Film of the 1940s*, Bloomington, Indiana University Press.

Doane, M. A. (1988–89), Masquerade Reconsidered, *Discourse*, 11:1, 42–54.

Douglas, M. (1975), *Implicit Meanings: Essays in Anthropology*, Boston, Routledge & Kegan Paul.

Douglas, M. (1988), *Purity and Danger: An Analysis of the Concepts of Pollution and Taboo*, New York, Ark Paperbacks.

Dyer, R. (1979), *Stars*, London, British Film Institute.

Dyer, R. (1986), *Heavenly Bodies: Film Stars and Society*, New York, St Martin's Press.

Flitterman-Lewis, S. (1992), Psychoanalysis, Film, and Television, in R. C. Allen (ed.), *Channels of Discourse*, Chapel Hill, University of North Carolina Press, 203–46.

Freud, S. (1960), *Jokes and Their Relation to the Unconscious*, trans. J. Strachey, New York, W. W. Norton.

Frye, N. (1948), The Argument of Comedy, in D. A. Robertson, Jr (ed.), *English Institute Essays, 1948*, New York, Columbia University Press, 58–74.

Frye, N. (1957), *Anatomy of Criticism: Four Essays*, Princeton, Princeton University Press.

Frye, N. (1965), *A Natural Perspective: The Development of Shakespearean Comedy and Romance*, New York, Harcourt, Brace and World.

Henley, N. M. (1977), *Body Politics: Power, Sex and Non-Verbal Communication*, Englewood Cliffs, New Jersey, Prentice-Hall.

Mellencamp, P. (1983), Jokes and Their Relation to the Marx Brothers, in S. Heath and P. Mellencamp (eds), *Cinema and Language*, Frederick, Maryland, University Publications of America, 63–78.

Mellencamp, P. (1986), Situation Comedy, Feminism and Freud, in T. Modleski (ed.), *Studies in Entertainment*, Bloomington, Indiana University Press, 80–95.

Mellencamp, P. (1992), *High Anxiety: Catastrophe, Scandal, Age & Comedy*, Bloomington, Indiana University Press.

Millman, M. (1980), *Such a Pretty Face: Being Fat in America*, New York, W. W. Norton.

Mirza, C. (1990), The Collective Spirit of Revolt: An Historical Reading of Holiday, *Wide Angle*, 12:3, 98–116.

Modleski, T. (1982), *Loving with a Vengeance: Mass Produced Fantasies for Women*, New York and London, Methuen.

Mulvey, L. (1975, 1989), Visual Pleasure and Narrative Cinema, in her *Visual and Other Pleasures*, Bloomington, Indiana University Press, 14–26, originally published in *Screen*, 16, 6–18.

Mulvey, L. (1985, 1989), Changes: Thoughts on Myth, Narrative and Historical Experience, in her *Visual and Other Pleasures*, Bloomington, Indiana University Press, 159–76, originally published in *Discourse*, 7, 6–18.

Newcomb, H. M. (1984), On the Dialogic Aspects of Mass Communication, *Critical Studies of Mass Communication*, 1, 34–50.

Orbach, S. (1982), *Fat is a Feminist Issue 2*, London, Arrow Books.

Orbach, S. (1986), *Hunger Strike: The Anoretic's Struggle as a Metaphor for Our Age*, New York, Norton.

Parker, P. (1987), *Literary Fat Ladies: Rhetoric, Gender, Property*, New York, Methuen.

Roberts, S. (1993), 'The Lady in the Tutti-Frutti Hat': Carmen Miranda, a Spectacle of Ethnicity, *Cinema Journal*, 32:3, 3–23.

Robertson, P. (1993), 'The Kinda Comedy That Imitates Me': Mae West's Identification With the Feminist Camp, *Cinema Journal*, 32:2, 57–72.

Rowe, K. K. (1990), Roseanne: Unruly Woman as Domestic Goddess, *Screen*, 31:4, 408–19.

Rowe, K. K. (1995), *The Unruly Woman: Gender and the Genres of Laughter*, Austin, University of Texas Press.

Russo, M. (1986), Female Grotesques: Carnival and Theory, in Teresa de Lauretis (ed.), *Feminist Studies/Critical Studies*, Bloomington, Indiana University Press, 213–29.

Stam, R. (1987), Bakhtin, Eroticism and Cinema, *CineAction!*, 9, 13–20.

Stam, R. (1989), *Subversive Pleasures*, Baltimore: Johns Hopkins University Press.

Stallybrass, P. and A. White (1986), *The Politics and Poetics of Transgression*, Ithaca, Cornell University Press.

Suleiman, S. R. (1990), *Subversive Intent: Gender, Politics, and the Avant-Garde*, Cambridge, Mass., Harvard University Press.

3

Common knowledge: the 'nature' of historical evidence

JANET THUMIM

Questions

The term 'common knowledge' implies things so well known that they don't need to be spoken, or written, about, yet the assertion that knowledge is common frequently conceals a claim for the dominance of one set of interests over others. One of the more important insights of the women's movement in the 1970s and 1980s, that 'the personal is political' exercised me particularly and I tried, in the juggling act familiar to so many women of my generation, to keep it in mind as I negotiated the various demands of my students, my colleagues, my children and my friends and in the way I understood and interpreted the material of art history and film history which constituted my academic subject matter. The fragmentation of daily experience – nappies and shopping, lectures, tutorials, course planning and assessment, family dinners and the procession of private and public rituals which make up 'social life' – worked directly against what I understood to be the unifying trajectory of the women's movement injunction and led me, gradually, to reconsider the 'facts' of history. I began to wonder, as others did, why some facts rather than others, why some expressive forms, were deemed to be serious and therefore worthy of study while others were not, and where my own life experiences might fit into the cultural history of the modern period which I explored with my students. The teaching of cultural history – in particular the visual histories of art and of film – tended to focus on the exceptional, the 'masterpiece', the 'auteur', and on the interpretation of artist's intentions, albeit with reference to the exigencies of their historical context, but there was a lack of consideration given to what I came to consider as the 'use-value' of the objects of study to successive generations of consumers. The question of use-value encouraged a gradual emphasis, in my teaching, on the forms of culture explicitly addressed to the mass scale audiences of the twentieth century where audience activity was, arguably, harder to discount, and, logically, to a focus on film and, more recently, television.

It began to be clear to me that there is nothing 'natural' about historical evidence any more than there is anything 'common' about knowledge, rather both knowledge and evidence are the stuff through which hegemonic struggles are conducted.[1] This led to two profoundly useful insights which, as this chapter will show, were fundamental to the methodologies I developed in my doctoral thesis, a version of which was published as *Celluloid Sisters* (1992). First, that controversies in the discussion of cultural products – paintings, films, television programmes – are indicative of disagreement over their worth or their meaning, usually both, hence suggest struggle over the issues raised in or by the work in question. Second, and conversely, that lack of controversy is indicative of a general acceptance of proportions made in, or about, the work, thus of a widely held assumption that the propositions are 'true', that they are 'common knowledge' and *therefore* require no discussion.

These insights, combined with my attempts to live out the women's movement proposition that the personal is political led me not only to begin to redefine, to broaden, the scope of what I took to be politics but also to query the ideological work performed by widely held social assumptions which didn't tally with my personal experience. I began to realise that the rhetoric of equality of opportunity, particularly in education, which had informed my own education during the 1950s and 1960s, combined with the rhetoric of individual freedom and the valorisation of the authentic characteristic of the 1960s – the famously 'permissive' decade – had in fact produced permissions with very different consequences for women than for men. In the 1970s I found myself the major wage earner of the family, the mother of two small children, and found also that I still carried the major share of the domestic burden – once the novelties of the first baby, the first steps, the first words, had worn off. Two very different events combined to bring these disjunctions into sharp focus, and to provoke the work which, eventually, enabled me to articulate, and therefore to begin to understand not only the social dynamics which produced the disjunction but also, much more importantly, my own collusion in what had seemed an inexorable, inevitable, 'natural' path – the path of common knowledge.

In 1980 I saw the film *Rosie the Riveter* (1980) which dealt with the American State's propagandist soliciting of women to join the workforce during the Second World War and their re-positioning within the domestic sphere and consequent barring from 'men's jobs' in the immediate post-war period and I knew, from my teaching about documentary cinema in Britain in the 1930s and 1940s, that a similar pattern occurred in this country. The second event was the sudden and unexpected shattering of my marriage, which coincided with the birth of our third child and left me, once the dust had begun to settle a few years later, with seemingly endless reserves of anger to fuel my search, if not for answers, at least for some understanding of the cultural determinants which lead so many women into what seems a cruel impasse. The immediate question which formed itself from these disparate events, one cultural, one personal, both political, was how did we women allow ourselves to be re-placed in the devalued domestic sphere after our equality of citizenship, rights and duties had been so publicly celebrated during the war period? How had we allowed such disgraceful inequities in the social balance of gender power to become so entrenched in the mere twenty years after the end of the 'people's' war in 1945? And why is 'the domestic' devalued, anyway?

Many factors combine, it seems, to produce action – particularly sustained action such as that required for part-time graduate study combined with full-time wage earning and full-time parenting. In my case anger was certainly one such factor, but it was tempered by economic necessity – my career path took on a whole new significance once I realised my income must provide indefinitely for four – and above all it was channelled by curiosity. I wanted to understand what part cultural artefacts, popular culture, mass entertainment forms – call them what you will – going to the movies, perhaps, played in personal identity formation, in the establishment and maintenance of 'common knowledge', of the 'natural' in history, above all what part popular culture plays in securing the collusion of disadvantaged groups in their subjection. Because of *Rosie the Riveter*, because of my age (I was born just after the war, at the very beginning of the peace in late 1945), because of my already existing scholarly interest in popular cinema, and because of a pragmatic recognition that I could lighten my load somewhat if my graduate study could feed into my teaching, I decided to explore the question of the representation of women in films enjoying the widest circulation in British society during the immediate post-war period, a period I conceived of initially as 1946–1957.

Like all questions, this one instantly suggests a number of more or less contentious, or problematic issues, and I want to take the opportunity afforded by this book to suggest what these initially seemed to me to be, how they became refined and focused during the course of the work, and how the context of my studies, outlined above, inflected my particular development of the theoretical models which seemed to have some relevance to my questions. My interest in the expectations of and about women in society required attention to popular filmic representations of women, but also, through consideration of women's spectatorial activity, to the readings made by women in the film audiences. Two questions arise here: one concerns the business of representation itself, its forms and conventions and the ways in which these had already 'educated' the reader to have certain competencies with respect to the text; the other concerns the notion of the popular, particularly what criteria might legitimately be employed to define some films rather than others as belonging to 'popular cinema'. In considering representations of women I might have attended to the production histories of the films selected for analysis but, since my primary interest was in the consequences of the cinematic experience I decided to take the film as an already existent thing-in-the-world and to concentrate on the reading strategies employed in its interpretation. Similarly, there are many different and sometimes even contradictory ways of apprehending 'the popular' but, because of my concern with the establishment and maintenance of what I came later to understand as the hegemonic significance of cinema during this period, I opted for mass circulation and took this to be expressed in the terms of box office success. In short, I defined the popular in quantitative terms, taking the popular object to be one that is well-liked by the largest number of people. A further question arises concerning the choice of period for analysis. I was of course narcissistically absorbed by my own formative years, by the social climate in which my mother raised her children, and by the apparent volte-face in 'the woman's place' following the Second World War. As a film historian I was also aware that the immediate post-war period was characterised by a huge popular audience for the cinema which began a rapid decline, in the mid-1950s, from which it has never recovered. So, while I hope that the product of my researches has some relevance to the women of the 1990s and beyond because of the cultural mechanisms I uncovered, I chose to conduct my research apropos the post-war period because of its particular relevance to my personal trajectory and because in this period the cinema audience unarguably qualified for the term 'mass'.

The terms I have outlined so far are, broadly, the same as those in which I originally conceived my project. But the practical steps which followed were not so clear. Had I had any idea of the scope of my undertaking I probably would not have ventured on it at all. I assumed, in blithe ignorance, for example, that it would be a simple matter to know which was the top box office hit in each of the post-war years, that these films would be easily available for my perusal, and that any ancillary information I might subsequently require would be similarly available. The fact that none of these assumptions held led me, in a kind of stubborn refusal to abandon my questions which became all the more alluring as I recognised their difficulty, into a painstaking and laborious, though never tedious, process of historical detection. In the course of this, the preliminary part of the work in which I established a sample of films on which to perform the analytic task I had originally envisaged, I learned the truth of Carr's (1961) dictum that historians find the facts they are looking for. Historical evidence, like the representation of women in film, is subject to the dominant discourses of the day and history itself, far from being a procession of verifiable though sometimes forgotten narratives, is in fact in itself a trace of those discourses.

I had some sense that this would be the case, forewarned both by my own teaching and by Carr's essays, and was consequently scrupulous in the kinds of material I drew on both in arriving at definitions of the popular, and in the second part of my task, analysing the representations in their contemporary discursive fields. I tried, particularly, to avoid the dangers inherent in pollution by hindsight, dangers to which oral history in its reliance on individual memory is, I think, particularly susceptible.[2] For in my analyses of filmic representations of women, what I came to term the 'construction of the feminine', I was interested not only in the films themselves, their narratives, the trajectories of their heroines, the details of *mise-en-scène*, lighting, camera angles and so forth in producing the visual images constituting the representations, but also in the discursive context through which these representations were consumed. Here were many pitfalls of which 'pollution by hindsight' was certainly one.

In order to arrive at a sample of the films seen by the majority of the audience at any particular historical moment I needed to look to the data collected at the time rather than subsequently, and, similarly, in order to understand the terms in which such images were discussed as they appeared I needed to confine my attention to material – largely ephemeral – published at the time. Memoirs, summaries, critical appraisals and so forth written later already involved exactly the kind of reconstruction from which I aimed to 'protect' my research – though it is clearly the case that this was an ideal in many ways impossible to achieve since the 'provenance' of my questions – my personal history – would nuance my readings of both text and context in specific and idiosyncratic ways. It seemed to me, however, that the more systematic my sampling method, the more I would be able to distance myself from any excessively partisan slant to the sample. As I began to assemble my lists of films achieving the biggest success at their contemporary box office, as I collected names of the most popular stars of the day, it became clear that there were considerable differences between my 'data' and the film titles and star names enshrined in film histories. To summarise – what I aimed to do, by consulting material contemporary to the film, both to determine the popular and to gather traces of its original discursive contexts, was to avoid the canon established by successive generations of film historians and critics[3] of both sexes and, in doing this, I became aware of the gender, class and race interests at work in the establishment and maintenance of the canon and increasingly aware, too, of the canon's own function as part of the dominant discourse securing patriarchal hegemony. In order to challenge dominant discourse by showing how the filmic construction of the feminine has been (and, there-fore, how the cultural construction of the feminine certainly still is) subject to the hegemonic requirements of the patriarchal order in which we did, and do, live, I felt obliged to piece together my evidence from fragments of the ephemera of popular culture, reconstituting traces of the cinema experience of another time. But the trace alone isn't enough and to this I added, unashamedly, speculations about the reading process itself, derived from psychoanalytic and semiotic models currently in use, as well as interrogations of my own and other women's negotiations of the texts of popular culture with our lived experience to produce propositions which might account for the fact that huge numbers of women did, and do, gain pleasure from the consumption of material which systematically devalues the feminine. In this way I hoped to demonstrate one of the ways in which patriarchal hegemony has secured the collusion of its female subjects.

Research tasks

My original questions translated into three distinct practical tasks. First, by collecting various contemporary assessments of box office success, I defined and selected a sample of films for analysis. Second, I developed an analytic method which would allow detailed attention to all representations of women to be found in the sample films, would acknowledge the readerly activity of individual audience members, and which would also permit comparisons between different films made at the same time as well as between films made at different times. Third, I collected and devised a means of collating contemporary reviews from a variety of published sources in order to permit access to the discursive field within which the films and their fictional women were read by contemporary audiences.

The question of method in arriving at a sample was crucial if my conclusions were to be applicable to film culture as a whole. A quick glance at the index of various film dictionaries and encyclopaedias, for example, revealed an extremely partisan approach to the question of value and betrayed what for my purposes was an excessive dependence on canonical imperatives derived from an implicit high vs. low 'art' model. Bordwell *et al.* (1985), clearly improving on this in their *Classical Hollywood Cinema*, employed a random sampling method on a list of all extant Hollywood films (made before 1960) to yield a sample of 851 titles of which they studied one hundred in order to arrive at their invaluable definitions of Hollywood's film language.[4] But my own intentions were different since my interest was in what the mass-scale audiences chose from the titles available. An indicator of films' profitability was no help (even were such figures to be available which, because of the dynamics of the industry, they were not) since profitability includes production costs in its calculations, not to mention performance over time. I didn't want to know how much money individual titles had made, but which titles were seen by the most people on the films' first release. I wanted to take account, too, of the importance of individual actors, the stars, who were often the reason why one film was selected over another in making a choice about Saturday night's entertainment. After considering the various available monthly and annual assessments of popularity made by the national press, the film journals and trade papers, and the fan magazines, and considering, too, the differing interests which they served I selected three sources, using their most consistent and relevant data.[5] These were the British trade journal *Kinematograph Weekly*, serving British distributors and exhibitors, from which I took the annual 'Top Box Office Hits', 'Most Popular Star', and 'Best Individual Performance' lists; the American trade publication *Motion Picture Almanac*, serving American distributors by summarising the annual performance of American products in the international market, from which I took the 'Top Ten Pictures' and 'Top Ten Stars' listed in respect of the British market; and the fan magazine *Picturegoer* which published, following a poll of its readership, annual lists of the 'Top Ten Actors' and 'Top Ten Actresses'. I collated these eight listings for each year in the period 1945–1963,[6] producing tables which showed the number of mentions any title received, and a separate set showing mentions of stars.

Bearing in mind the fact that stars are often as big a draw as the films themselves, I devised a 'scoring' method which took account of stars' popularity (indicated by the number of mentions they had received) as well as that of individual films, and this yielded a set of figures which enabled me to assess the relative popularity of the twenty or so titles which appeared in my correlation for each year.[7] But instead of there being one clear 'hit' as I had originally supposed, I found that generally a group of five or six titles were markedly more popular than others, and also noted that, owing to the vagaries of release dates it generally made sense to consider two years together. My intention was to engage in detailed analyses of the hit films, looking, amongst other things, for changes in the typical representations of women over the period in question – 1945–1963.[8] Clearly it would not have been feasible to contemplate in-depth work on about a hundred films (five or six films a year for twenty years), and since pairs of years appeared to yield more reliable lists of the most popular films, and I was interested in change, I opted for groups of six films taken from a two-year period at three 'moments' separated by about ten years – 1945–1946, 1955–1956 and 1963–1965.[9] This plan gave me a choice of about twelve titles from which to select six for my study, and this selection was governed by availability, generic diversity, and a mix of British and American titles reflecting that available to British cinema audiences.[10]

The next task was the analysis of the films. Here I required a method which would allow attention to the particular narrative development, genre and style of the discrete film, as well as focusing attention on the presentation, treatment and narrative experience of female characters. The former was a relatively straightforward, if time-consuming task, the latter needed, for my purposes in connection with the female audience members, to take particular account of filmic 'positioning' of the audience *vis-à-vis* the female characters. In order to develop my methods I took another set of six films[11] and analysed them experimentally[12] until I devised a schema which satisfied my requirements, and then applied the procedures to each set of six films in my main sample. Thus the first phase of the analysis yielded information about the themes, representations and presence of women in six of the most popular box office films of one two-year 'moment', while the second phase allowed comparisons between the three 'moments', enabling me to recognise and consider the significance of both change and lack of change in themes and representations over the period, and to begin speculations about the relation between my observations and other relevant contextual material. I found that all the characters, male and female, could be assigned to one of four groups according to the twin criteria of *narrative function* and *audience access to the character's point of view*. Accordingly, for each film I performed the following tasks: I wrote a long synopsis outlining the story, the particular ways in which this appeared to be visually ordered, the dominant themes and, where appropriate, the effect of genre: these synopses varied between *c.* 1000 and *c.* 5000 words, tending to get longer with subsequent films as I became more alert to textual nuances. I listed all characters appearing on screen, both male and female, noting their order of appearance. Then I assigned all the characters to one of the four groups, and once I had completed this work for each set of six films I tabulated them according to character

Character groups: female **F** in six top box office films, UK 1955/56 (numbers in brackets indicate order of appearance)

	The Dam Busters (UK 55)	Doctor at Sea (UK 55)	East of Eden (US 55)	Rebel Without a Cause (US 56)	Reach for the Sky (UK 56)	The Searchers (US 56)
Central	**F** = 0 **M** = 2	**F** = 0 **M** = 1	**F** = 0 **M** = 1	**F** = 0 **M** = 1	**F** = 0 **M** = 1	**F** = 0 **M** = 1
Major	**F** = 0 **M** = 0	**F** = 0 **M** = 0	Kate (2) **F** = 2 Abra (7) **M** = 2	Judy (2) **F** = 1 **M** = 1	Thelma Edwards (13) **F** = 1 **M** = 0	Debbie Edwards (3) Laurie Jorgensen (6) **F** = 2 **M** = 1
Minor	Barnes Wallace's wife (2) **F** = 1 **M** = 6	Wendy Thomas (1) Miss Mallett (8) Helene Colbert (9) **F** = 3 **M** = 4	Sally (4) Anna, maid at Kate's place (6) **F** = 2 **M** = 4	Plato's nanny (5) Jim's mother (6) Jim's grandmother (7) Judy's mother (14) **F** = 4 **M** = 6	Sally (2) Nursing sister (5) Nurse Brace (10) Bader's secretary (16) French resistance supporter (23) **F** = 5 **M** = 12	Martha Edwards (1) Lucy Edwards (2) Mrs Jorgensen (5) Look/wild goose/Mrs Panley (8) **F** = 4 **M** = 11
'Figures'	B. W. daughters[2] (1) F in Whitehall (3) Researcher at testing tank (4) Chorus line at London show (5) Singer at London show (6) F in poultry farmer's cottage (7) Waitress (coffee) in mess (8) Waitress (badon + eggs) (9) WAF officer serving coffee in London operations (10) Waitress (coffee) in mess after raid (11) **F** = 10 **M** = 28	Wendy's mother (2) Rosie Jenkins, ship's cook's wife (not seen) (3) F in crowd at Bellos Docks (4) F in red dress aboard ship at Bellos (5) F on ship, Bellos, (6) Rosita (7) Guests at nightclub, Bellos (10) Nightclub pianist (11) Diner in nightclub (12) F at bar in nightclub (13) F in Bellos brothel/'dive' (14) F in blue dress in 'dive' (15) 1st F with 3rd officer trail at ship's dance (16) 2nd F with trail at dance (17) Dancing couples (18) **F** = 15 **M** = 35	F + girl, outskirts Monterey (1) People in street, Monterey (3) 2 F watching Kate as she leaves Monterey Bank (5) Trask maid (8) F in bar at Kate's Place (9) F + girls at lettuce harvest (10) Mexican girl at harvest (11) Abra's dead mother (not seen) (13) Crowds at Salinas station (14) Crowd at war parade (15) F in black crossing street (16) Girl at bean field (17) Old F at fair (18) Crowds at fair (19) Bereaved F (20) Crowd at brawl (21) Mrs Albrecht (22) Nurse attending Adam (23) **F** = 19 **M** = 30	Girls at police station (1) Nurse at police station (3) F police officer (4) Plato's mother (not seen) (8) 2 children in street with Judy's brother (9) Girl in 'wheels' gang (10) Girls in street, going to school (11) Students at Dawson High School (12) Schoolteacher at observatory lecture (13) Bertha, maid at Judy's house (not seen) (15) Girls at chicken run (16) **F** = 11 **M** = 21	Spectators, Cranwell cricket (1) Couples, Kenley dance (3) Nurses with Bader stretcher (4) Nurse in surgeon's office (6) Operating theatre staff (7) Bader's mother (8) Bader post-op nurses (9) Ladies at tea rooms (12) Waitress, tea rooms (14) Couples, restaurant (15) People, air-raid shelter (17) F in mess bar (18) Guests at mess party (19) Staff in bomber command (20) Lucille, maid in P.O.W. hospital (21) Nurse in P.O.W. hospital (22) Ground watching as Germans capture Bader (24) London grounds at peace declaration (25) **F** = 19 **M** = 54	Mourners (4) Indian women (7) Deranged young **F** (10) Indian F captives (9) F companion to (10) (11) 2 girls in Fort chapel (12) Corpses at Fort (13) Carmen, Mexican bar (14) Mamacita, kitchen at Mexican bar (15) Scar's wives (16) Guests at Jorgensen wedding (17) **F** = 4 **M** = 16
Totals F/M	**F** = 11 **M** = 36	**F** = 18 **M** = 40	**F** = 23 **M** = 37	**F** = 16 **M** = 29	**F** = 25 **M** = 67	**F** = 17 **M** = 29

groups so that I could see at a glance how many of each group appeared in each film. For each of the female characters in groups 1 and 2, that is those characters with whom the audience is invited to empathise by such means as voice-over, flashback or fantasy showing the character's memories or desires, or simply close-ups in which the audience alone is privy to the character's reactions or emotions as revealed through his or her facial expression, and who are implicated in or affected by the narrative resolution of the film, I wrote an additional synopsis tracing the particular narrative of that character. By these means I was able to note the relative importance of male and female characters, the frequency of particular narrative events or devices in respect of female characters and, importantly, other details about the films' representations of women such as their age, appearance, occupation, the locations in which they are first seen, their narrative trajectories and their narrative resolutions.

When I came to the second phase of the analysis, the comparison between the three two-year 'moments' separated by a ten-year interval, I was able to tabulate the detail of female representations by character group and by three other factors which were *presentation*, *definition*, and *resolution*. *Presentation* entailed noting the location in which the character was first seen, whether or not she was performing an action (and if so, what action), whether or not she was speaking (and if so, about what), or whether she was first introduced off-screen, as it were, through an introduction by another character. *Definition* entailed the summary of all knowledge the audience received about the character during the course of the film and I summarised this as her age, class, race and nationality; her sexual status (virgin, bride, wife, mother, 'committed' or 'available') noting also whether the character moved, as many did, from one state to another during the course of the narrative; and her aims and/or occupation (if any). Finally in *resolution*, which by definition applied only to characters in groups 1 and 2, I noted what happened to the character 'in the end', and whether or not she had fulfilled her aims. This tabulation allowed me to note typical narrative resolutions and their relation to the characters' narrative experiences, to compare the narrative importance of female characters at different historical moments, and to assess the prevalence of some fictional situations and trajectories over others. This is an example of the kind of reading 'competence' so ubiquitous that we hardly acknowledge it as a skill at all yet, by the same means, other ubiquitous propositions are also made, such as those concerning the merits of one social practice in relation to another. Many such propositions contribute, I would argue, to the 'common' knowledge that I aimed to 'make strange' in order to be able to see what it is.

The third and final stage of my analytic procedures was the collection and collation of discursive materials. I collected reviews from a range of sources from specialised trade papers, through film journals and fan magazines to national press and women's magazines. Though the greater part of the material was British I did also look at some American and French publications in order to get a sense of the discursive 'climate' in a period where there was considerable traffic between these three countries both of films and of publications relating to the cinema. My intention here was, by surveying the language and content of reviews or related discussion of my sample films, to get some sense of what aspects of the films – their themes, their resolutions, their characterisations – were admired or thought contentious and, further, whether there was any unanimity on these points. Admiration, it seemed to me, signified agreement with the appropriateness of the issue in question and might be expressed through praise of a performance.[13] Conversely, denigration of performance frequently masked disapproval of a narrative trajectory, of the aims or experiences of a character.[14] Where there was widespread agreement among different sources regarding the critical assessments of film and performance I took the points in question to be the subject of widely held assumptions undisturbed by their filmic portrayal, but where I found radical disagreement it seemed to me that I had evidence of something which was currently under scrutiny, the subject of debate or unease, something in flux in society as a whole.

In this way I was able to move from the fine detail of particular films – even of scenes or images within one film – to speculation about the significance of such details to the audiences who found them pleasurable and therefore, I would argue, useful, secure in the knowledge that though I might simply have discovered what was obvious in the first place it *was*, nevertheless, a discovery because I had arrived there by a systematic process attending first to structure and only then to the qualitative and arguable material constituting the field of interpretation.

Thought

Now this account of my research procedures may give the impression that I knew what I was up to – but though hindsight enables the logical patterns of such work to be outlined clearly, in an orderly manner, so to speak, it certainly wasn't so clear during the processes themselves. I knew what my questions were, and at each stage was just about able to organise my data and procedures so that the next set of questions might be posed. It was never answers, really, that interested me so much as a better idea of the processes in play, the mechanisms which seemed to be operative in the hegemonic production of ideology. In forming the successive questions, then, which constituted the work, I was guided by a combination of insights and methodological suggestions from various sources and it is these which I want now to indicate. I read widely and, as the following may suggest, eclectically, during the long and often relatively mechanical processes outlined above, and I also wrote – summaries of my procedures, detailed discussion of propositions which I needed to test, as it were – much of this writing being, precisely, exploratory, didn't find its way into my thesis but was nevertheless invaluable for its part in enabling the development of my ideas. I didn't always know what would turn out to be significant or useful until, in the course of writing or of contemplating my various lists, tables and charts, some ideas would come to the fore demanding further consideration.

When I began to consider films not just in terms of their form and content, their genres and the production and authorial strategies which they evidenced, but also in terms of their appeal to audiences – in other words once I was alert to the mass audience's work in reading popular cinema – I became aware that the actors, particularly the stars, were a crucial factor. Reviews, publicity and general discussion of viewing centred, it seemed to me, just as much on the performance and 'persona' of the star as it did on the film itself. Here John Ellis's (1975) proposition that 'the film is one text, the star is another text passing through it' was fundamental to my conception of the reading moment as an intersection of numerous and disparate 'texts' including not only those of the film and the star but also the cinema in which the viewing takes place, the production history of the studio responsible for the film, not to mention the experiential history of individual spectators. Pursuing this idea in the course of a study

of Katharine Hepburn's star persona and its consequences for
readings of the films in which she appeared in the 1940s and
1950s (see Thumim, 1986), I found Richard Dyer's (1979) work
particularly useful in its demonstration of the discursive field
within which, typically, readings take place.[15] His insistence on
considering ephemera and his scholarly discussion of the commodification of personality which, in *Stars*, he shows to be a
consequence of the capitalist industrialisation of cinema were,
it seemed to me, key to the articulation of this field. Michele
Mattelart's (1986) study of the international flow of cultural
commodities – of cultural imperialism – attending as it does
to issues of both race and gender, enabled me to conceive of the
hegemonic determinants at play on the largest scale. Her deconstruction of political activity suggested 'This zone of mass culture
is the privileged space where authority does not need to speak
politically in order to act politically' (p. 24) and echoed, as I read
it, Brecht's dictum that 'there is no such thing as a-political art',
by which I understand that cultural production of any kind, if
not overtly oppositional, must be deemed to support the *status
quo*. My understanding of the important concepts of ideology
and hegemony in their cultural operations was derived from a
long-standing interest in the development of Marxist politics
during the twentieth century, from Raymond Williams's (1976)
comments on this development, particularly the valuable summaries in his *Keywords*, and from the writings of Marx himself
as well as Engels, Gramsci and Althusser.

From these insights about the broad cultural operations of
cinema I move to their corollary, the discrete activity of the
individual spectator and here, in common with many feminist
scholars (including Kathleen Rowe and Jackie Stacey in this
volume), I found myself confronted by Freud's work as purveyed
through psychoanalytic theory. Freud, of course, is a problem.
His account of the early formation of identity is predicated on a
masculine subject and doesn't account for female subjectivity,
yet his assertion of psychic reality and its effectivity in the subject's later experience of desire and fantasy – both crucial to
spectatorial activity – seems to me to be too valuable to reject
on account of its masculinist provenance. It's a problem that
accompanies much philosophical speculation, but since we *do*
live, breathe, speak, think, desire and fantasise in terms evolved
and ordered in a patriarchy, it is also a problem that cannot be
escaped. In considering its consequences for the spectatorial

activity of the female reader I found Christine Gledhill's (1988) discussion of the reader's 'negotiation' of the text particularly helpful in steering my way out of the impasse. Her insight, that the reading process entails an active and conscious negotiation of often contradictory imperatives – the textual proposition may contradict the reader's knowledge and experience and operate against her interests, yet still be pleasurable – seemed to me to suggest an optimistic sense of the possibility of the subject's independence in the face of the (patriarchal) text. This optimism also recalled Janice Radway's (1984) work on romance readers and her account of the use-value, often in opposition to the romance texts themselves, which they derived from their readings. Levi-Strauss's (1967) propositions about the function of myth in revealing significant relations *between* social groups was fundamental to my approach, as was its development in Will Wright's (1975) study of the western, and in Barthes' work (1973, 1974, 1984). The analyses of contemporary ephemera in *Mythologies* and the essay on the production of myths and meta-myth were profoundly enabling, all the more so because they were developed in such remarkably imaginative detail in *S/Z* and *Camera Lucida* dealing, respectively, with the story and the photographic image – which together constitute cinema. Each of these scholars offered means which I could profitably adapt to my own concern with gender politics. In this endeavour I was encouraged, too, by the feminist writings of Rosalind Coward (1983) and Toril Moi (1985). Coward's conclusion that '... in our society there is an ideological investment to effect the equation between anatomical division and sexual identity' (p. 286) confirmed my own recognition of the elisions at work in the maintenance of patriarchal hegemony. Moi's suggestion that 'the real', far from being 'common knowledge' is continually under construction – as she put it 'the real is not only something we construct, but a controversial construct at that' (p. 45) – seemed to me to justify my pursuit of the obvious. Above all, however, there were two writers to whom I continually returned, finding their insights and propositions ever more germane to the material unfolding before me. Lorraine Code's *Epistemic Responsibility* (1987) not only enabled my recognition that knowledge is *not* common, but also, in her discussion of the responsibility inhering in 'knowing', provided a positive exhortation that my pursuit of the obvious, far from being simply my pleasure, was in fact an important political act – a duty, one might say. All these ideas, from Levi-Strauss,

Barthes, Coward, Moi and Code seemed to me to be in play as I read and re-read Foucault – particularly his *History of Sexuality Vol 1: An Introduction* (1970) and his *The Order of Things* (1974). For both his account of the development of the human sciences during the eighteenth and nineteenth centuries, and his discussion of the developing social consequences of what he effectively described as the policing of sexuality in the same period reveal the discursive *construction* of 'common knowledge'. The fact that he was unequivocally speaking from the position of the male subject as the second and third volumes of his history of sexuality *The Use of Pleasure* (1984) and *The Care of the Self* (1984) make abundantly clear, since they deal exclusively with male sexual pleasure and the masculine self, in no way diminishes the usefulness of his insights. He shows how assumptions about the 'self evident' nature of 'truths' to be derived from the empirical data characteristic of the natural sciences came to inform the very structure of language and, therefore, the modes of thought dominant in the twentieth century.

Foucault himself was writing about the relation between the individual and the State, but his insights, it seems to me, are invaluable to a feminist analysis of gender politics, because, as he himself notes more than once, knowledge is power. If knowing, as Code claims, entails responsibility, then so does power – but this doesn't simply mean that those with power carry responsibility for those subject to their power. Far more profoundly, I think, it suggests that knowledge, above all knowledge that carries a claim to commonality, must constantly be checked against actual experience and that historical evidence, far from being natural, is (usually) man-made. The articulation of collective experience entails a combination of negotiation and assertion and, in the inevitable reduction that a coherent account requires, results in a claim that one 'set of ideas' is appropriate to the ordering of the account. But a 'set of ideas' *is* ideology, and the processes of negotiation and assertion are hegemonic processes. This is what the women's movement dictum that 'the personal is political' means in practice. In the texts of popular culture in patriarchal order women and the feminine are presented and defined in a manner which serves patriarchal interests. It is this self-evident but none the less fundamental observation that my research and writing unpacked – in the case of cinema and its mass audience at a specific period. It is clearly important that feminists, at least, insist on the articulation of women's personal experience in relation to cultural representations of it because in so doing we can attempt to intervene, in the interests of female subjects of post-industrial, post-modern, patriarchy, in hegemonic struggle.

Notes

1 I am using the term hegemony in a post-Gramscian sense to refer to the circulation of ideas in society in which 'social practice is seen to depend on consent to certain dominant ideas which in fact express the needs of a dominant class', thus hegemony depends 'not only on its expression of a ruling class but also on its acceptance as "normal reality" or "commonsense" by those in practice subordinated to it' Williams (1976/1988). I use the concept of ideology and the ideological to refer to a coherent set of ideas which consciously inform social practice, conforming with Marx's 1859 usage: 'the distinction should always be made between the material transformation of the economic conditions of production ... and the legal, political, religious, aesthetic or philosophic – in short, ideological – forms in which men become conscious of this conflict and fight it out' (Williams, 1976/1988, p. 156). Thus hegemony refers to *a process* whereby the consequence of *a thing* – is set of ideas – is enacted. Through hegemonic processes an ideology achieves dominance.

2 My use of the term *pollution*, here, doesn't imply that there can ever be an ideal or *un*polluted – pure – reading, but that the processes of memory are likely to affect readings in a particular way, introducing material and inflections whose provenance may be subsequent to the text in question. Jackie Stacey, in this volume, attends to this question and to the status of various types of memory.

3 There were both male and female critics writing during the period but the criticism itself is largely indistinguishable in terms of gender. From this I deduce that all critics, men and women, aimed to satisfy what they understood to be the requirements of dominant discourse in the public sphere of published journalism to which they contributed.

4 They used the list published in the *1961 Film Daily Yearbook* (Bahn, 1961), of 29,998 titles released in the USA between 1915 and 1960, and after 'eliminating all titles not from an American studio' used a random number table to select 851 titles of which they located one hundred of detailed study, claiming that: 'Our selection procedures represent the closest a researcher can come to random sampling when dealing with historical artefacts. The point remains that our choices were not biased by personal preferences or conceptions of influential or masterful films' (Bordwell *et al.*, 1985, p. 388).

5 See Thumim (1991) and Thumim (forthcoming) for a more detailed discussion of my correlation.

6 There were some exceptions, detailed in Thumim (1991), pp. 258–9.

7 There were of course far more films on release in each year: my correlation included only those receiving at least one mention in the listings cited.

8 I extended the period I had originally envisaged, 1945–1957, in order to offer a longer and therefore, apparently, more marketable timespan in the book, *Celluloid Sisters*, which I was in the process of negotiating with Macmillan Ltd. I had, and have, some misgivings about this extension – though my editor's point about marketing the book was a sound one – because the cinema audience in the late 1950s and 1960s was qualitatively different than that of the 1940s and earlier 1950s, being much smaller and possibly not qualifying for the term 'mass audience'.

9 My original plan was for five-year intervals to 1957, viz 1945–1946; 1950–1951; 1956–1957.

10 See Thumim (1991) for lists of possible titles indicating which I selected for analysis.

11 These were chosen from the ten or so films most popular at the British box office in 1954 according to my correlation. They were *The Glenn Miller Story* (Anthony Mann, US, 1954); *Doctor in the House* (Ralph Thomas, UK, 1954); *On the Waterfront* (Elia Kazan, US, 1954); *Hobson's Choice* (David Lean, UK, 1953); *Rob Roy the Highland Rogue* (Harold French, UK, 1953); and *The Million Pound Note* (Ronald Neame, UK, 1954).

12 I did this by writing a short synopsis of all female characters' progress through the six narratives, considering what narrative means were called on to present and define the characters and to position the audience in relation to each character. Then I considered what these narrative methods from six different films had in common and how their consequences for character construction might be categorised.

13 For example Kate (Jo Van Fleet) in *East of Eden* (Elia Kazan, US, 1955), whose unsatisfactory mothering was noted as a prime cause of the hero Cal (James Dean)'s distress, came to a sad end: her performance was widely praised suggesting that her fate was thought to be deserved.

14 For example Barbara (Margaret Lockwood), *The Wicked Lady* (Leslie Arliss, UK, 1945), whose transgressive behaviour earned her death in the narrative closure but whose exploits were widely enjoyed at the box office, and Marnie (Tipi Hedren) in *Marnie* (Alfred Hitchcock, US, 1964), whose subversive but articulate and appealing refusal of male support was revealed, in the narrative closure, to be the pathological consequence of a repressed childhood trauma.

15 See Dyer (1979, 1980, 1987).

Bibliography

Bahn (ed.), *N.Y. Film Daily*, New York.

Barthes, R. (1973), *Mythologies*, London, Paladin.

Barthes, R. (1974), *S/Z*, New York, Hill and Wang.

Barthes, R. (1984), *Camera Lucida*, London, Flamingo.

Bordwell, D., J. Staiger and K. Thompson (1985), *The Classical Hollywood Cinema: Film Style and Mode of Production to 1960*, London, Routledge, Kegan and Paul.

Carr, E.H. (1961), *What is History?*, London, Macmillan.

Code, L. (1987), *Epistemic Responsibility*, Hanover and London, Brown University Press, distributed by University Press of New England.

Coward, R. (1983), *Patriarchal Precedents: Sexuality and Social Relations*, London, Routledge, Kegan and Paul.

Coward, R. (1984), *Female Desire: Women's Sexuality Today*, London, Paladin.

Dyer, R. (1979), *Stars*, London, BFI.

Dyer, R. (1980), *Star Dossier One: Marilyn Monroe*, London, BFI.

Dyer, R. (1987), *Heavenly Bodies*, London, BFI/Macmillan.

Ellis, J. (1975), Made in Ealing, *Screen*, 16:1.

Foucault, M. (1970), *The History of Sexuality. Volume One: An Introduction*, London, Allen Lane.

Foucault, M. (1974/1989), *The Order of Things*, London, Tavistock/Routledge (1st pub. Gallimard, 1966).

Foucault, M. (1984a), *The Use of Pleasure*, London, Penguin.

Foucault, M. (1984b), *The Care of the Self*, London, Penguin.

Gledhill, C. (1988), Pleasurable Negotiations, in D. D. Pribram (ed.), *Female Spectators*, London, Verso.

Levi-Strauss, C. (1967), *Structural Anthropology*, New York, Doubleday.

Mattelart, M. (1986), *Women, Media, Crisis: Femininity and Disorder*, London, Comedia.

Moi, T. (1985), *Sexual/Textual Politics: Feminist Literary Theory*, London, Methuen.

Radway, J. (1984), *Reading the Romance: Women, Patriarchy and Popular Fiction*, Chapel Hill, University of North Carolina Press.

Thumim, J. (1986), 'Miss Hepburn is Humanised': The Star Persona of Katharine Hepburn, *Feminist Review*, 24, 71–105.

Thumim, J. (1991), The 'Popular', Cash and Culture in the Post-war British Cinema Industry, *Screen*, 32:3, 245–71.

Thumim, J. (1992), *Celluloid Sisters: Women and Popular Cinema*, London, Macmillan.

Thumim, J. (forthcoming), Film and Female Identity: Questions of Method in Investigating Representations of Women in Popular Cinema, in D. Petrie (ed.), *New Scholarship Working Papers*, London, BFI.

Williams, R. (1976/1988), *Keywords*, London, Fontana.

Wright, W. (1975), *Sixguns and Society: A Structural Study of the Western*, Los Angeles, University of California Press.

4

Finding a place from which to write: the methodology of feminist textual practice

LYNNE PEARCE

For the last twenty-five years literary critics have been burdened with the theoretical question of who, or what, is responsible for a text's 'meaning'. Is it the *author* (the base-line for all those who depend upon biographical and other extratextual data to 'explain' the text), the *text* itself (the view favoured by 'New Critics', Formalists and Structuralists), the *reader* (the opinion of 'reader-response' and reception theorists), or some more complex combination of two or three of these (the position held by the majority of post-structuralists)?[1]

Negotiating a position for oneself within this complicated set of author/text/reader relations is, I wish to propose, one of the key methodological concerns that besets the textual critic every time she embarks upon the analysis of a visual or verbal text. Indeed, for literary critics, who have great difficulty in understanding exactly what is meant by 'methodology' in a discipline so unlike the data-based research of the social sciences, the decision of where to situate oneself in this author-text-reader matrix may justifiably be thought of as *the* methodological issue. Apart from establishing a rationale for why a certain text or group of texts has been selected for study (e.g. author/genre/historical period), most of the factors that inform the course of a textual reading are *theoretical* rather than methodological: selecting a theoretical framework with which to read a text is one step on from this more basic decision of *who or what it is that one is investigating* (i.e. author/'means of production', text, or audience/readership).

For feminists, moreover, this is a methodological choice with profound political implications. Adopting the formalist/structuralist principle of locating all meaning *within* the text can, for example, make it extremely difficult to explain what is problematic about it in the broader context of its production and consumption (a point particularly charged for those working in the field of pornography and representation). Similarly, research focused on the *reception* of texts by female readers and viewers (where readings are often made 'against the grain' of the texts' dominant discourses) may overlook the extent to which those texts are nevertheless 'positioning' their readers in terms of gender and sexuality.

In this chapter I explore the political implications of this a priori methodological decision by focusing upon my own changing perception of the author-text-reader relationship.[2] I reflect upon the way in which these theoretical shifts made me feel, at different points in my career, both 'more' and 'less' powerful as a feminist reader and critic, and how that dynamic translated into a fast-changing set of textual practices. Part of my 'method' here, therefore, is to use autobiography to reveal the positioning of the feminist textual critic by contemporary theoretical debates and to prompt all 'readers' (from whatever disciplinary background) to reflect upon their own changing relationship to the author-text-reader matrix in the production of textual meaning.

Needless to say, this story of 'readership' is also a story of 'writing', since my own ability to put pen to paper has necessarily depended upon my ability to negotiate a position for myself *as critic vis-à-vis* the matrix. This is not to say that I was permitted a voice only at those points in my career where I perceived the reader to be dominant, but that I have always had to find some means of establishing my critical authority: as will become clear, this is usually *via* identification with a set of discourses which privileges one or other of the three terms (e.g. liberal humanism's championship of 'the author').[3] It is also worth mentioning that, despite the complexity of current debates over the construction of meaning, the self-reflexivity that has become central to my own critical practice means that there is *always something to say* even if it is merely an expression of one's own readerly 'defeat'!

While the narrative which follows takes in the full course of my history as a gendered reader, there is a particular focus on the crisis of reader-power that emerged as a consequence of my work on *Woman/Image/Text: Readings in Pre-Raphaelite Art and Literature* (1991). As will become clear, this was the moment at which I began to question the political and ethical legitimacy of reading texts 'against the grain' of the dominant historical and cultural discourses by which they were clearly inscribed, and began to attend, instead, to the way in which we, as female/feminist readers, must negotiate the way *in which they position us*.

What is now clear to me in terms of methodology (partly through my own experience, and partly through the supervision of my research students) is that the question of which element (author/text/reader) holds the balance of power is an issue on which we have to take a stand and then, in our textual practices, be(come) consistent. In too many critical texts (and postgraduate students are by no means the only ones guilty of this!), authors slide unwittingly from 'text' to 'reader', from 'reader' to 'text', as the 'source' of meaning. In feminist critiques of male-produced texts, in particular, one is repeatedly asking whether it is the text or the reader that is being subversive. Did a film like *Thelma and Louise* become popular with feminists because Ridley Scott (the director) gave it a 'feminist message', or simply because it can be read 'on behalf of feminism'? Although we may ultimately decide that such interpretations arise as the result of a complex interaction of text *and* reader, it is vitally important that we signal how this interaction is achieved at every stage of our textual analysis. The story of my own struggles to achieve this degree of methodological clarity will hopefully assist the readers of this book to arrive at their own positions rather less painfully.

'In the beginning' which, in my case, lasted until at least halfway through my first degree, the thing that shall henceforth be known as 'the text' had one sure source of meaning, the author's, and one sure reader: me. As a student of literature, my role was to attempt to reach the author through his words (and, of course, I use the masculine pronoun advisedly); to reconstruct his meanings and intentions through a process of sensitive and polite probing.

The most curious thing I now remember about this time was my fondness for the pronoun 'we'. Despite the elitism of my 'sensitive' engagement with the text, I was always happy to share my responses with a group of anonymous but like-minded readers: as in the instance of my brave attempt to empathise with Stephen Daedalus in James Joyce's (1916/1977) *Portrait of the Artist as a Young Man*. My senior school essays on *A Portrait* abound with sentences like: 'Chapter two is essentially a period of transition with regard to *our feelings* toward Stephen' and 'Unless the reader has himself reached the years of cynicism, bitterness is not an attractive quality (!)'. Looking back over the essays, it is evident that I had to work extremely hard to empathise with Joyce's representative of male adolescence, but the 'anonymous' 'we' clearly gave me the means to grit my teeth and try. In this resolve I was flying in the face of a class-background in which no other family member belonged to any sort of 'reading community', and my engagement is therefore striking evidence of how successfully we can be 'recruited' by a discourse (in this case, humanist literary criticism) not our own. The fact that I was also sublimating my *gendered* identity never occurred to me: English literature as it was taught at school meant becoming a 'transvestite-reader' on a permanent basis. No matter how complex the reader-positioning of the texts concerned, we were trained to respond as universalised male subjects and to assume this critical perspective in our writings.

It is also a significant comment on the limitations of English literature as it was taught to me at university that my perception of the existence of a balance of power between author, text and reader only really became clear when I began my doctoral research. My Ph.D., on the nineteenth-century peasant poet, John Clare, was undertaken at Birmingham University where the sudden blast of critical theory offered by the staff-postgraduate seminar (then led by David Lodge) turned me from a passive reader into a textual activist. It was the early 1980s: the time when the British academic system was desperately scrambling to catch up with Roland Barthes, Jacques Derrida, Michel Foucault, and, to my own particular peril, Mikhail Bakhtin. Suddenly the author was dead, the text 'untied', its meaning multiple, and the reader in a position of unprecedented power. With reckless confidence I set about releasing all the hidden voices from John Clare's now manifestly 'polyphonic' texts; employed deconstructive strategies to reveal their loss of faith in Romantic theories of language and the imagination.[4]

For those coming from non-literary backgrounds, a word or two is probably necessary here to explain how my new positioning as a reader affected my productivity as a *writer*. The short answer is that the deconstructive and 'symptomatic' approaches I have just described actively depend upon the reader to release the covert, 'hidden', and contradictory meanings within a text.[5] Criticism changes from being a *descriptive* or *reconstructive* practice ('reconstructive' in the sense of reconstructing the 'author's intentions') into something vastly more creative. While cynics from other disciplines might see these interventions as tantamount to 'making the text mean anything', in practice the critics are working very closely with it *in order to see* what is 'written between the lines'.

Powerful as I now was as a reader, however, I had yet to catch up with a sense of my gendered identity. Although I was teaching overtly feminist courses by this time, the material I was working with elsewhere failed to seem relevant to my work as a reader of John Clare. In terms of the text-reader equation, I can now explain this as the direct result of the 'false-consciousness' of my readerly supremacy. These were the years when I subscribed to the [Stanley] Fishian maxim that it is the method that the reader brings to bear upon the text that enables it to be heard and seen, which meant that I was entirely oblivious to the fact that the text might, in any way, be positioning *me*.[6] Hence I achieved the strange feat of talking extensively about the polyphonic and heteroglossic coexistence of different voices in Clare's poems, without considering the fact that they were all *male voices* which, although frequently addressed to a female subject *within the text*, nevertheless assumed a male reader. Because I thought it was I, the reader, who had made these voices audible by bringing my Bakhtinian theory to bear upon the text, both their gender and mine were irrelevant. It didn't bother me that these texts were excluding of a female reader in terms of their positioning because I (as an existential female reader) had already bent them to my will. Looking back, this was the period of both my greatest power and my greatest blindness.

Thankfully the megalomania didn't last. At the same time that I, the postgraduate reader, was playing Faustus, another self was in the throes of a belated radical-feminism. A generation removed from the revolutionary events of the early 1970s, I am one of those who read Kate Millett and Germaine Greer alongside Catherine Belsey, Cora Kaplan, and Terry Eagleton: who caught up with the theory of 'second-wave' feminism at the same time that its followers were charting its demise.[7] This sense of critical and political 'belatedness' has, in itself, caused me considerable anxiety over the years. Like others of the post-revolutionary generation, I have often felt I lack the political 'authenticity' of those that were there 'at the beginning'. In terms of my reader's history, moreover, I can see that what this new feminist consciousness produced was a peculiarly anarchic form of 'reader-schizophrenia'. I, the reader, would read differently in different situations. Thus during the same period that I was completing my Bakhtinian liberation of Clare, I had also begun a fairly crude 'images of women' assault on Pre-Raphaelite painting. While one self was oblivious to the gendered positioning of a text because she thought herself free to do what she liked with it, another was steaming through the exhibition rooms of the Tate Gallery furious at the blatant exclusiveness of these male-authored icons. In one context I felt so powerful; in the other, so powerless.

My earliest work with the Pre-Raphaelites, then, which centred on a number of adult education courses I taught on Victorian art and literature, was very much an attempt to expose and vilify the 'negative representation' of women in such texts. It is interesting to reflect how unproblematically 'the author' crept back into the equation at this point: 'John Clare' might have been consigned to permanent quotation marks, but the most reprehensible authorial intentions were ascribed to Dante Gabriel Rossetti. I, the reader, meanwhile assumed the role of heckler, instigating groups of cultured, middle-class female adult education students to mock and despise the texts that they were only permitted to view from the margins. It was a readerly scenario exemplified by Lucy Snowe's visit to the art gallery in Charlotte Brontë's *Villette* (1984): the Pre-Raphaelite images of women, like Lucy Snowe's 'Cleopatra', were rejected on the grounds that they had been wrought for the salacious pleasure of a male audience. My most memorable statement as a reader from this period was a reference to the Pre-Raphaelite Brotherhood's 'penchant for sick and dying women'. Satire, I confess, had become a rather enjoyable reading strategy, and as it spread its seeds amongst my students, inculcated in us a sense of dissident group-power. The same spirit invaded my writing, and early versions of what was to become *Woman/Image/Text* – in the form of the lectures and conference papers I gave at this time – remain the most exuberantly polemical texts I have written.[8]

Indeed, with the trashing and ridiculing of sexist and/or misogynist texts having noticeably declined in recent years, I am sometimes overwhelmed with nostalgia for the pleasure of such ribald malice. In an academic context it has disappeared, of course, because we are no longer so sure about who or what to ridicule: discourses, not authors, are now responsible for the anti-feminist world in which we live, and patriarchy is no longer the monolithic white elephant we can blame for all our ills. For today's feminist reader everything, everywhere, is almost oppressively subtle, complex and contradictory. Things (regret-tably?) have gone beyond a joke.

As it happens, the book that finally came out of my work with the Pre-Raphaelites, *Woman/Image/Text*, is not entirely without jokes or the occasional flippant aside. However, any feminist aspiring to scholarly credibility in the late 1980s could not afford to be too cavalier. I, the reader, finally got round to putting pen to paper just as the paranoia over 'essentialist-thinking' really began to set in: the term 'woman' had by now become an epis-temological minefield and, as all certainty over gendered identity fell apart, so, too, did the anxieties around reading increase. If it was no longer tenable to represent women as a group, where did that leave the woman reader, or, indeed, the feminist reader? Could there be any such thing as a reading position that was gendered, simplistically, male or female? How could a text direct itself to a male or female audience when those terms, in them-selves, are inclusive of so many differences and contradictions as to render them meaningless?

The grim burden of these questions caused me, like many of my contemporaries, to moderate my polemic and to develop a new style of writing predicated upon the 'caveat'. It is a style characterised by long and agonised sentences, sub-clauses, parentheses and footnotes. Theses, now, proceed with infinite caution: one step forward is followed by two steps back. Entire books are likely to end with a sentence which puts into question all that has gone before. We, as a community of feminist readers and critics, have found ourselves with a cleft stick which requires us to advance new theories (which are always demanding of *some kind* of generalisation), at the same time as recognising the thing that we are theorising – in my case, 'gendered reading' – is impossible to generalise about. The skill that we all most aspire to is therefore circumspection: how to succeed in getting through a book or article without tripping oneself up: a second's lapse of concentration and the essentialist assumption will be out, and you, the guilty party, will be shot down.[9]

On this last point it is interesting to speculate to what extent a rhetorical style can actually be said to constitute a methodology? Clearly parallels could be drawn between the acute self-reflexivity (and resistance to totalising discourses) I have just been describing and the call for 'situated knowledges' in other disciplines.[10] A recent meta-theoretical study of feminist thought, Kathy Ferguson's (1993) *The Man Question: Visions of Subjectivity in*

Feminist Theory brings theory and rhetoric together in just this way by arguing that *irony* (as a rhetorical *strategy*) is the only means ('method'?) by which today's feminist can live with the contradictory demands of what she refers to as the 'genealogical' and 'interpretive' schools of feminist thought.[11] While the full implications of such an argument are too complex to go into here, it is worth noting that if rhetorical styles were conceived of as methodological strategies in this way, it would also be possible to *re-legitimate* other writing practices (like polemic) which have been discredited.

In terms of my own scholarly history, the rhetorical circumspection of 1980s feminism had a major impact on the way in which I approached my writing, and in many ways *Woman/ Image/Text* may be seen as the moment when I, the reader, lost my nerve. Its readings of eight poem-painting combinations are a strange mixture of textual dexterity (reflecting the confidence I had gained through my post-structuralist training), methodological angst of the kind I've just described, and, most importantly, an increasing uneasiness about whether my readerly practices could be ethically and politically justified. I shall explain.

Alongside the growing demand for ever-greater critical complexity, 1980s feminist theory also required 'a positive approach' to textual analysis. Here, I have memories of publishers asking for a more 'up-beat' ending to books or chapters of books.[12] Practising feminist criticism might be getting increasingly hard, but it must still be seen to be fun. Through the work of poststructuralist critics in literary and cultural studies, the fashion had been set for making the most recalcitrant of texts complex, exciting, and, of course, politically redeemable. Terry Eagleton's (1986) attempt to read Richardson's *Clarissa* 'on behalf of feminism' is a classic case in point, while in Kate Belsey's (1986) hands the manifest misogyny of Milton's *Paradise Lost* is blasted away to reveal exquisite points of doubt and contradiction.

Thus by the time I actually came to write *Woman/Image/ Text* (summer 1989), I was obliged to put aside the feelings of gendered exclusion that many of the texts inspired and set about seeing how they could be positively re-read. The question I posed myself, and which for a long time functioned as the working title for my introduction, was 'what can the C20th feminist reader/viewer do with C19th male-produced images of women?' Drawing upon the full range of 'deconstructive' reading strategies (methods) by then available to the feminist reader (e.g. post-

Althusserian Marxism, discourse theory, and recent work on spectatorship and pleasure in film and media studies) I found ways of undermining the dominant ideologies of the texts concerned and of inserting myself, the feminist reader, in their 'gaps and silences'.[13] By this means, a radical collusion could be wrought between myself and the women represented in the texts. Beata Beatrix might be dying (or, as Rossetti put it, 'rapt visibly towards heaven'), but her ghostliness and two-dimensionality are, in the last analysis, part of the discourse of masculine fear and impotence. The erotic threat presented by women in Pre-Raphaelite painting is circumscribed only by a formal and symbolic denial of their existential reality. Beatrice, as I suggest in my chapter, exults in her own ghostliness; smiles in our direction (Pearce, 1991: 46–58).

Yet even as I used my post-structuralist reader-power to prise apart these texts and reappropriate them, I began to have grave doubts about the ethics and politics of doing so. To redeem the images concerned meant, more often than not, to read them out of context: to extract the text from the circumstances of its historical production and consumption. On the one hand this was reader-power being put to the most subversive of feminist uses, but on the other, it completely ignored the dominant reading position offered by the text itself.

Although *Woman/Image/Text* brought this dilemma to consciousness and made it part of its central thesis, the whole book was predicated upon the assumption that, as long as we, as readers, are aware of what we are doing, such breaking of the rules is acceptable. In retrospect, I am less sure. When I come back to the paintings again now it is my sense of gendered exclusion which prevails. That I can, and indeed, have, read them against the grain of their historical production does not alter the fact that they have a *preferred reader* who is not me. The text I pretended was mine was all the time in dialogue with someone else.

The consequence of this loss of confidence in my readerly power was to turn away from male-authored texts altogether; and whenever I get lost in the sophistications of whether there is such a thing as 'women's writing' I hold on to this 'readerly response' as evidence that there must be. Indeed, as I thought more about the force of my own reaction I concluded that here, if anywhere, must be the definition of what we mean by women's writing: not writing by women, or about women, but, more especially, writing *for* them. However complex the categories 'male' and 'female' have become, texts *do* gender their readers, either explicitly or implicitly. While there will, of course, be some texts that are less specific in their address than others, at the two extremes there are many texts produced fairly exclusively for men or for women. Thus having spent so long attempting to redeem the former, I turned with joy and relief into the pages of the latter.

My attempts to formulate a theory for the specificity of address in contemporary women's fiction took me back, once again, to the work of Mikhail Bakhtin. In an essay entitled 'Dialogic Theory and Women's Writing' (Pearce, 1992) I have argued that recent work on Bakhtin's theories of dialogic activity can be used to support the notion of a gendered exclusivity within certain female-authored texts. Through linguistic strategies of direct and indirect address, through intonation and extra-literary context, it is evident that several women writers have successfully defined their audience as both female and feminist. Thus, once again, albeit for a short time, everything seemed very simple. There may be millions of texts from which, as a woman reader, I am excluded, but with an ever-increasing library of contemporary feminist writing, it became obvious where my energies should be directed. I resolved only to trouble myself with texts which spoke to me as a woman and as a feminist.

Unfortunately this second wave of readerly euphoria lasted little longer than the first. The texts I thought to be addressed especially to me turned out not to be so. What I had experienced as an intimate relationship between the chosen text and myself, turned out to be but one of many. I soon saw that I could only ever occupy but *one* of the multiple positionings denoted by the category 'woman reader'. The text I had thought of as 'mine' was talking to others as easily as it talked to me. All the time I was reading, I kept overhearing scraps of conversation between the text and readers differently situated from myself. I became jealous and suspicious. I wanted to know what the text was saying to *them*: to the Black women, the heterosexual women, the working-class women; to the women who were ten years older, or ten years younger, than myself. Once again I, the reader, felt excluded and unwanted. With so many *different* readers jostling for the position of preferred reader, I found it difficult to accept my own insignificance. De-essentialising the category 'woman' (as I knew I must) had de-essentialised me.

I have since discovered a number of texts which have helped explain the nature of this 'reader-jealousy' to me, as well as suggesting a possible way forward. One of these is Martin Montgomery's (1986) 'D-J Talk'. Part of Montgomery's analysis is concerned with the way in which the radio D-J's monologue is continually addressing different segments of the audience through 'identifiers' which include or exclude particular groups. For example, horoscope features identify and privilege the different star-signs in turn. The effect of this, as Montgomery explains, is that any individual listener will be positioned differently at different times and that: 'It is quite common for an audience to be in a position of overhearing recipient of a discourse that is being directly addressed to someone else'.

While Montgomery welcomed this constant realignment of address as evidence that no discourse 'speaks from a single authoritative position' I, the erstwhile privileged reader, received the evidence with gloom. It was clearly true that none of my favoured feminist texts could exist in an exclusive relationship with any one reader-positioning, and my status as addressee was as tenuous as it had always been.

Since this 'second splitting' of the reader's ego I have, however, come to realise that my jealousy was somewhat misplaced. While it may be true that my favoured feminist texts have more readers than I originally thought, this does not irredeemably alter my special relationship to them. Indeed, after reflecting some more on Montgomery's model of shifting address, I realised that mutability does not necessarily equal promiscuity. 'Polyphony' which, in the Bakhtinian sense, demands that a text be comprised of a 'plurality of consciousness with equal rights', is not my *reader's* experience of contemporary feminist writing any more than it is my experience of the male literary canon.[14] The text may be comprised of many voices; it may effect multiple text-reader positionings, but this does not mean that it does so without preference or discrimination. As Stuart Hall (1980) observed in his work on encoding and decoding in television discourse as long ago as 1973, 'polysemy must not, however, be confused with pluralism'.

Therefore, even as I showed in my work on John Clare that the voices *within* the polyphonic text can be hierarchised according to the balance of power between speaker and addressee within the text, so, too, do I now propose a (mutable) hierarchy of reader-positionings.[15] Viewed in this way, a text like Alice Walker's

The Color Purple becomes the site of a struggle for reader-privilege. Readers of different classes, races, and sexual orientations may turn hungrily from page to page for a sign of their own preferment. Sometimes their desire will be appeased; sometimes it will be disappointed. But either way, by the time they finish reading, a judgement will have been cast and they will know their place in the schema of the text's reader-positionings.

While, on the one hand, the existence of such textual preferment helps to explain why reading books, watching films, or looking at paintings continues to be such an exciting but nerve-racking occupation, it also offered me, the jealous reader, perverse consolation. Realising that one text might privilege me, even if another did not, confirmed that the dialogue between text and reader was, after all, a 'real' relationship; that it was subject to the same laws of selection, rejection and reciprocity as our inter-personal relations. If I, as a reader, have to learn to live with the continual possibility of rejection, then I may also enjoy the possibility of preferment. Acknowledging that the relationship between text and reader is inscribed by a volatile power dynamic in this way, permits desire even as it engenders fear. We may look forward to opening a new book, even as we are apprehensive of it. Moreover, by recognising this emotional dimension within the reading process we may come to a new understanding of its politics.

This equivocal position, which is where my story ends, is the reader space/place that I have occupied for the past two years. In terms of the thesis I have been pursuing – the question of whether, in the production of textual meaning, it is text or reader who holds the balance of power – it is clear that I have now conceded renewed authority to the text. While I, the reader, exist in dialogic relationship with the text (any text), I am nevertheless *positioned by it*, and the challenge and excitement of the reading process depends upon my not knowing, in advance, if it will embrace me or reject me: position me as an ally or as an antagonist.[16]

How this theoretical resolution (or quasi-resolution) translates into an effective methodological practice is, however, another matter. How does this acknowledgement of the *provisionality* of one's position as a reader – the fact that one might feel in-cluded/excluded, empowered/disempowered by a text in turn – translate into acceptable critical analysis? Surely there is a tension here between the 'personal' experience of reading a text as demanding, say, as Toni Morrison's *Beloved* (1987), and the 'professional' demands of literary criticism which require us (no matter how complex our emotional and intellectual engagement) to appear 'in control' of the texts we analyse? But then again, *how* can we speak about texts which, wholly or in part, refuse dialogue? These are, I feel, some of the toughest questions facing literary critics today, and it is, of course, no coincidence that I chose as my last example a text (*Beloved*) that has challenged the interpretive 'rights' of its white feminist readership in just this way.

Faced with such acute ethical dilemmas amidst so much theoretical complexity, the only methodological recommendation I feel able to make to today's feminist reader/critic is for even greater self-reflexivity. This is not to say that I believe we should all engage in the intellectual macramé of those post-structuralist writers who, as I mentioned above, frequently seem unable to make *any* positive statement without qualifying it, but rather that we should admit our *lack of control* in the reading process and somehow write this into our scripts. Indeed, by signalling the provisionality and precariousness of our positioning as readers we may become bolder in our pronouncements. By recognising both our 'situatedness' as readers and the dialogic nature of any textual encounter (the text positions us even as we position it), it may actually become easier to give voice. 'Knowing our place' as readers means *finding* a place from which to write.

Notes

1 'New Criticism', which became the dominant model of textual analysis in the United States from 1930 to the 1960s and centred on the work of John Crowe Ransome, I. A. Richards and William Empson, 'repudiated "extrinsic criteria for understanding poems" ' and proposed that the value of 'great literature' lay in its organic synthesis of form and content (see Baldick, 1990: 149–50), Formalist criticism, derived from the work of the Russian Formalists (see Baldick, 1990: 195–6), focuses on 'artistic technique' rather than 'subject matter', while Structuralist criticism, deriving from the linguistic theories of Ferdinand de Saussure (see Baldick, 1990: 213–14) sees the text as 'an objective structure activating various codes and conventions which are independent of the author, reader and external reality. Structuralist criticism is less interested in interpreting what literary works mean than explaining *how* they can mean what they mean' (Baldick, 1990: 214). Reader-response theory is 'not a single agreed theory so much as a shared concern with a set of problems involving the extent and nature of the reader's contribution to the meanings of literary works, approached from different positions including those of structuralism, psychoanalysis, phenomenology, and hermeneutics' (Baldick, 1990: 184). Post-structuralist literary criticism, deriving from the work of Roland

Barthes, Jacques Lacan, Jacques Derrida, Louis Althusser and Michel Foucault, has 'emphasized the instability of meanings and of intellectual categories' in the analysis of texts, and has foregrounded 'a non-hierarchical plurality of "free-play" of meanings' (Baldick, 1990: 175–6).

2 An earlier version of this chapter, focusing more exclusively on my history as a 'gendered reader', is published in Penny Florence and Dee Reynolds's edited collection *Feminist Subjects, Multi-Media* (1995).

3 'Liberal humanism' is the term used to refer to the type of literary criticism which 'centres its view of the world upon the notion of the freely self-determining individual. In modern literary theory, liberal humanism ... has come under challenge from post-structuralism, which replaces the unitary concept of "Man" with that of the subject, which is gendered, "de-centred" and no longer self-determining' (Baldick, 1990: 102–3). In terms of textual practice, humanist beliefs translate into a particular value system which assesses texts on their ability to portray convincingly the 'eternal truths' about individuals and human existence. Believing in the autonomy of individuals, liberal humanists also believe in the power of authors to control a text's meaning; hence, the notion of 'author intentionality' which has been widely challenged by structuralists and post-structuralists.

4 See Pearce (1987). Part of my thesis focused on the polyphonic nature of Clare's asylum poem 'Child Harold' (written as a continuation of Byron's poem of the same name). In the Bakhtinian vocabulary, 'polyphony' means simply 'many voices' and my reading of this text analysed the many different personae adopted by the narrator and his fluctuating power *vis-à-vis* his 'addressees' within the text. A shortened version of this analysis was published as an article entitled 'John Clare's "Child Harold": A Polyphonic Reading' (Pearce, 1989b).

Dialogic theory, as it has been developed by literary and other critics following in Bakhtin's footsteps, is predicated upon the general principle that no utterance (either written or spoken) is made in isolation, but is always dependent upon the anticipated response of an (actual or implicit) *addressee*. The reciprocal nature of this relationship is summed up in the following sentence from V. N. Voloshinov's *Marxism and the Philosophy of Language* (1973): 'A word is a bridge thrown between myself and another. If one end of the bridge belongs to me, then the other depends on my addressee. A word is a territory shared by both addresser and addressee, by the speaker and his interlocutor' (p. 86). This principle of reciprocity is implicit in the work of all Bakhtinians whether they are dealing with 'the utterance' as a small, linguistic unit (the individual word or sentence) or in terms of larger discourses.

For further information about the work of Mikhail Bakhtin and dialogic theory see Katerina Clark and Michael Holquist's *Mikhail Bakhtin* (1984) or my own *Reading Dialogics* (1994a).

5 'Symptomatic reading' is a method of textual practice associated with the work of the Structuralist-Marxist critic, Pierre Macherey (see Macherey, 1978). It encourages readers to identify the 'gaps and silences' in a text in order to reveal its covert (as opposed to its overt) ideological agenda.

6 Stanley Fish is America's most celebrated reader-response critic. See in particular *Is There a Text In This Class and Other Essays* (1980). See also the Introduction to *Gendering the Reader* (1994) edited by Sara Mills.

7 Kate Millett's *Sexual Politics* (1977) (originally published in the US in 1969) and Germaine Greer's *The Female Eunuch* (1971) were two of the key texts which fuelled the modern Women's Liberation Movement. Catherine Belsey's influential *Critical Practice* appeared in 1980, and Cora Kaplan wrote an important critical response to Millett's *Sexual Politics* which is reproduced in her collection of essays *Sea Changes* (1986). Terry Eagleton's work, from the 1970s onwards, has provided a model for much Marxist and feminist criticism: see in particular his *Literary Theory* (1983).

8 At this point it is important to register the importance of my teaching in the production of *Woman/Image/Text*. The fact that the design of the book, structured around the analysis of eight poem-painting combinations from the Victorian period, derived directly from the lectures and seminars on my adult education course, reveals its 'dialogic' origins. Many of the views I was able to express about the way in which these texts positioned a twentieth-century female reader came from the participatory observations of my students.

9 For an account of how anxious feminists have become about committing the 'sin' of essentialism see the 'round table discussion' between Marianne Hirsch, Jane Gallop and Nancy K. Miller in 'Criticizing Feminist Criticism' (Hirsch and Fox-Keller, 1990).

10 The concept 'situated knowledges' is used by Donna Haraway (1988) to identify the partiality and multiplicity of the positions we take up in response to domination. It is used to challenge the traditional use of the concept of 'objectivity' by claiming a politics of positionality for the production of any knowledge.

11 Ferguson employs 'genealogy' to refer to those theories focused on the 'deconstruction' of the category 'woman', and interpretation to refer to those focused on articulations of women's experience.

12 The publishers of the introductory guide to feminist criticism, *Feminist Readings/ Feminists Reading* (1989a) of which I was a co-author advised us repeatedly to adopt an 'up-beat' tone in order that the textual practices we were demonstrating appeared attractive and accessible to student readers. We were advised against making too much of the problems involved in all the approaches we described, and to avoid implying that feminist criticism was at an impasse (or, indeed, in crisis).

13 'Gaps and silences': another reference to the 'symptomatic reading practice' of Pierre Macherey (see note 5 above).

14 'A plurality of independent and unmerged voices and consciousnesses': see Mikhail Bakhtin (1984), p. 6.

15 For my discussion of the power-relationship existing between speaker and addressee in John Clare's 'Child Harold', see Pearce (1987).

16 See Anne Herrmann, *The Dialogic and Difference: 'An/Other Woman' in Virginia Woolf and Christa Wolf* (1989). In this fascinating application of Bakhtin's dialogic theory Herrmann compares the way in which Wolf's texts position their reader as a female 'ally', and Woolf's as a male 'antagonist'.

Bibliography

Bakhtin, M. (1984), *Problems of Dostoevsky's Poetics*, ed. and trans. D. Emerson, Manchester, Manchester University Press.

Baldick, C. (1990), *The Concise Oxford Dictionary of Literary Terms*, Oxford, Oxford University Press.

Belsey, C. (1980), *Critical Practice*, London, Methuen.

Belsey, C. (1986), *John Milton: Language, Gender, Power*, Oxford, Basil Blackwell.

Brontë, C. (1984), *Villette*, Oxford, Clarendon Press.

Clark, K. and M. Holquist (1984), *Mikhail Bakhtin*, Massachussetts and London, Harvard University Press.

Eagleton, T. (1983), *Literary Theory*, Oxford, Basil Blackwell.

Eagleton, T. (1986), *The Rape of Clarissa: Writing, Sexuality and Class Struggle in Samuel Richardson*, Oxford, Basil Blackwell.

Ferguson, K. (1993), *The Man Question: Visions of Subjectivity in Feminist Theory*, Berkeley, University of California Press.

Fish, S. (1980), *Is There a Text in This Class and Other Essays*, Cambridge, Mass., Harvard University Press.

Florence, P. and D. Reynolds (1995), *Feminist Subjects, Multi-Media*, Manchester, Manchester University Press.

Greer, G. (1971), *The Female Eunuch*, London, Paladin.

Hall, S. (1980), Encoding/Decoding, in S. Hall (ed.), *Culture/Media/Language*, London, Hutchinson.

Haraway, D. (1988), Situated Knowledges: The Science Question in Feminism and the Privilege of Partial Perspective, *Feminist Studies*, 14:3, 575–99.

Herrmann, A. (1989), *The Dialogic and Difference: 'An/Other Woman' in Virginia Woolf and Christa Wolf*, New York, Columbia University Press.

Hirsch, M. and E. Fox-Keller (eds) (1990), *Conflicts in Feminism*, London, Routledge.

Joyce, J. (1916/1977), *Portrait of the Artist as a Young Man*, St Albans, Panther.

Kaplan, C. (1986), *Sea Changes: Culture and Feminism*, London, Verso.

Macherey, P. (1978), *The Theory of Literary Production*, trans. G. Wall, London, Routledge.

Millett, K. (1977), *Sexual Politics*, London, Virago.

Mills, S. (ed.) (1994), *Gendering the Reader*, Hemel Hempstead, Harvester Wheatsheaf.

Montgomery, M. (1986), D-J Talk, in R. Collins (ed.), *Media, Culture and Society*, London, Sage.

Morrison, T. (1987), *Beloved*, London, Chato & Windus.

Pearce, L. (1987), John Clare and Mikhail Bakhtin: The Dialogic Principle – Readings from John Clare's Manuscripts 1832–1945. unpublished Ph.D. thesis, University of Birmingham.

Pearce, L., S. Mills, S. Spaull and E. Millard (1989a), *Feminist Readings/Feminists Reading*, Hemel Hempstead, Harvester Wheatsheaf.

Pearce, L. (1989b), John Clare's 'Child Harold': A Polyphonic Reading, *Criticism*, 31:2, 139–57.

Pearce, L. (1991), *Woman/Image/Text: Readings in Pre-Raphaelite Art and Literature*, Hemel Hempstead, Harvester Wheatsheaf.

Pearce, L. (1992), Dialogic Theory and Women's Writing, in H. Hinds, A. Phoenix and J. Stacey (eds), *Working Out: New Directions for Women's Studies*, Brighton, Falmer Press.

Pearce, L. (1994a), *Reading Dialogics*, London, Edward Arnold.

Pearce, L. (1994b), 'I' the Reader: Text, Context and the Balance of Power, in P. Florence and D. Reynolds (eds), *Feminist Subjects, Multi-Media*, Manchester, Manchester University Press.

Voloshinov, V. N. (1973), *Marxism and the Philosophy of Language*, New York, Seminar Press.

5

The lost audience: methodology, cinema history and feminist film criticism

JACKIE STACEY

> Except for the legendary viewers who dove under their seats at the sight
> of Lumiere's train coming into the station; the countless immigrants
> to the U.S. who, we are told, learned American values in the sawdust-
> floored nickleodeons of the Lower East Side; and those who, to a
> person it would seem, applauded Al Jolson's 'You ain't seen nothing
> yet' in 1927; film history had been written as if films had no audiences
> or were seen by everyone in the same way, or as if however they were
> viewed and by whomever, the history of 'films' was distinct from and
> privileged over the history of their being taken up by the billions of
> people who have watched them since 1894. (Allen, 1990: 348)

There are numerous histories of female cinematic spectatorship
which have yet to be written. Within feminist film criticism there
has been much work on textual spectatorship, but almost none
on the ways in which cinema audiences understood specific films
in particular cultural locations. Speaking very generally, feminist
film theorists have tended to investigate cinematic spectatorship
within semiotic/psychoanalytic textual analyses, with little
attention to the social identities of particular audiences. Within
cultural studies, on the other hand, audiences have been studied
within the specific locations of their consumption practices; but
here the focus has been mainly on non-cinematic forms: popular
fiction, television or video.[1] There remain few historical investigations of cinema spectators within feminist film criticism.[2]

This chapter offers an account of how and why I embarked on
a research project which attempted to investigate that slippery
category 'the female spectator', not through readings of textual
positionalities, but through spectators' own accounts of the
cinema and its appeal. The first part of the chapter offers a retrospective account of the trajectory of the research process: how I
came to choose to focus the study in the way I did and what other
possibilities I rejected and why; the second part of the chapter

discusses more fully the methodological problems and theoretical tensions raised by this particular focus: what kinds of interpretations of this material could be made and what were their limits? However, in the retelling, it is almost impossible to separate fully the methodological questions from the theoretical and epistemological ones: the choice of the object of study, the method of collecting the material, the theoretical frameworks used to interpret the material and the assumptions embedded within those interpretations, all interconnect. It is thus difficult to explain why I chose to abandon some sources and follow up others, without offering a brief summary of the content of the material such sources provided. Thus, interspersed between the narrative stages of my account are considerations of the methodological issues raised by choosing certain kinds of material over others and some discussion of the content of what I found, as well as of its relationship to existing theoretical debates. Similarly, some of the theoretical issues raised towards the end of the chapter relate back very closely to the focus of the study and the methods used to collect the material. In other words, embedded within the apparently perfunctory decisions about what we study are as many epistemological assumptions as there are in the more abstract debates we have about theoretical interpretation. My movement between these different methodological and theoretical levels, then, is an attempt to analyse the intellectual processes involved in working through these interconnecting problems.

When I began the research I had very little idea of what its focus would be; instead I had a desire to intervene into the debates about female spectatorship which seemed to have been so centre-stage in film theory for so long. Whilst convinced by many of the feminist criticisms of the patriarchal character of Hollywood cinema, I saw three main problems with this approach: the universalisms of its claims (especially those based on psychoanalysis); the emphasis on sexual difference as the central (and often only) signifier of cinematic meanings; and the dismissal of audience (in favour of the text) as having anything important to say about popular cinema. My starting-point, then, was a desire to find out whether another kind of story about Hollywood cinema might be told. My 'research questions', then, followed from my doubts about the existing theoretical debates: were the forms of spectatorship generated by Hollywood so limited and monolithic; how did women read images of femininity in this culture of the 'male gaze', and would audiences' accounts of

Hollywood cinema confirm the text-based claims, or might they offer insight into other readings unimagined by the film critic? My aim, however, was not to abandon the psychoanalytic insights altogether because I had (and continue to have) little doubt that unconscious processes are crucial to an understanding of how patriarchal culture reproduces itself and how and why certain visual images continue to have such strong appeal in their ever-increasing repetitious circulation. But it seemed to me that the account of the unconscious stemming from psychoanalysis had almost come to stand in for the whole of 'culture' at the expense of other processes which are central to the formations of gendered identities and the construction of particular kinds of visual images. Pushing against the textual determinism of so many accounts of spectatorship (both in terms of psyche and of film), then, I embarked on a research project which might in some way extend existing feminist accounts of Hollywood. The risk, of course, was that it might not: perhaps looking to cinema audiences would simply confirm these accounts and thus reinforce the model of Hollywood as a patriarchal monolith.

My historical focus was in part an attempt to locate the processes of spectatorship which had hitherto been so universally cast: one way perhaps to counter such universalistic tendencies would be to see whether or not these general claims about the female spectator made sense within a more specific time and place. I chose the 1940s and 1950s since it seemed to be a time of transition in which the battle over definitions of femininity were brought into particularly sharp relief by the wartime and post-war social change; the cultural construction of 'woman as image' also took on particular significance during the 1950s consumer boom. Furthermore, this period had been a key focus of feminist work on Hollywood (for example, film noir of the 1940s and melodrama of the 1950s). My choice was also a result of the significance of this period of films in my own relationship to Hollywood, both through my mother's retelling of this period and my own second-hand experience of it through television screenings of Hollywood classics (especially the Sunday matinée).

In retelling the story of this research I am aware of the temptation to represent the research project as a seamless narrative in which the next step seems inevitable. The dead-ends, the U-turns, the frustrations and the despair tend to get written out as the logic of the research project is imposed retrospectively. Such stories have been seen as problematic for the ways in which they reproduce the dominant narrative of 'history' (and, indeed, of much Hollywood cinema), in which events follow each other in a cause and effect logic, and in which the end point is shown to be the enlightened place of conclusion from which to assess the mistakes of the past. For the writer, this narrative offers structure and form to organise what are often rather haphazard and arbitrary steps in the research process; for the reader, it offers the pleasures of discovery, of recognition and of resolution; for both, order is imposed upon what once seemed chaos, and process becomes product. Within the conventions of academic presentation, this process aims to justify the specific research project, show the limits of previous ones, and point to the way forward. Working within, and yet against, these conventions, feminists have constantly had to strike a balance between challenging some academic conventions and adhering to others. In this chapter, I am both conforming to certain conventions of retrospective reconstruction, and yet undermining the smoothness of the finished product usually presented under such circumstances. Some of the narrative pleasures will therefore be offered to the reader: a chronological sequence, a move towards resolution and the retrospective interpretation of the meaning of baffling evidence by the authorial 'voice-over'. However, I hope to disrupt this streamlined linearity by focusing primarily on the *processes* of this research and the methodological issues they raise and by including some discussion of the less fruitful avenues I pursued as well as those which ultimately led in more productive directions.

Finding lost objects

The investigation of the historical reception of film raises important questions about the relationship between the cinematic institution and the female spectator. What do spectators bring to films from their own specific historical and cultural locations which then inform their readings? How do the discourses of particular historical conjunctures limit the possible readings a spectator may make of a film? Challenging both the supremacy of the text, and of the individual spectator, as the singular location of meaning production, Janet Staiger has argued that:

> What we are interested in, then, is not the so-called correct reading of a particular film but the range of possible readings and reading processes at historical moments and their relation or lack of relation to groups of historical spectators. (Staiger, 1986: 20)

As Staiger goes on to highlight, however, the investigation of the historical spectator presents the film researcher with a whole series of complex methodological and theoretical questions: what status do spectators' accounts of films have; how are these to be found; and which interpretive frameworks might be useful in analysing such accounts?[3]

Methodologically, important questions about what should count as 'data' and how this material should be treated by the researcher are raised by the historical study of cinema spectators. Finding the material in the first place is a problem, since availability is clearly difficult in the historical study of film reception. But in addition, questions of interpretation are complex, since the material cannot be seen to 'speak for itself' as if it were separate from discursive and institutional forces. What audiences tell researchers will always be shaped by the discursive factors of the interview context and will produce a very particular set of selective knowledges. This leads to theoretical questions about subjectivity and meaning: should it be assumed that the conscious retelling of the response to a film tells us how this film works? What about the processes of spectatorship which are less directly accessible? Staiger argues that such problems mean that even in the cases where film studies work has engaged with historical concerns, it has tended to focus on the institutional factors which may have shaped spectators' readings of particular films and to ignore audiences' responses.[4] According to Staiger, this evasion has been for good reason: the result of the practical, theoretical and methodological complexities that such studies pose. In addition to the problems Staiger raises, there are more specific reasons for the reluctance on the part of feminist film theorists to venture into the area of audience research.[5] A feminist analysis of cinema spectatorship of the kind I undertook, then, is a potential minefield of methodological, theoretical and political problems to which I shall now turn in more detail through an account of the research process.

The first place I searched for material for my research on cinema audiences was the Mass Observation Archive at Sussex University which held large amounts of historical material from the 1940s and 1950s and some of which concerned the cinema.

The collection of papers on the cinema includes some fifty reports on cinemagoing in Britain between 1939 and 1945. The topics range from general material, such as 'Report on Audience Preference in Film Themes', or 'The Film and Family Life', to detailed observations on responses of audiences to particular films, or descriptions of people's behaviour in a cinema queue (see Richards and Sheridan, 1987). Together with box office statistics of cinema attendance, these reports can give us an indication of which films, and perhaps which stars, were popular and when (see Thumim, 1992 and this volume). However, interesting as this material may be, it was not the kind of qualitative detail I sought in order to begin to make arguments about how female spectators might have made sense of the cinema during this period. I was particularly troubled by the mismatch between the subjects represented here and the existing debates in the field I sought to address. The questions put on the agenda by feminist theory seemed to bear no relation whatsoever to the questions of general cinemagoing habits of women at different times. For example, two striking issues emerged from this historical material: first, the great significance of the cinema in women's everyday lives in Britain in the 1940s, especially during the Second World War, and secondly, the rivalry between British and American cinema. Most feminist literature on Hollywood cinema and female spectatorship, however, paid little attention to the battle over national identities in relation to the cinema (at that time anyway, this is less true today).[6] In *retrospect* these seem interesting and theorisable questions; however, early in my research, they led to confusion and disorientation not least because they seemed *so* disconnected from the theoretical concerns of feminist film criticism.

Fortunately, my summer at the Mass Observation Archive proved more fruitful than these early explorations might have suggested. The Archive also holds all the letters (1,536) which were written to *Picturegoer* between May and November in 1940. Looking through these letters, I seemed at last to have some kind of lead. It was through the analysis of these letters that a more focused topic for this research emerged. Nearly 50 per cent of the letters concerned film stars and of the letters about film stars sent to *Picturegoer* at this time, 59 per cent were from women. Their overwhelming interest in the stars convinced me that the focus for this research should be female spectators and Hollywood stars. In addition, the absence of feminist work on stars at the time was a striking contrast to the female spectators' interest in them.[7]

The possibility of using this source, however, raised important methodological questions about the status of letters from cinema weeklies at this time. After all, as Janet Staiger argues, this material will necessarily be partial and shaped by the interests of the institution in which it was produced:

> Audience response research is invariably linked into commercial and academic institutions, already mediated by economic and theoretical projects at odds with any political goals of de-centering dominant practices or discourses. Marketing analyses, audience opinion polls, film reviews, interviews and letters to editors of periodicals are bound up with an apparatus of perpetuating the pleasure of the cinematic institution. Even if we acknowledge mediation and distortion these stumbling blocks can never be fully overcome. (Staiger, 1986: 21)

In the case of the *Picturegoer* letters it is clear that many of them are written in response to articles and features in the magazine, suggesting that the agenda for legitimate topics is largely framed by the producers of the magazine. Thus whilst letters pages in magazines such as *Picturegoer* might seem to provide suitable material for the study of star consumption, further consideration of the framing of the content of such letters demonstrates the complex overlaps between production and consumption in this case. A second problem with this source is that the opinions of more marginal groups may not be expressed within the established pages of such mainstream publications; letters printed can thus not be read as 'representative' of all spectators (Staiger, 1986: 20–2). In the case of the Mass Observation material, however, the situation is rather different. Holding all the letters from one particular period, some of which had been published and some had not, the editor's selection would not have influenced the material available, although editorials may have prompted their concerns. Furthermore, the Mass Observation letters confirm that audiences/readers do actually write to magazines, contradicting the understandable academic scepticism about whether the letters are 'genuine' or fabrications of magazine office staff.[8]

Although this finding sheds some light on the question of the validity of readers' letters, however, it does not detract from some of the other limitations of using them as a source for the study of the historical reception of film. These letters cannot be analysed outside a consideration of how the discourses of the cinema and of stardom are organised within the specific magazines. In addition, the generic conventions of letter writing for publication would need to be taken into account. Particular types of letters, such as complaints, criticism, appreciation, humorous anecdotes, and so on are recognisable forms for readers and editors, and knowledge of such forms will shape the kinds of letters written and selected for publication. To argue that this material should therefore be discounted by film historians, however, would be mistaken. Janet Staiger's claim that 'even if we acknowledge mediation and distortion, these stumbling blocks can never be fully overcome' (Staiger, 1986: 21) implies the possibility of an unproblematic source of audience response beyond such stumbling blocks. 'Mediation' and 'distortion' suggest that there is pure cinematic experience beyond the limitations of representation. I would argue that all audience researchers must deal inevitably with the question of representation, but not as a barrier to meaning, but rather as the form of that meaning. Given that language itself is a system of representation, any expression of taste, preference and pleasure is necessarily organised according to certain conventions and patterns. Perhaps some material is less defined by the institutional boundaries of the film industry, but all audience 'data' has its textual formations, produced within particular historical and cultural discourses. The problem with the Mass Observation *Picturegoer* letters for my purposes, then, was not their '*inauthenticity*', but rather that they all came from one year and thus offer few points of comparison. Since my general aim was to analyse historical change and continuity, these particular letters were unlikely to offer any conclusions. However, I left Mass Observation with a more focused topic for my research project, and with the intention of finding some comparative material of a similar kind elsewhere.

The second archive I used in my investigation of the cinema audience was the library and archive at the British Film Institute in London. Following my leads from the Mass Observation Archive, I began by surveying all the cinema magazines available at the time in the hope of finding letters pages for comparative purposes. All the letters written by female spectators about female stars in the issues of *Picturegoer* from 1940, 1945, 1950 and 1955 were analysed. Since this was a weekly magazine, I decided to sample those particular years, rather than attempt a comprehensive analysis of the letters from each issue. Articles on female stars were also analysed, since these often became the subject of the letters the following week.

Analysing the letters brought me up sharply against some of the methodological issues of using letters pages discussed above. These letters are interesting cultural texts in so far as they cut across the usual cultural divides of public and private, production and consumption; they are a conventionally 'private' form – the letter – and yet written for public consumption. However, they were clearly heavily edited and this became increasingly so as the 1950s progressed. In addition, they were often written in response to agendas set by film magazines which are part of the film industry. I therefore decided to look for further sources to supplement the letters from *Picturegoer*. Reading these letters, I had thought repeatedly about fan mail written to stars during this period. This seemed an appropriate addition to the letters I had analysed, since both took letter form and were written at the same time. Nevertheless I anticipated considerable differences between the 'private' fan mail and the 'public' letters to editors. Sitting on a shelf somewhere, I fantasised, were hundreds of old letters, like those I had found in the Mass Observation Archive, written to favourite stars and articulating the likes and dislikes of female spectators. I wrote to every possible source I could think of to find out addresses of fan clubs here and in America. I was unsure where the old letters would be, given the Second World War, the breakup of the studio system, and other intervening factors. I managed to find the addresses of about ten Hollywood stars and I wrote asking if any fan mail remained, and whether I could have access to it. Clearly fan mail would again be a very specific form of information about cinema audiences. Most obviously it is from fans rather than a cross-section of the audience, some of whom would be keener on Hollywood than others. Reading fan mail as evidence of a typical audience's feelings about the cinema, then, would be problematic. There would also be little information about dislikes, in contrast to letters pages which give a wide range of complaints as well as praise. However, my anticipations of such difficulties were wasted, since I received no positive responses to my requests. Some letters were returned unopened, others never produced a reply. A postcard from Doris Day, however, saying sorry, no, she could not help, but good luck with the project meant my search had not been completely in vain. I decided to give up on the fan clubs. I had come to the end of the road in terms of finding historical material written in the 1940s and 1950s about female stars. It was time for a rethink and a change of course.

My final option seemed to be to follow the lead of others in the field and advertise for women to write to me about their memories of their favourite film stars. As long ago as 1950, Leo Handel used the method of advertising for audiences to recount their cinemagoing experiences. More recently, Helen Taylor (1989) and Richard Dyer (1986) advertised for audiences to write to them with their accounts of their fandom of *Gone With the Wind* (1939, Victor Flemming) and of Judy Garland respectively. Initially, I had wanted to look at the discourses which existed at the time, rather than those reconstructed retrospectively, but it became increasingly clear that if I wanted fuller qualitative material I would have to be willing to consider memories of Hollywood stars as a possible source.

I sent a letter to the four leading British women's magazines whose readerships were generally women of fifty and over: *Woman*, *Woman's Own*, *Woman's Weekly* and *Woman's Realm*. These were the most popular magazines in terms of having high sales, and also caught a readership of the age group who were likely to remember the cinema in the 1940s and 1950s. 'Keen cinemagoers' from this period were invited to write to me about their favourite Hollywood stars and were asked to request a questionnaire if they were interested. Two magazines, *Woman's Realm* and *Woman's Weekly*, published my letter and I had an overwhelming response. Altogether I received over 350 letters, and they continued to arrive from Canada, Australia and New Zealand, where the magazines come out some months behind Britain, two years later. The letters varied enormously: some were ten pages long offering remarkably rich details, others were simply requests for a questionnaire.

A questionnaire was then compiled from the themes emerging from the letters. Thus the material from respondents generated the structure and content of the questionnaire. It was the specific interests and concerns of these female spectators which shaped the future direction of my research at this stage: rather than just asking about stars, which had been my original intention, I decided to situate the stars' questions within a broader remit. Rather than simply being asked detailed questions about stars cold, respondents were first asked to answer questions about their general cinemagoing habits at that time. The more practical details of cinemagoing, how often, with whom, how this changed, reasons for visit, and so on were designed to enable respondents to write about film stars in relation to their cinemagoing practices more generally, as they had done in their letters. The form of the questionnaire was a mixture of structured and more open-ended questions. This was finally decided upon by referring to existing work using questionnaires, such as those of Radway (1984) and Taylor (1989), and advice from experts in the field.[9] The structured, multiple-choice questions were designed to offer a contrast to the open-ended questions, and to offer respondents the pleasure of quick, easy selection of categories in which they recognised themselves. The more open-ended questions were to encourage them to provide the qualitative material I was interested in for more in-depth analysis.

Of the women who requested a questionnaire only twenty decided not to return it. This high return rate is clearly due to the fact that these questionnaires were requested by a group of cinema enthusiasts, and not a group of randomly chosen respondents. Many sent me diaries, scrapbooks, old photos and leaflets, as well as their completed questionnaires. On the whole, the questionnaires were completed very fully, and the description of favourite stars often went on to two or three extra pages, if not more. The group of respondents was a relatively homogeneous one. This is not surprising since all the women were readers of the same two leading women's magazines. In general, my respondents tended to come from similar class backgrounds in the 1940s and 1950s, though many of them have since shifted to more middle-class positions through marriage or changes in education, training and employment.

Class position is notoriously difficult to ascertain for women, since women's class position is frequently defined through their husband's paid employment, and the category 'housewife' which many women use to describe themselves is one which does not explicitly indicate class position. However, based upon information such as ownership of accommodation, educational qualifications and employment of the respondents and their spouses, typically respondents came from predominantly the same class backgrounds which are, not surprisingly, the same class of women which the magazines appeal to (primarily C1 and C2, 'Lower middle class and skilled working class', according to the magazines' readers' profiles). This is also consistent with the statistics available on the composition of the cinema audience during this period. Furthermore, the respondents to my advertisement were all white women. This is not surprising, given the magazines which agreed to print my request; both *Woman's Weekly* and *Woman's Realm* appeal predominantly to a white readership. Thus the study remains a study of white British female spectatorship in relation to Hollywood stars. It is a study of white fantasy and the relationships between white female spectators and their white ideals on the Hollywood screen. A further study would be necessary to look at Black women's relationship to Hollywood stars and such a study would doubtless reveal a specific set of issues for Black female audiences.

The outcome of this fourth investigation, then, was a proliferation of material from a very specific group of female spectators. The shift from a scarcity of historical material to an abundance of memories of Hollywood and its stars was very sudden and very striking. I now had over 350 letters and 238 questionnaires (each 12 pages long) to analyse. The sheer volume was daunting, if exciting, and the methodological implications increasing in their complexity. I therefore abandoned the idea of going back to the material I had already collected on Hollywood stars, since these letters and questionnaires proved such a rich source of material that it became increasingly clear that this should be the main focus of the research project.

Producing the past

> 'History' is a record of subjective readings of the past; it exists only in the perspective of the lens through which it is viewed ... History is not simply a study of the *past* by official historians. We are all historians of the *present*; 'popular memory' is produced socially and collectively as a précis of the past and everyone is a kind of historian. (Taylor, 1989: 203)

> Memory alone cannot resurrect past time, because it is memory itself that shapes it, long after historical time has passed. (Steedman, 1986: 29)

The question of the relationship between memory and history is a tricky one. Yet it is a crucial one for those interested in the historical reception of film, if we are seriously concerned with the history of cinema audiences and not just the history of films (Allen, 1990). The history of audiences necessitates some consideration of memory if it is not to remain at the purely quantitative level; in other words if film history is to engage with ethnographic methods of audience analysis, as well as detailing cinema attendance statistically, then memory has to be of central consideration, since audiences always 'retell' their viewing experiences to researchers retrospectively. However, in this research, the length of the gap between the events and their recollection (forty or fifty years) highlights the question of the processes of memory especially sharply.

Spectators' memories of Hollywood stars, then, need to be considered within a critical framework highlighting these processes of memory itself. Memory is not a straightforward representation of past events to which we have direct access and which we can in turn retell to others. Instead it involves a set of complex cultural processes: these operate at a psychic and a social level, producing identities through the negotiation of 'public' discourses and 'private' narratives. These histories of spectatorship are retrospective reconstructions of a past in the light of the present and will have been shaped by the popular versions of the 1940s and 1950s which have become cultural currency during the intervening years.[10]

As is true of all the sources discussed in this chapter, the rules of the enquiry frame the kind of information elicited. The form of the request for audiences' recollections of Hollywood stars will have shaped the memories sent to me. The kind of advertisement for responses clearly had a determining effect on the material I received. Answers to an advertisement asking for recollections of favourite stars inevitably produce a particular set of representations resulting from a specific cultural context. Advertising for 'keen cinemagoers of the 1940s and 1950s', for example, addressed potential respondents as a distinct group; in recognising themselves in this category, respondents were constructed as a particular kind of authority: the 'amateur expert'. The private pleasures of collecting cinema memorabilia and of having film star expertise is thus given a kind of public importance in such research. In turn, my recognition of their 'expertise' could have been perceived to be flattering, and indeed to have set up an expectation that their 'keenness' as cinemagoers in this period had to be demonstrated either through the detail of their accounts, or through an expression of the significance of cinema in their lives.

The request for information about a period at such historical distance also shaped the material I received: respondents may have felt recognised as a valuable source of historical information, and thus endeavoured to give as much detail as they could remember. Furthermore, my advertisement suggested an academic recognition, or indeed, validation, of women's pleasure in Hollywood cinema during this period, thus combining two things rarely taken seriously or given much status: popular culture and its female spectators. In other research, women had expressed shame in their pleasure because they were aware of its low status (Taylor, 1989: 204).

The kinds of selections respondents made when remembering what Hollywood stars meant in their lives would also have been framed by the subsequent histories of the stars in question: which stars were remembered and how they were remembered must have been influenced by the cultural constructions of those stars since that time. For example, audiences may have remembered stars differently depending on whether the stars were still alive, and if not, how they had died (such as Marilyn Monroe) and indeed when they had died (Bette Davis died during the time the questionnaire was with respondents); whether they still had a fan club (such as Deanne Durbin); whether the star had continued to have a successful career (such as Katharine Hepburn and Bette Davis); whether their films had been shown frequently on television and indeed whether the stars had gone on to have a television career (such as Barbara Stanwyck).

In addition to these factors, memories are recollections of the past through changing historical discourses. Assessments of stars will inevitably have been affected by changing notions of acceptable femininity and female sexuality. The different constructions of femininity within Hollywood, such as the power and rebelliousness of Bette Davis or the sexual attractiveness of Marilyn Monroe, or the clean-livingness of Deanna Durbin may have had particular appeal in retrospect, and they may have come to mean something over the years which they did not in the 1940s and 1950s. For example, what effect did the 'permissive' 1960s have on discourses of stardom and glamour? To what extent might stars have been re-evaluated through a post-1960s understanding of female sexuality? How might women's increased participation in the public sphere have transformed the discourses through which Hollywood's 'independent women' stars have been read? To what extent might the increased visibility of lesbians and gay men in society have encouraged a re-evaluation of early 'attachments' to stars of the same sex?

What gets remembered and what gets forgotten may depend not only on the star's career and changing discourses since the time period specified, but also upon the identity of the cinema spectator. The kinds of representations offered will have been informed by issues such as the respondents' own personal histories. The ways in which their lives had changed, and the feelings they had about their past, present and future selves, will have been amongst the factors determining the memories produced for the purposes of this research. There is thus a specificity to the production of the memories of Hollywood stars which form the basis of this research and the conventions through which knowledge about the past is formed. Rather than seeing these conditions and conventions as *barriers* to 'the real past', as if it existed separately from our retelling of it, I highlighted them as an integral part of the research. What is important here is to recognise the factors shaping these women's memories of Hollywood stars and to analyse the conventions through which such material is represented.

Textual spectators?

The question of the textual conventions of popular forms is one which bridges debates about popular memory and those about ethnography, since both involve the problem of the interpretation of personal accounts. This is, however, a general issue in the analysis of media reception, be it of interviews, letters or questionnaires. For feminists, this presents problems of long-standing concern about the politics of interpretation in research. In particular, the power of the feminist researcher to interpret other women's feelings and thoughts from a position of expertise in the academy is highlighted. There are certainly fewer moral dilemmas for feminists who continue to analyse film texts to which they are never held accountable in terms of the politics of methodology. This dilemma may be a reason for the reluctance of feminist film critics to engage with audiences, as well as their anxieties about committing the cardinal sin of 'empiricism'. Those who have criticised the method that treats audiences' accounts as texts may argue that it is patronising to the women concerned. It may seem more 'democratic' simply to let women speak for themselves, since, many have argued, women are rarely listened to in this culture. Indeed, much early feminist oral history and documentary film aimed to 'give women a voice' and to make visible their experiences. However, some kind of interpretive framework is inevitable in academic research, and avoiding analysis of women audiences because of embarrassment or anxiety about imposing such a framework merely perpetuates their absence from feminist film theory. The role of the researcher is to interpret the material that audiences produce within a critical framework which is appropriate to the material and which is made explicit and can therefore be contested. Thus a dialectical relationship emerges between the material studied and the theory used to analyse it. In my own research, female spectators' accounts of the cinema were used to critique or confirm existing film theory, and indeed to produce new or refined categories which could usefully add to our understanding of how audiences watch films.

How, then, might audiences' accounts be considered as texts, and yet maintain a different status from the texts of film theory? How might we move beyond the simplistic ascription of audiences' responses as the 'authentic truth' about media meaning, whilst avoiding treating them as simply another kind of narrative fiction? How might some aspects of the psychoanalytic conception of the subject be retained, if modified, within studies of 'real audiences'? The material I received from my respondents presented me with just such dilemmas. In aiming to produce a historical study of women's memories of Hollywood stars in the 1940s and 1950s, I wanted to address some of the questions generated by the psychoanalytic feminist film theory, such as those about image and identity, using methods drawn from the very different traditions in cultural studies audience research. However, what interested me when I began this research was the extent to which the psychoanalytic and the historical investigation of female spectatorship were *necessarily* incompatible. In film theory, any engagement with audiences has been dismissed as crudely or naively empiricist, and in film history there have been few 'ethnographic' analyses of audiences; instead studies have tended to focus on the institutional reception of films or on quantitative material about cinema audiences in the past. For some the most obvious reason for this incompatibility between psychoanalytic film criticism and ethnographic cultural studies is the issue of the unconscious. These two approaches, it has been argued, are contradictory because ethnography deals with 'conscious and easily articulated response' and ignores the unconscious, whereas psychoanalytic readings would mistrust audiences' accounts emphasising instead the importance of unconscious processes to the meanings of visual images (Feuer, quoted in Morley, 1989: 24). However, my aim was to move beyond the standard binarism of conscious, empirical description versus psychoanalytic insights into the unconscious patterns of the psyche.[11]

David Morley has defended his ethnographic method of interviewing television audiences as 'a fundamentally more appropriate way to attempt to understand what audiences do when they watch television than for the analyst to sit at home and imagine the possible implications of how other people might watch television, in the manner that Feuer suggests' (Morley, 1989: 24). The suggestion is not that audiences are the only source of meaning, but that if we are concerned with questions of reception and cultural consumption, then the study of audiences will provide material not otherwise available to media researchers. Similarly, I would argue that if we are interested in female spectatorship then it is important to find out what female spectators say about Hollywood. In other words, I am arguing for the importance of putting spectators back into theories of female spectatorship.

As I have argued, audiences' responses are not self-evident truths about what the media means; this would completely ignore the ways in which subjectivities are constituted through ideological discourses. The Althusserian and Lacanian work in the 1970s may have ascribed too much power to the dominant ideology and the symbolic order respectively, negating any notion of the historical agency of subjects, but to ignore issues of power relations in the name of celebrating popular taste is equally misguided. Thus, in my research these memories of Hollywood stars were treated as texts in so far as they are forms of representation produced within certain cultural conventions. I would argue that the analysis of any form of representation requires a consideration of these conventions. Indeed, these conventions should not be seen as a barrier to the real meaning underneath, but rather as forming *part of the meaning itself*. In this research, for example, the processes of self-narrativisation discussed above would be one such convention which needs to be seen as part of the mechanisms of memory formation. To take such an approach, however, is not to argue that what my respondents wrote to me is purely fictional, and thus of only relative significance to other fictions. Taking account of the narrative formations of audiences' memories is not to rob them of their specificity, and to treat them as fictional narratives like the films they were watching. This would be to confuse the categories of narrative and of fiction.[12] To argue that audiences produce narrative accounts of their responses to Hollywood is not to say that they may as well have made them up! Indeed, the importance of taking account of the cultural conventions of audiences' stories is precisely intended here to deal with them *in their specificity*. Audiences' memories of Hollywood stars, then, are obviously texts, but they are specific kinds of texts produced within a specific set of conditions. The readings of Hollywood that they produce need therefore to be situated within the context of their production. What I have highlighted, then, is the importance of audiences as a source for the study of the reception of film, without rendering them supreme, or transparent conveyors of historical truths.

However, I *am* arguing for a method of analysis which takes what audiences say seriously. There is little point in gathering such material simply to analyse what is in excess of its textuality. In other words I did not seek to take on the role of analyst in relation to these accounts of the past. There are particular implications here for the politics of the power relations between the researcher and those being researched. To analyse their responses in terms of their unconscious psychic structures which the researcher, but not the researched, can identify is to impose the greatest degree of power difference between the two parties. The assumption behind such a method of interpretation is that audiences have offered information, but that the researcher can read between the lines for the latent meanings which reveal unconscious responses that are more significant than those apparently offered by the respondents. In some ways the question of the use of psychoanalytic theory here only intensifies the general problems of the power of the researcher to interpret audiences' responses. After all, critical analysis of the narrative structures of, or personal investments in, memory also involves highlighting hidden or implicit mechanisms. The question of the unconscious puts these issues into particularly sharp relief: it could be argued that psychoanalysing audiences' responses invests the researcher with maximum power and the audience with least agency. In analysing these memories I thus felt a constant tension between taking seriously what had been written and uncovering some of their more hidden implications and assumptions. Furthermore, I wanted to represent these accounts respectfully and in their full complexity, rather than just as an abstracted means to an end, and yet also to be able to make critical interpretations from my point of view as a feminist researcher with an interest in challenging the terms of patriarchal culture. It should also be remembered that many of the methodological (and often 'ethical') problems concerned with the use of psycho-analysis in media interpretation apply to textual analysis, as well as to audience studies. Thus, another problem with this rigid division between ethnographic empiricism and theories of the unconscious is that it somewhat evades the methodological issues involved in the psychoanalytically informed textual analysis of film (rarely discussed in film studies) which similarly speculates about the unconscious of the spectator 'without the benefit of the therapeutic situation'.

In my research the boundary between empirical audience research and psychoanalytic textual analysis could not be drawn as straightforwardly as Feuer (in Morley, 1989) suggests. Instead my material demanded a consideration of cultural processes such as those of memory, identify formations, fantasy and day dreaming which involve unconscious processes, but also need to be analysed in terms of the conscious everyday meanings they have for cinema spectators. There are indeed many modes and levels of perception significant to the analysis of spectator/star relations in the 1940s and 1950s. A consideration of psycho-analytic theory and ethnographies of media audiences, therefore, needs to take account of the potential complexity of the relationship; it may be that methods of interpretation, theoretical perspectives, object of study and research questions cannot be collapsed into straightforward choices between the psycho-analytic and empirical traditions of film and cultural studies.

However, I would not want to deny the difficulties of com-bining a psychoanalytic with a historical approach. My own perspective then could be summed up as follows: in this research I continued to address issues generated by psychoanalytic film theory, and I did so from a critical perspective which also sought to question its universalist claims about female spectatorship and Hollywood cinema. What the project aimed to offer was an investigation of the ways in which psychic investments are grounded within specific sets of historical and cultural relations which in turn shape the formation of identities on conscious and unconscious levels. In short, my investigation analysed the relationship between psychic and social formations, challenging the ways in which the latter has so often been ignored at the expense of the former within feminist film criticism.

Notes

A longer version of this chapter first appeared in *Star Gazing: Hollywood Cinema and Female Spectatorship* (Stacey, 1994a). It is reprinted here with a new introduction.

I would like to thank all the women who wrote to me with their memories of Hollywood stars for contributing to this study. I am also indebted to those who read earlier drafts of this work, most especially: Richard Dyer, Sarah Franklin, Hilary Hinds, Richard Johnson, Celia Lury, Maureen McNeil and Lynne Pearce.

1 Most notably: Dorothy Hobson (1982); Tania Modleski (1984); Janice Radway (1984); Ien Ang (1985) and Ann Gray (1992).

2 Although not based upon audience studies, both Miriam Hansen's book (1991) and Angela Partington's work (1991) investigate questions of cinema history and spectatorship.

3 See Janet Staiger's book on the question of cinema history and methodology, Staiger (1992). See also Janet Thumim (1991, 1992) in which important questions about methodology and cinema history are raised.

4 See, for example, Philip Corrigan (1983), Thomas Elsaesser (1984), Janet Staiger (1986, 1992) and Mary Ann Doane (1987, 1989).

5 See Brunsdon (1991) and Stacey (1993).

6 The work of Antonia Lant (1991) is an exception to this.

7 Recent publications on stars which have filled this gap to some extent include Gledhill (1991) and Butler (1991).

8 I am grateful to Jane Gaines for pointing out to me the problem of the 'authenticity' of the letters sent to editors of film weeklies.

9 I am indebted to Phil Levy and David Clarke in the Department of Information Studies at the University of Sheffield for their guidance and advice on the structure and question formulation in the questionnaire compiled for this research.

10 There is insufficient space here to pursue questions of memory and historical methodology; however, these have been written about elsewhere, see, for example, Popular Memory Group (1982); Frigga Haugg (ed.) (1987); and Stacey (1994a, b).

11 For an example of research which brings together psychoanalysis and ethnography, see Walkerdine (1986).

12 Christopher Norris made a useful distinction between history as narrative and history as fiction in his paper, 'Deconstruction vs. Postmodernism' at the *Literary Studies in a Postmodern World* conference, held at Lancaster University on 4 May 1991.

Bibliography

Allen, R. C. (1990), From Exhibition to Reception: Reflections on the Audience in Film History, *Screen*, 31:4, 347–56.

Ang, I. (1985), *Watching Dallas: Soap Opera and the Melodramatic Imagination*, London, Methuen.

Brunsdon, C. (1991), Pedagogies of the Feminine: Feminist Teaching and Women's Genres, *Screen*, 32:4, 364–81.

Butler, J. (ed.) (1991), *Star Texts: Image and Performance in Film and Television*, Detroit, Wayne State University Press.

Corrigan, P. (1983), Film Entertainment as Ideology and Pleasure: A Preliminary Approach to a History of Audiences, in J. Curran and V. Porter (eds), *British Cinema History*, London, Weidenfeld and Nicholson.

Doane, M. A. (1987), *The Desire to Desire: The Woman's Film of the 1940's*, Bloomington and Indianapolis, Indiana University Press.

Doane, M. A. (1989), The Economy of Desire: The Commodity Form in/of the Cinema, *Quarterly Review of Film and Video*, 11, 23–33.

Dyer, R. (1986), *Heavenly Bodies: Film Stars and Society*, Basingstoke, Macmillan.

Elsaesser, T. (1984), Film History and Visual Pleasure: Weimar Cinema, in P. Mellencamp and P. Rosen (eds), *Cinema Histories, Cinema Practices*, American Film Institute Monograph Series, 4, Frederic, Maryland, University Publications of America.

Gledhill, C. (ed.) (1991), *Stardom: Industry of Desire*, London, Routledge.

Gray, A. (1992), *Video Playtime: The Gendering of a Leisure Technology*, London, Routledge.

Handel, L. (1950), *Hollywood Looks at its Audience*, Urbana, Illinois, University of Illinois Press.

Hansen, M. (1991), *Babel and Babylon: Spectatorship in American Silent Film*, Cambridge, Mass., Harvard University Press.

Haugg, F. (ed.) (1987), *Female Sexualisation*, London, Verso.

Hobson, D. (1982), *Crossroads: The Drama of a Soap Opera*, London, Methuen.

Lant, A. (1991), *Blackout: Reinventing Women for Wartime British Cinema*, Princeton, New Jersey, Princeton University Press.

Modleski, T. (1984), *Loving With A Vengeance: Mass-Produced Fantasies for Women*, London, Methuen.

Morley, D. (1989), Changing Paradigms in Audience Studies, in E. Seiter, H. Borchers, G. Kreutzner and E. M. Warth (eds), *Remote Control: Television, Audiences and Cultural Power*, London, Routledge.

Partington, A. (1991), Melodrama's Gendered Audience, in C. Lury, S. Franklin and J. Stacey (eds), *Off Centre: Feminism and Cultural Studies*, London, HarperCollins/Routledge.

Popular Memory Group (1982), Popular Memory: Theory, Politics and Method, in R. Johnson *et al.* (eds), *Making Histories*, London, Hutchinson.

Radway, J. (1984), *Reading the Romance: Women, Patriarchy and Popular Literature*, Chapel Hill, London, University of North Carolina Press.

Richards, J. and D. Sheridan (eds) (1987), *Mass Observation at the Movies*, London, Routledge and Kegan Paul.

Stacey, J. (1993), Textual Obsessions: Method, Memory and Researching Female Spectatorship, *Screen*, 34:3, 260–74.

Stacey, J. (1994a), *Star Gazing: Hollywood Cinema and Female Spectatorship*, London, Routledge.

Stacey, J. (1994b), Hollywood Memories, *Screen*, 35:4, 317–35.

Staiger, J. (1986), *The Handmaiden of Villainy*: Methods and Problems in Studying the Historical Reception of Film, *Wide Angle*, 8:1, 19–28.

Staiger, J. (1992), *Interpreting Films: Studies in the Historical Reception of American Cinema*, Princeton, New Jersey, Princeton University Press.

Steedman, C. (1986), *Landscape for a Good Woman: A Story of Two Lives*, London, Virago.

Taylor, H. (1989), *Scarlett's Women: 'Gone with the Wind' and its Female Fans*, London, Virago.

Thumim, J. (1991), The 'Popular': Cash and Culture in the Postwar British Cinema Industry, *Screen*, 32:3, 245–71.

Thumim, J. (1992), *Celluloid Sisters: Women and Popular Cinema*, London, Macmillan.

Walkerdine, V. (1986), Video Replay: Families, Films and Fantasy, in V. Burgin, J. Donald and C. Kaplan (eds), *Formations of Fantasy*, London, Methuen.

6

Writing *Femininity in Dissent*

ALISON YOUNG

In early 1994, a review of *Femininity in Dissent* was published in *Social and Legal Studies*. The reviewer stated:

> For all her emphasis on the definitions, metaphors and re-presentation applied to Greenham Women, Alison Young denies them any voice which is theirs. They are absent from her study, their experiences seemingly marginal to the deconstruction – and reconstruction – of the press discourse. They have no presence, no access to the text, to the analysis, to the post-structuralist reconstruction of their lives, their actions, their politics. What did they think, feel, know about the media portrayals, press manipulations and re-presentation of their lives? We don't know from this text – they weren't asked. What is more, the text itself practises and purveys an exclusionism of which the academic traditions, so masculinist in their underpinnings, would be proud. (Scraton, 1994: 191)

Earlier in the review, he writes:

> Alison Young is physically distanced from the direct action of Greenham Common, engaged in an entirely different project. Here is a third level construct, not discussing media representation with the women, not discussing media representation with reporters, sub-editors or editors but, rather, recounting 'how a women's peace protest could be represented as a criminal activity, a witches' coven, a threat to the state, the family and the democratic order ... (Scraton, 1994: 189)

Reading reviews of your own book is always a traumatic experience; but this review seemed to me to be more painful than usual. Its publication coincided with my reflecting upon the writing of *Femininity in Dissent*, for the purposes of writing this piece. Having been asked to consider the 'hows and whys' of the project, the discovery of a review which so mis-stated the book's aims, intention and methodology impelled me to address explicitly certain aspects of the project. The book originated as my doctoral thesis. It was completed as a thesis in 1988 and re-written for publication during 1989. Its stated purpose was 'to look at the discourse constructed by the national press around a particular form of defiance, an anti-nuclear protest by women at the Greenham Common missile base' (Young, 1990: viii). To that extent, it could have been deemed a 'third level' or meta-commentary, in that its main aim was to analyse years of press coverage and to render such a discourse open to criticism by virtue of various techniques of textual analysis (elaboration of its main themes, its metaphorical structures, its narrative form and its political and institutional underpinnings). Its intention was indeed to be academic, in that it began life as a Ph.D. and ended up as an academic book, but my aim was always to write, within that form, a political text: political in seeking to ask '(the often ignored) questions about the construction of categories' (1990: ix) in seeking to resist the construction of truth and self-evidence present in press reports (1990: viii) and, most important-ly for me, in analysing an instance of the representation of sexual difference as one of 'the key ways in which the normal is marked out from the deviant' (1990: ix).

The Greenham Common peace camp was a protest by women outside a Cruise missile base in Berkshire, England.[1] It began in August 1981, and some of the protesters remain at the Common at time of writing. Its unique dynamic was a demand for dis-armament linked to an analysis of patriarchy. Their unique methods of 'doing politics' won them an international following (appropriate to such an international issue: the presence of American missiles in England as part of NATO's European 'defence' policies). Support for the camp was immense: women from many different countries visited it; women from the camp travelled through the Pacific nations and the United States. At least two other peace camps were inspired by Greenham Com-mon (Seneca Falls in the United States and Pine Gap in Australia) while dozens of permanent and temporary camps were set up in Britain, following the Greenham example. Thousands of women joined in their demonstrations and hundreds lived at the camp, some for years on end. Still more were made aware of issues relating to disarmament through the Greenham women's own information networks and through media coverage of the protest. The Greenham women took legal action in the United States against the American government. In Britain, they challenged the legitimacy of local by-laws. They engaged in non-violent direct action ranging from mass demonstrations to protests by individual women. They breached the perimeter fence on count-less occasions and on others turned it into a gallery of women's creative artwork. These unique political strategies made the Greenham protest highly visible. In Britain, the protest came to epitomise peace politics (for both sympathetic followers and more hostile observers). The news media established the Greenham women as the focal point of their coverage of peace politics. However, the protest came to represent much more than this. The women were alternately ridiculed, revered, castigated, humiliated and reviled. In later years, they were simply ignored. The media created a mythology around the camp which centred on the fact that the protesters were *women* and elaborated this into an account of their *deviance*.

My aim, as a Ph.D. student in Cambridge and later in writing the book, was to ascertain how such a mythologising was possible. In going about this, I made various excursions through criminol-ogy, media studies, feminist theory, sociology of deviance, dis-course analysis and social theory (in a manner very much typical of Ph.D. students and first books). The result was a range of theoretical concepts with which I not only proceeded to analyse the press reports but also retrospectively reconsidered the precepts of my education to date, particularly the legalistic dogma no law student can avoid. (Around this time I distanced myself from any interest in 'the law', finding it to be the horror from which, through social theory and feminist theory, I had escaped. Later, after writing *Femininity in Dissent*, I became aware of reasons why law constitutes, now, the primary object of my research: this is partly a result of teaching would-be lawyers and feeling appalled by the unquestioning conviction many hold that law is an un-problematic social institution, and partly to do with a desire to resist, through writing, law's construction of feminine identity.)

The theoretical concepts which were to prove so important to me were drawn from discourse analysis (particularly from Bakhtin and Pecheux), from legal theory (especially the work of Goodrich), post-modernism (Lyotard on *l'impresentable*), post-structuralism (Derrida on *difference*) and certain feminist writings (Irigaray, Cixous and Kristeva, who were, in the mid-1980s, an almost inseparable trinity). To that extent, my interests fitted in to dominant trends in academic writing in the mid to late 1980s, although as a student I did not realise that at the time. I remember feeling shocked when I found out that the work of

Irigaray and Kristeva (which I tended to consider my 'discovery' – due partly to the isolation experienced by a student registered in one disciplinary area and working with materials which were being freely discussed in other departments, and partly to the possessiveness with which most of us view our ideas) was the subject of a weekly reading group for feminists in Cambridge.

From discourse analysis I derived concepts which demanded an analysis of the press as institutional, historical and linguistic constructs, rather than a content-based counting of atomised words and phrases. Through reading post-structuralism and post-modernism I saw that history did not have to be seen as an inevitable progression towards or from Enlightenment, that difference was positive, that resistance and power went together. These ideas were extremely useful in enabling me to view the Greenham women as creating acts of resistance to the press, the police, the government, the local residents, and to view the press as products of their institutional positionality and history and thus limited, rather than overwhelming. This latter point was very important since on occasions after a day of reading *The Sun* at the library I would feel the considerable weight of the media invective. Finally, from Kristeva, Cixous and Irigaray, I was able to find a way through the maze of feminist theory that debated equality, difference, sameness, heterosexuality, lesbianism. I wanted to talk about femininity as a *category*, contingent, productive and able to exist discursively, without any essential relation to women as individuals. This seemed important not only in order to understand the press representation of Greenham women as Woman, but also in order to be able to admire the Greenham women's political methods without necessarily adopting their views as *if* they represented all women.

My theoretical interests influenced many of my analytical and methodological choices: for example, through reading Bakhtin, I became interested in Blanchot and Ricoeur; from there it was a short hop to realising that I wanted to study narrative form in the press discourse (not merely the narratives contained in individual press reports, but also the overarching narrative constructed when an event is covered in the press for several years). Similarly, reading my way slowly through Derrida (as almost every postgraduate student at Cambridge was then doing), brought me one day to his essay 'White Mythologies' and its startling account of metaphor. I then began thinking about the substance of the press reports, now faithfully transcribed on hundreds of index cards. I saw that the themes I had identified in the press discourse (the Greenham women as threat to the state, dirt and disease, mother, lesbian, hysterical woman) did not simply exist as a *surface* in the press discourse, but rather obtained most of their condemnatory purchase (and they were used as condemnation) through foundational metaphorical structures which ensured that a motif – for example, mother – was to be read *negatively* instead of positively. Metaphors therefore worked actively to fix the necessarily unstable meanings in an abstract theme, and to fix them in ways derogatory to the protest.

It is difficult to describe in any coherent way how this process of reading and analysing developed. I remember the experience of being a postgraduate student as one of openness: within the formal limits of the thesis, it seemed that I was surrounded by an abundance of materials. As I read my way around, there were punctuating moments when my half-thought ideas condensed and crystallised. The first such occasion occurred after a long period of reading what my supervisor (a male Marxist with views much like those of the reviewer cited above) had directed me to. Bored with the dominant ideology thesis, I was foraging in the Feminism section of the library in the Social and Political Sciences Department (attempting interdisciplinary work meant being departmentally un-homed and spending most of my time outside my own – criminology – department) when I came upon Marks and de Courtivron's *New French Feminisms*. After reading this book, I could find no expression to describe to friends its effect on me other than 'it blew my mind'. Something in the fragmented, diverse pieces gave voice to my sense of feminism and its place in the research. I found that its heterogeneous voices, with their shared emphasis on the powers of discourse and of feminism, gave me a way to describe what I wanted my project to do: to analyse the relationship between sexual difference, language or discourse, and social structure.

Since the project was about the press discourse (and not about the protest *per se*), my empirical work involved, for the most part, reading newspapers in the university library. It took several weeks to transcribe about a year and a half of press reports on to index cards. Reading newspapers in a library for research purposes is a strange experience. I came across some reports that I had actually seen, years ago, when they were originally published as 'news'. Indeed, one of the most unpleasant reports, in *The Sun* ('Pigs' Jibe At Police And Gays Hit Nukes Demo', 14 December 1982), I read on that very day in a newspaper at my parents' house. At the time I had read the story very uncritically (and I could recall very sharply how I felt very distanced from and condemnatory of the women and their protest as represented in the report). Years later, as I sat in the library in July 1986 re-reading the report I was filled with anger at the representation, and at its effect on me all those years ago. In between those two readings had developed – through studying feminist theory and Foucault, through being a Scottish female who did not go to public school at male, upper-class, anglicising Cambridge – a sense of feminism, of inequality and injustice. In many ways, my own certainty as to how a press report could influence its reader was based, not on reader-response theory, but on a memory of my own reactions. In *Femininity in Dissent* I had written of my desire to provide readers with the tools to resist the powerful discourse of the press, stating that '[the book] will have achieved its ends if it can provide its readers with the means to resist the discourse on deviance generated in the press' (1990: 152) and that 'I have attempted to take part in ... a struggle against the force of ... condemnatory representations' (1990: 152). At these points, I had in mind one archetypal reader: my earlier self.

Throughout the writing of the Ph.D. and the book, I was conscious that I did not want to write *on* the Greenham women; I wanted to write *on* the press reports' *representations* of the Greenham women and thus open up the space of representation to analysis. This seemed a crucial distinction. The press routinely denied any voice or autonomy to the women as subjects; they were indeed thoroughly objectified in the most base ways by the press discourse. One of the most depressing aspects of the research, for a *Guardian* reader, was finding that no newspaper really escaped this criticism. Even the most liberal broadsheet newspaper indulged in versions of the techniques that were foregrounded in the tabloid press. Even where a Greenham woman was directly quoted (to give 'balance'), her views were often positioned at the very end of the report, or surrounded by representatives of the dominant order (police officers, members of Parliament, residents of Newbury). Doing this research meant the end of any simple reading pleasure in newspapers.

It therefore was important to me not to repeat the denial of subjectivity to the Greenham women. More than this, I wanted to try to represent their voices within my own text. I did not wish to *judge* the protest, to offer an opinion as to whether their political choices were appropriate or even feminist. That seemed to be part of some other project. However, since I had been so appalled by the nature of their representation in the press discourse, I strove to allow their own voices, albeit mediated through *my* discourse, to be heard. This was not done with any intention of claiming that my research contained *their* reality: that would have been to repeat the arrogance of the newspapers (and I was also critical at various junctures in the research of those media scholars who claimed to offer 'reality' in contradistinction to the mere 'representation' of the press, forgetting to acknowledge the mediation their own texts produced). My aim was to show the powerful persuasiveness of the press and at the same time to afford the Greenham women an opportunity to tell a different story.

> [R]ecounting, as much as possible, the stories, ideas and hopes of the women participants. Due to the hierarchical and exclusive structuring of methods of information dissemination, the views of the Greenham women are not often heard [in the press] ... The views of the proponents of the necessity of nuclear deterrence are easily accessible; alternative ideological or political positions are less available. It has therefore been a determined political choice to employ as information almost solely the words and ideas, in short, the *discourse* of the Greenham women. (1990: 15)

To do this, I obtained as much material as I could that was produced by Greenham women themselves: pamphlets, songs, films, books, newsletters, posters. I also went to Greenham Common on several very wet days and spoke with women there. This proved to be a very mixed experience: my first encounter was at Blue Gate, where the women seemed resentful of outsiders and even hostile to my presence (were they tired of reporters, of any kind of assessing eyes?). At Green Gate, the women were immensely welcoming (and they laughingly referred to Blue Gate as my 'baptism of fire'). Sitting under tarpaulins in the freezing rain and slick mud, they told me of planned actions within the base and discussed the tactics of the police. Yet they too evinced no interest in the idea that I was writing a Ph.D. about the press coverage of their protest. One woman said that if I wouldn't come and live at the base and take part in their struggle, then I was as good as 'against' them. Without hostility, they were simply of the opinion that political action did not include research. This is one reason why my research did not include large amounts of data gained from interviews with the Greenham woman:

they were not interested. But that is not to say – as the reviewer did – that they were not asked. They were asked, and, in the main, they did not wish to speak to me about it.

Some individual women were extremely helpful. Interestingly, these were women whom I met away from the base. Jean Hutchinson, who had lived at Greenham for several years, spent hours with me talking into a tape recorder about 'awful little men from *The Sun*' and her views of the years of scornful press coverage. Jane Hickman, a lawyer for the women, also spoke to me at some length about the protest. All the women's contributions were acknowledged in the book; many of the footnotes detailed information that had come from interviews or correspondence.[2] And yet, the review cited at the beginning of this essay confidently asserted that I had not asked any of the women (or any other person, such as a journalist) for their opinion. How is such a mis-reading possible? My guess is that it is a consequence of the book's theoretical scaffolding. A text which states its aims to be the 'excavation of a discursive site' (1990: 3) and reading the 'factors at work in the preconstruction of dialogue' (1990: 8), permits sceptics or critics to interpret that as an abrogation of political duty. That duty is to be critical; to be critical is to be engaged; to be engaged is to live in the real world (and the academy is not in the real world). Texts are easily seen as literary, second order phenomena. A critical text, according to this syllogism, would have recounted verbatim the views of the Greenham women, adding my own comments as analytical afterthoughts. It is as though those views would count as critical analysis of their own.

Textual analysis should be as much a part of political action as going on protest marches. Much of feminism has been directed against the perpetuation of hierarchy – such as men over women, reason over emotion, activity over passivity. It seems crucial that hierarchy should not be permitted to enter feminist or critical theory 'by the back door', through the derogation of textual analysis. Reading months of coverage of the Greenham protest in *The Sun* and the *Daily Express* left me feeling dirty, defiled by association. The representation of the Greenham women in the press was infinitely generalisable: such was the heart of its power. My commitment was to analyse not just how the Greenham women suffered under the burden of newspaper representation, but also how these representations refer inevitably to Woman, to every woman. The malice and venom in the newspaper writings reached me, sitting in the library. I wanted to create a means of reading against the construction of femininity as always already deviant and in so doing to emphasise that, for all its institutional and financial power, for all its discursive persuasiveness, the press discourse is always contestable.

My reading of the press coverage is therefore considerably concerned with the underlying assumptions and structures of criminology. However due to its interdisciplinary methodology, it brushes up against a number of other perspectives. These are media studies, social theory and feminist theory. For the moment, I need only say that my project was *not* part of traditional media studies, which emphasises the gap between representation and reality or between truth and lie in the media message. The project was similarly *not* purely linguistic in orientation: it is informed by a sense of political urgency and horror which demands that structure and state be part of the analytic frame. Conversely, what follows *does* draw very strongly on recent developments in social theory, particularly that of deconstruction within post-structuralism, a means of reading which emphasises difference and dialogue, pointing out the factors at work in the preconstruction of discourse. In addition, my work *is* informed utterly by my own position as a feminist critic and by evolutions within feminist theory. For me, examining the press coverage of the Greenham protest provided an important means to fight back at the structures of oppression.

Such was the generating dynamic behind the production of the book. For my role in it I can offer the following names: 'feminist', 'critic/deconstructionist', 'woman'. Do these naming devices give me definition? Although not one of the 'Greenham women' as such (responsive to but not captured by their cause), I found the period of learning about their protest to cause many resonances within me. Not a 'Greenham woman', but then what 'am' 'I', that this experience of critical exposition has had such importance for me? First, as a woman, and therefore (however much privileged by also being white and middle class) continually confronted by oppressive masculinist practices which operate to subjugate my 'womanhood', the privileged position of critic has brought with it some feeling of concrete resistance, a resettlement of power, a short-term ability to fight back at the discursive formations and processes which (seek to) repress and confine. The position of 'critic', of 'theoretician' has been one of the (re) claiming of (phallic) power (the power to speak). This critic wants to win change, to transform, to overcome, to affirm for the side of women, to side with women. Anger, hope and a determined vision of an 'otherwise' keep this critique in continual engagement with the patriarchal order, which is both rejected and yet is also necessary as the medium in which a critique can find its voice. Bound to patriarchy for an object of criticism, tied up in it through the institutional structure in which I have chosen to work, this is the negative experience of the critical difference. Working within the academy, in a phallocratic order of rationality, the woman-critic finds herself on the margin once more, or ghettoised and barely tolerated.

Within the academy as critic, yet 'critic' is not here the sole determinant of subjectivity. The production of both powerlessness and exhilaration associated with the liberation of criticism is tied also to the perceived fact of the status of womanhood. My marginal(ised) position is not simply a handicap but also points to a freedom to discover an 'elsewhere', is an incentive to speak ('as a woman'), (to be) radically other, different. An important part of this self-constitution as a woman is a strong link to feminism; perceived both by others (I will be thought of as 'a feminist' by others, either approvingly or pejoratively) and by myself: my self-definition as 'feminist' is crucial to my work, and also in the day-to-day negotiation of the academy in particular and the social in general.

As a feminist, I work to transform, specifically, the relations of power, representation and signification between men and women (the production and evaluation of masculinity and femininity as categories). Those commitments are at all times consciously present in this project. Such an explicit inscription of commitment carries a risk: of dismissal as yet another 'biased' product, too subjective, irrational, emotional. This would provide a neat means for a reader not to take its points seriously. However, feminism *is* serious: the question of (the suppression of) sexual difference is one of the most crucial questions in contemporary society (and perhaps, as it is in the Greenham protest, linked to the possibility of global destruction, it becomes undismissable). If, as Heidegger (1967) writes, every epoch has its own utopia, then sexual difference and its operation is the utopia of the current age.

Woman-feminist-critic: between these (interlinked) categories I move back and forth. This movement is echoed in the interdisciplinary shifts I employed in my reading of the press discourse.

Not comfortably part of 'criminology' with its recurrent dominant concerns (empiricist, individualised, offender-based), my
project was set adrift between departments. Dissatisfied with
criminology's blinkered amnesia, I sought resources elsewhere:
sociology, philosophy, literary criticism. Too ex-centric for one
department, my work has taken place on its margins with forays
('sorties') into others. This situation produces unease, discom-
forts, insecurity, but also a tension which galvanises insights
and expands horizons. An uncomfortable position, but I would
want it no other way, for in always being 'somewhere else', I am
forever 'having it both ways'.

Methodology

I would contend that the mode of reading I developed is considerably different from previous analyses of deviance in the media.
The difference consists in the interconnectedness of perspectives
at work in my methodology: to this I gave the name *synergism*.
The synergistic reading which I made of the press coverage utilised a variety of disciplines and approaches, all working together in
mutual tension and co-operation. The result is a mode of reading
which could be called feminist, post-structuralist and post-
modernist. In a rejection of methodologies which regard the text
as complete, ahistorical and unified, I have utilised the insights
of philosophy, social theory, discourse analysis and semiotics
to argue for a conception of the text which acknowledges its
historical and social stratification and the foundation of its
monologic nature upon the exclusion of alternative accounts.
As well as reading the substance of the press reports, it is also
necessary to consider the interrelationship of that content with
the form and organisation of the discourse, from narrative structure and metaphorical configuration to the underpinning political
strategies of its preconstruction. Through these means, my
research sought to provide critical powers for reading and deconstructing the inscription of sexual difference within the press
discourse.

As a preliminary and explanatory comment, I should state that
my use of the term 'commonplace' at various points recalls its
roots as a sub-division of one of the skills of rhetoric, *inventio*,
which is the finding or discovering of material pertinent to an
argument. A 'commonplace' was first defined as those topics of

argument which occur in more than one subject area; later it was applied to any expression taken as pithy, serviceable and true (and thus it was similar in use and form to the maxim). The employment of this term in relation to the discourse of the press engenders an association with rhetoric: a discursive dimension which is generally suppressed within a representational form dependent for its success on an attribution of naturalness, truthfulness and acceptability. Crucial to my criticisms of traditional 'media studies' has been the recognition of their failure to put the possibility, status and self-constitution of the media text into question. 'Meaning' is taken as forever present; analysis begins after 'meaning' has been achieved. I see the issue here as a certain 'blindness' to or forgetfulness of the processes of 'making to mean' or 'becoming meaning'. I used here a conceptualisation of the media text as ontological category, whereby critique of the processes or potentials of representation concerns itself also with the constitution of representation as a social practice. The traditional view of the media text as belonging to a unitary code incorporating certain necessary if submerged truths, should be rejected in favour of a mode of reading inflected by attention to context and the condition of the text's existence as a social and discursive practice constituted by certain institutional frames and directed to bring about certain effects.

Analysis of the newspaper text as discourse is an important heuristic tool. It opens up a possibility of reading the text as contextual, contingent and socially constructed. It reveals the operation of hierarchies, the polarisation of values and the powers of an authoritative monologue which pretends to universal necessary truths to seduce and capture its reader. As Bakhtin (1982) writes: 'The authoritative word demands that we acknowledge it, that we make it our own; it binds us, quite independently of any power it might have to persuade us internally; we encounter it with its authority already attached to it' (p. 342). This is quite distinct from a claim that 'meaning' is forever present in the text: meaning is always-already negotiated, whereas the construction of authority within the newspaper text fixes the proferred version of meaning as 'true' or 'real'. An analysis which approaches the writings of newspapers as such an authoritative discourse, while not in any sense a 'theory of the press', can provide an account of the means of its preconstruction and the predetermination of its meaning-effects.

In my reading of the press coverage of the Greenham protest, I used the concept of the press report as discourse. This had important effects, which I will show by means of a contrasting example. Heidensohn (1985) examined 'images of women's deviance'. In her investigation of the thesis that 'ensuring female conformity has been a near-universal goal of male-dominated society', she turns for evidence to support this '... as any good anthropologist would expect, in the cultural artefacts, the pictures, books, films, plays and programmes in which are expressed the key images and symbols of our own society' (p. 106). Heidensohn is thus prey to the modernist attribution of privileged inherent value to the artefacts; she invests the artefact with meaning and status. It holds the cultural message, a unique symbolic message to be freed through the absences of other conceptions. Whatever the object of a discourse, the object has always-already been said.

In writing about the representation of desire, of women's bodies, of Woman, there is a difficulty whereby any attempt to rescue an omission or the repressed becomes yet another 'image of woman' to be redefined in masculine terms. Irigaray attempts to avoid this by seeking the blank spaces (the blind spots) of masculine representations. She writes:

> [Women] must not pose [the question] in the form 'What is woman?' They must through repetition – interpretation of the way in which the feminine finds itself determined in discourse – as lack, default, or as mime and inverted reproduction of the subject – show that on the feminine side it is possible to exceed and disturb this logic. (1977: 75–6)

Femininity in Dissent attempted to realise these ideals. In addition, without wishing to literalise or ignore the metaphorical aspect of Irigaray's points, it can be argued that the Greenham women are *living out* exactly such an excess and disturbance of patriarchal logic. In many ways, in the terms of their own discursive production, in their activities, in their very presence at the weapons base, they constitute a confounding of the phallocratic or masculinist ideology.

The book was produced as part of a commitment to feminism; just as the focus on Greenham Common reflects this, so the project itself and its analytic strategies are formed by an awareness of the need to recognise sexual difference, to make it operative *other* than in a hierarchised opposition.

'A commitment to feminism', however, is ambiguous in its lack of definition, since 'feminism' consists of a diversity of aims, strategies and theoretical underpinnings. It is my hope that the various sections of *Femininity in Dissent* constitute a synergistic method. My analysis was strengthened by the contributions made by each individual form of investigation: however, none of them can be singled out as being the most important or indispensable. Its interdisciplinarity is important: showing how the disciplinary boundaries that we take for granted are not fixed, but shift back and forth. From such a perspective, we can come to new understandings of the manipulation of concepts such as criminality or 'law and order' by criminology and the sociology of law. Finally, I hoped to achieve something in resistance to the very real devastation that can be wreaked by the press discourse. The Greenham protesters suffered enormously as a direct result of the press coverage they received. By detailing the means by which the press brought this about, I tried to resist the force of its discourse. This may have been 'academic' research, written by someone within the academy, but its political aims were never limited by such a beginning. It will have achieved its ends if it can provide its readers with the means to resist the discourse on deviance generated by the press.

With the opportunity for retrospective reflection that has come with writing this chapter, I now imagine my ideal reader to have been something of a hybrid. Such a reader would have no overwhelming and determining disciplinary affiliations, no commitment to criminology or law or women's studies that would lead her to dismiss the book or any part of it as 'too criminological' or 'too feminist'. The space occupied by this ideal reader is, of course, also the space that I sought to occupy, in my attempts to read beyond the boundaries that are imposed by institutions, grants, supervisors, disciplines. And it is a location that I still seek, as reader/writer, in this article and in my current research, where I am still trying to achieve work that transcends some of the limits experienced in or associated with academic research. *Femininity in Dissent* was written with the aim of thinking through those limits, in relation to a group of women who spent years rejecting the limits that had been imposed upon them by the discourse of the press. *Femininity in Dissent* was also written in admiration of the Greenham women, in the hope of learning – from their commitment – about writing as a feminist, and in opposition to the press, who sought to make their criticisms of the Greenham women applicable to feminists and women everywhere.

Notes

1 The protest did not begin as a women-only one; it originated in August 1981 as a march from South Wales to Greenham Common, undertaken by women, men and children. The protest became women-only in March 1982, for several reasons, including a desire for a woman-centred political space, a belief in the political tactics that women could develop on their own, and a resistance to the traditional male/female division of labour that quickly developed at the camp. For a more detailed description of the decision to become women-only, see *Femininity in Dissent*, Chapter Two.

2 The same should be said of the journalists who helped me: especially Alan Rusbridger, Paul Brown and Mark Hollingsworth; while others wrote in response to my queries. See pp. 173, 174, 177, 178, 186.

Bibliography

Bakhtin, M. (1982), *The Dialogic Imagination*, Austin, University of Texas Press.

Heidegger, M. (1967), *Being and Time*, Oxford, Oxford University Press.

Heidensohn, F. (1985), *Women and Crime*, London, Macmillan.

Irigaray, L. (1977), Women's Exile, *Ideology and Consciousness*, 1, 61–76.

Marks, E. and I. de Courtivron (eds) (1981), *New French Feminisms*, Brighton, Harvester.

Scraton, P. (1994), Book reviews of P. Green, *The Enemy Without* and A. Young, *Femininity in Dissent*, *Social and Legal Studies*, 13:1, 187–92.

Young, A. (1990), *Femininity in Dissent*, London, Routledge.

PART TWO

responses and texts

7

Mothers watching children watching television

ELLEN SEITER

In 1993, I published a book entitled *Sold Separately: Children and Parents in Consumer Culture*. Missing from that book is the participant ethnography of a parents' support group that served as one of my primary motivations for doing the work. Manuscript reviewers and editors deemed my sample too small and the study too anecdotal for inclusion in the book. They argued the study was contaminated by my own participation in the group of parents studied. One of the ironies of this critique was that in writing the final draft I was later encouraged to personalize the chapters, to speak in the first person throughout, to find my own voice. But the self-reflexive style of participant ethnography was unacceptable. I would like to describe that study here, the reasons I embarked upon it, and the place I think such work may hold in feminist research and television research.

Advice literature in women's magazines and educational hand-outs from pediatricians and teachers incessantly urges parents – and this, of course, means mothers – to monitor and control their children's television viewing. I wanted to show the trickle-down effect of the academic representation of children's (and women's) viewing as passive, and therefore, bad, and its consequences for the labor of middle-class mothers. How do mothers determine what is okay for children to watch and what is not? How are these decisions and rules shaped by class background, educational aspirations, and mothers' own struggles with the combined load of housework, child care and, very often, paid work outside the home? How much are they influenced by a particular ideology of childhood embedded in developmental psychology? What is the relationship between adult women's viewing habits and the television viewing of their children? These questions appeared to be largely untouched by empirical research, and yet they were everywhere in my personal life and the consumer culture that surrounded me.

In 1988, shortly after I finished co-editing *Remote Control*, a book of essays on television audience research, I gave birth to my first child and joined a parents' support group in Eugene, Oregon. The group was organized by a private social service agency whose mission is child abuse prevention. A facilitator contacts all new parents while they are in the obstetrics ward at the hospital to invite them to join a monthly meeting. The group had met about once a month for two years – and the fathers' attendance had become more infrequent than the mothers' – when I asked them in 1990 if they would be willing to become a focus group for my research. The reaction of the group was positive, enthusiastic. In our group discussions (for which I ordered pizza and paid two teenage girls to supervise the children), children's television viewing easily fitted into an agenda of perceived problems facing parents, taking its place alongside feeding, toilet training, fire safety. One of the most impressive lessons for me in doing this research was the very ease with which television was accepted as a suitable topic; it was deemed by everyone to be eminently appropriate – and was clearly already cast as a 'problem' warranting discussion, and if possible expert advice. Whenever we talked about television there was an outpouring of often anguished feelings about television's impact on child-rearing and marriage – a type of discourse at odds with the current optimism in cultural studies about popular pleasures and television viewing as resistance.

Doing audience research with my support group was in part a matter of convenience and in part the result of convictions I had developed doing audience research with strangers whom I saw only once or twice. The availability of the group made it possible for me to do research in a thrifty manner. My own time was constrained as a mother of small children and a full-time academic and I preferred activities like the support group where the children could come along. There was no grant support for organizing such research, because it employed ethnographic methods and approached television as a cultural topic rather than a behavioral phenomenon urgently needing intervention and because my research subjects were not so-called 'at-risk' families. Convenience, then, was part of my motivation, but there were also negative consequences that followed on turning the support group, a socially acquainted group unconnected to my professional life, into a group of research subjects. Attendant on that decision were a host of personal and ethical dilemmas, for changing that relationship involved a professional gain and a personal loss.

When I decided to use the group for research purposes I had a different kind of self-interest in seeing the group continued. As feminist researchers have noted there is 'a usually unarticulated tension between friendships and the goal of research. The researcher's goal is always to gather information; thus the danger always exists of manipulating friendships to that end' (Acker et al., 1991: 141). I was always conscious of ulterior motives in the efforts I undertook (telephoning, inviting over, chatting at the grocery store) to sustain and nurture these relationships (especially after the birth of my second child in 1991, when the strains of the double day became more acute). In some ways by doing research with this group I lost one of the great personal gains for me in having mothers to talk to in a space entirely separate from the world of work. One of the original appeals of the group was simply to have other mothers my age to talk to. I was often lonely as an employed mother working with faculty and students the vast majority of whom had no small children living in their households, or did not talk about them if they did. I was fascinated to learn about the lives of stay-at-home mothers and envious of how connected they were in a network of other women caring for small children – a group it was difficult for me to get to know.

The advantage for me was that by turning my own research focus to the topic of children, mothers and television, I was attempting to coordinate my own identities: the professional, cloistered world of the university where no one was a mother; and the public, everyday world of malls and grocery stores and the public library where everyone appeared to be. In some ways I was merely making explicit the kind of observations I was doing anyway: I already viewed the group with a sociological eye and deliberately attempted to foster conversation about television. One of the great advantages for me was that as a participant in the group, I had an opportunity for both formal and informal exchanges with other members, to gather solicited and unsolicited comments on the topic of television. I also had an opportunity to share, debate and discuss my work with them. That process allowed me to capture the ways that a particular kind of discourse on television was negotiated within the group, and to comment

self-reflexively on the methodology I employed, and my commonalities with the other women in the group as a mother, as
well as the differences that derived from my status as an intellectual with a relatively well-paid, comfortable job – and a hectic
schedule.

The decision to use my support group marked a return to
empirical audience research after a period of deep misgivings on
my part about the possibilities of doing this kind of work at all.
In 1985, I became involved with three researchers, from the
University of Tübingen American Studies Division. Two of them
were feminists and doctoral students, Eva-Maria Warth and
Gabriele Kreutzner; the other, Hans Borchers, was in a position
of authority over my two German women colleagues, and was
a Professor. Several grants and some years later, we found ourselves interviewing soap opera viewers in my home town of
Eugene, Oregon. We completed twenty-six interviews, with
viewers in groups of two to nine; fifteen were all-women groups.

My early training was in documentary and experimental film-
making, a background that has been surprisingly helpful in thinking through the problems of description, transcription, editing
and representation (of oneself and one's subjects) in dealing with
research interviews. My academic work had been devoted entirely
to feminist textual analysis, and I had been much influenced by
debates within feminist film theory on the position of the female
spectator (Bergstrom and Doane, 1990). My graduate training and
dissertation and much of my published writing had been textual
analysis of melodramas, soap operas and films by German women
directors. My work had used theories of ideology and semiotics,
rather than psychoanalysis, as their focal point. I found the heavy
emphasis on psychoanalysis in feminist film criticism of the
1970s and 1980s very alienating. I was persistently bothered by
the tendency toward universalism, and the extremely ethno-
centric nature of this work. Psychoanalysis shared with the
Althusserian theories of ideology I was schooled in a heavy emphasis on the ways subjectivity is locked in to the unconscious.
I saw qualitative interviews with television viewers as a means
of reintroducing the heterogeneity of experience (especially
experiences of family life) into accounts of spectatorship, as well
as the possibility of action, of conscious belief, of an active
feminist subject.

I wrote an analysis of a single interview that Borchers and I
did with two men viewers in *Cultural Studies*, and this piece was

cited a good deal and resulted in a number of invitations to do more writing on the subject. In that article I expressed my reservations about the lack of self-reflexivity in much qualitative television audience research. I was concerned to point out that most of the work done (our own included) was not really ethnography, because of the short contact periods, and the fact that the interviews tend to be focused on a single, isolated aspect of culture, namely television viewing. If anything, the attempt to limit discussion to television content proved the extent to which television viewing overlapped with all kinds of interesting things, gender roles in the family, political beliefs, social networks of kin and friendship, and routines of the clock in everyday life. Lines are continually drawn by the interviewer in discussions of television viewing, and subjects are steered away from certain 'extraneous' topics and towards others. The criteria are often implicit, unexamined.

I also argued for the need to attend closely to the self-selection elements in qualitative studies: it excludes people who will not have the time, or the trust to participate in such research. This is one reason that white media researchers repeatedly wind up with all-white samples: my support group is no different in this respect. It is likely that the self-selection factor in joining the group excluded some women of color who tend to have little free time for such activities and may be more suspicious than whites of the interventions of social workers (Cannon *et al.*, 1991: 113). Historically, social service agencies – and academic sociologists – have incurred much resentment in the Black community, for example, leaving many African–American women less than eager to volunteer themselves or their families for further surveillance.

Looking back on *Remote Control* I was worried over the way in which we typed working-class and middle-class women viewers in a casual, offhanded way. This is by now a truism: everyone complains about class definition but a method for doing things differently has remained elusive (Morley, 1992; Press, 1991). It was very difficult to sort through the extent to which home furnishings, clothing and speech patterns led us to classify our subjects impressionistically and simplistically in one of two categories. Often I had the feeling that, 'I know a working-class house when I walk in one'. These categorizations relied upon recognizing women's responsibility for consumption (choosing clothing and household decorations, for example). Clearly much of what we were doing can be explained in terms of Bourdieu's notion that 'taste classifies, and it classifies the classifier' (Bourdieu, 1984: 6). But it was impossible to begin to explore these issues in a project limited to generic readings and the soap opera as a text.

In *Remote Control*, our theoretical failure regarding class was exacerbated by our own sheepishness about asking for any kind of hard, cold sociological data: income, education, occupation, etc. (possibly related to the bourgeois taboo on talking about money). In the end, we resorted to a follow-up questionnaire, in an attempt to get some hard demographic data to feel more secure with than our impressionistic accounts of life stories and living rooms. But many of our subjects were resistant to the questionnaire approach. Some of our respondents with the highest educational aspirations resented this kind of questioning: we had created the impression that we were interested in their television analysis: and it came as a shock, and a tip-off of some unspoken agenda items when we began interrogating them on other topics.

The other way that our operating definitions of class seemed inadequate to the economic realities of the moment was the fact that people were frequently referring to drastically changing and shifting fortunes, such as unemployment, divorce, relocation. Whenever such disruptions were present we tended to categorize the subjects as working class. I believe that one salient bias of the middle-class academic stems from the relative stability of their class membership; whenever I do field work I am reminded that to be born into the middle class and to manage to hold on to a white collar job throughout one's adult life, leaves me ill-prepared to appreciate in the kinds of upheavals – the economic freefall – experienced by so many during the 1980s and 1990s. This problem – and the different vantage point of academics from working- and lower middle-class backgrounds – has been addressed in the work of Ann Gray (1992) and Valerie Walkerdine (1986).

I continue to struggle with the problem of how to define mothers of young children as a social group and as an audience. They do not fit easily into the definition of a sub-culture, which has been usefully employed in a number of ethnographic studies of media audiences (Jenkins, 1992; Bacon-Smith, 1992; McRobbie, 1991). Although mothers share some qualities of a sub-culture (generation, familiarity with shared texts, common experience with medical, educational and social service institutions), their media experiences are largely shaped by their role as gatekeepers of another consumer sub-culture, their children's (Seiter, 1993).

In the *Remote Control* study, aspiration often seemed to determine people's positions on television and television viewing: income and occupation could not indicate the ways that people imagined their class position; or imagined themselves in a more affluent future. I think that the case studies I located within my support group could exemplify the importance of examining the relationships between 'fields' and habitus as Bourdieu recommends: 'Social reality exists, so to speak, twice, in things and in minds, in fields and in habitus, outside and inside of agents (Bourdieu and Wacquant, 1992: 127). My extended contact with this group allowed me to factor in more specifically the work of mothering in producing habitus, in perceiving early childhood as a segment of the educational field, in the reproduction of competing class positions, in the maintenance of consumer distinctions.

By using the women in my support group as a research base, I was privy to a wide range of information about them, that I acquired without direct questioning. Their housing, their consumer purchasing, their decisions about going back to paid employment or having a second child, their educational background, their concerns about the household budget, the ways their fortunes changed over the four years I knew them. More directly, I engaged in dozens of conversations about children, desires for the child's future, and choices that were made for the child, that revealed more subtle aspects of family values, world views and aspirations.

Certain kinds of homogeneity, especially in terms of age (everyone was between 25 and 35 at the onset), allowed the group to function and sustain itself as a social unit. Most members of the group were highly similar in terms of age, educational level, type of housing. One family, whom I will call Lesley, Wade and Kelly, stood out because they participated marginally in the middle-class world of childhood (lessons, preschool centers, vacations), and in some ways, what I have done is document the struggles of this family in their attempt to catch up with the middle-class ideals of others in the group; while examining the ways that mothers situated more securely in the middle-class established time-consuming and difficult, if not impossible, norms for good motherhood.

Whereas I had formerly suppressed my academic background in our group discussions (although everyone was aware of my occupation), when I asked the group to be recorded as a focus group I was recasting myself in a new way. It was important, however, that I was already trusted and known before I broached the topic, and I think that the discussions bear a kind of intimacy and trust that is hard to get in studying television audiencehood. Most importantly, I was already accepted as a person with similar kinds of concerns and problems. I have been very direct with these women, saying that the academics whose work I read do not think television viewing is as bad for you, as morally and psychically corrupting, as the experts who they are likely to read about in the newspaper or in *Parents* magazine suggest. In the soap opera project we had been unable to describe what we knew about soap operas from an academic – or a feminist perspective: we were supposed to be listeners in an unstructured conversation, unable to share with them our own opinions on the subject. I felt that the only way I wanted to conduct research on mothers, and on this group in particular, was under circumstances where I would be permitted to speak about a feminist analysis of the topic under discussion: in this case, to use my expertise to impart a representation of child-rearing duties that is kinder and more considerate of the burden of mothering in contemporary society. This conviction grew from my own anxiety-filled reactions to advice literature – of which I read a lot – and which I knew persistently added to the burden of guilty feelings and limited time by suggesting new and more labour-intensive strategies for coping with family problems.

Before recorded interviews, I would ask them to think about the topic before they arrived (children's TV, advertising and toys; their own and their children's viewing). For Lesley, this reflection included tremendous guilt over her own TV viewing of sitcoms or *Star Trek* (although she repeatedly described herself as 'addicted' to TV), intense fatigue which she found television alleviated, and deep-seated worry over the effect of her example of television viewing on her daughter. Unlike the fathers of the families David Morley studied (Morley, 1986), Lesley's guilt stemmed from seeing her own TV viewing as a bad example for Kelly, for whom she wanted something 'more' (especially self-reliance) and an irritation for Wade (as well as a withdrawal from communication with him). In a prior interview, Lesley described her TV viewing in the most deprecating terms imaginable (perhaps feeling compelled, too, when others did not speak up about sharing her 'problem'), but she also reported that at her work, where a group of five women groom dogs at stations in the same room, the sitcoms were discussed each day. While this sitcom viewing did not give her anything to talk about within the support group, it was very useful for participating in her social life at work. She acknowledged that this was an incentive to view, at the same time that she repeatedly distanced herself from these others. When I introduced the question of their own viewing it was two years later, and Lesley was the first to speak, eagerly, about her guilt over viewing, her difference from the others at her job, and the tensions she felt she was causing by watching this way. When Lesley spoke up, Karen (K) was quick to come in as an interrogator, encouraging Lesley to see her situation as one that she should feel guilty about, and insisting on the need for her to take self-disciplined action.

> L: I have been doing so-o-o-o-o much thinking about this lately. Every night I come home and flip on the news – this is my justification for watching TV. I flip on the news, but I'm in the kitchen, so I can hardly hear it and I can't see it. Then, my junk show is *Star Trek*. So, that's seven (o'clock) to eight so I figure that's two, two and a half hours of television. So that's not like this maxxed out fifty hours of TV a week that they talk about, you know, with everybody going into this ozone.
>
> K: Who has time to do that, when do they do that?
>
> L: All night long and all weekend they just sit in front of the TV and watch sports shows ... and they're watching all kinds of sitcom stuff or, you know, whatever.
>
> ES: Do Wade (husband) and Kelly let you watch it?
>
> L: Wade hates it. He disappears downstairs to work. So our communication has gone completely to zero. I mean we don't talk about anything anymore and it's really bad.
>
> K: Maybe you should turn off *Star Trek*!
>
> L: But it's hard. It's an addiction. It really is. And this is what I'm combatting right now because it's completely eliminated my self-discipline.

In part it was Karen's greater authority in the group as a school teacher that helped to push Lesley from a description of her viewing as an understandable release at the end of the day to the metaphor of physical addiction. In all of our discussions, Karen mentioned how tempting it was to allow her children to watch two hours in a row of public television programs in the morning so that she could get work done around the house. Karen took a year's leave after the birth of her first daughter, then returned to work as a fourth grade teacher, stayed home for two years after the birth of her second daughter (something she found very difficult to do) and then got a new half-time job as a foreign language teacher at the high school (in the same working-class community Lesley worked in). In an early focus group, Karen's husband, Larry, spoke harshly of the passivity of television viewing and it was clear that he made his opinions felt in the rules for rearing the children. Karen had once challenged Larry on this topic during one or our discussions, after she was apparently emboldened by the fact that in the course of the discussion it became clear that everyone's children were spending a lot of time with TV. But in the absence of the fathers, Karen took the same position as her husband: openly critical of television viewing as passive, bad and destructive of family life. Despite the fact that other women in the group, especially Patricia (P), Tess (T) and myself – form a sort of chorus, attempting to 'grant permission' to Lesley's behavior, Karen is the voice to which Lesley responds most directly, and defensively.

P: But do you have to deal with Kelly through this? What's Kelly doing? You can follow the story line ...

L: By the time *Star Trek* comes on dinner's cooked. So that's the other thing ...

ES: Because it's in a different place?

L: No it's right there, with the living room and dining room are right there next to each other ... six feet away. But her attention span isn't on her food or concentrating on eating so she doesn't eat dinner, then she wants dinner at eight or nine o'clock.

K: Why don't you tape it and watch it late at night?

L: No, that's the thing I shouldn't. I need to stop watching TV altogether. My self-esteem has gone way down because my self-discipline ... the TV has sapped my ability to structure my own time.

T: I don't think so. You need a break, a reward.

K: But you can't have it on when you eat dinner.

ES: We always have it on.

L: I've been talking about it with my mom and she's ... English and reading and all that is her forte – I think I said that right – it's her forte. She agreed with me wholeheartedly, her husband died a few years ago and she's been watching a lot more TV and she said 'I have no desire to read anymore it's just so easy to go in front of the TV.' And when you do that enough it really saps the energy to pick up a book and sustain the concentration.

ES: Do you think you're kind of tired, though, when you're starting to watch *Star Trek* or do you think *Star Trek* is making you tired?

L: Well I'm tired after a full day's work because I'm standing there and we don't get this nice fifteen-minute break in the morning, fifteen-minute break in the afternoon and half-hour lunch in the middle. We're booking from eight to five straight through. And I come home and I just flip on the TV because it's so easy. But it's not constructive use of my time and I've found that I, that my discipline level has gone way down ...

T: (with disbelief) Discipline level?

L: Discipline level in just keeping the TV off, just cooking dinner, and you know, that's just kind of my junk show.

K: (speaking over Lesley, but no one picking up on it) We watch *MacNeill-Lehrer Report* ...

L: Because I don't have any desires to do anything constructive like spend time with Kelly and read a book or sing songs or ... maybe if I weren't watching TV I would have more energy ... I ...

T: Maybe not. You go through phases. I stay up late for the *Tonight* show. I'm really tired but ... it's almost a form of rebellion, like, I don't have any leisure time so I'm just going to take it ... I'm not dead, I still understand adult things ...

L: But see what I was thinking was I would probably be much better informed if I spent that time reading the newspaper instead of watching TV ...

T: But what do you want to do? How many have-tos are you already doing?

L: I want to have communication with Wade. I wanna you know ... He disappears because the TV's on then something's got to change.

ES: He disapproves of you watching it?

L: (emphatically) Oh, yeah.

ES: TV in general or just *Star Trek*?

L: TV in general.

P: So maybe you don't want to talk to Wade.

BIG LAUGHS all around.

I offer this excerpt as an example both of 'realistic' support group talk – the kind of conversation that happens about television among people who know one another fairly well; and as symptom of the discursive limits of talk about television. It reveals what Lesley can say about television and how she feels about it; but also what she cannot say about it. Concerns about television viewing were expressed differently at different times, and contradictory statements were often made in the course of one meeting. All women in the group were likely to change the tone of their statements radically after a remark from someone else, but the stakes – of self-esteem, of role-expectations for being a good mother, and a good wife – tended to remain the same.

Group discussions have a life of their own. Despite my attempts to communicate to the group the type of permissive attitude towards television viewing popular among cultural studies academics (when I boldly claim, for example, that we always have the television on during dinner), what this research has been perhaps most useful for is documenting the ways that admissions of television viewing – or any other kind of less-than-ideal parenting behavior – run the risk of drawing censure from other women in the group, as much as they have the potential to garner support. I tried to steer Lesley towards considering the level of fatigue and obligation she was shouldering, as when I asked if she was already tired before watching *Star Trek*, but Karen had only to give her a little push towards a derogatory interpretation – by mentioning public television, viewing together with her husband, the 'just say no!' approach of turning the set off – to switch Lesley into an attack on her own self-worth. Our group involved a great deal of implicit competitiveness and one-up-(wo)manship. Class issues were suppressed (we're all mothers together) and though the difficulty of carrying out the ideal project of middle-class childhood was continually addressed, rarely spoken about was how much more difficult it was for some than for others. None of the other mothers worked a 9–5 job, as Lesley did (she was the only other mother working full-time apart from myself). None of us had jobs demanding the type of physical exertion that Lesley's did. As a caste-like group, we were familiar with a long list of shared problems: the five o'clock 'arsenic hour' with children, the seemingly endless burden of household chores, the demands of young children for attention, the wife's burden to ensure proper communication and closeness within the marriage, the leisure gap. But the ability to free oneself from the 'have-tos' was differentially distributed along strict lines of education and income.

In every instance we need to recognize the deep-seated ambivalence most people hold towards being consumers of popular culture and the ways this varied with status (not just class and income, say, but different occupational and domestic cultures –

and crucially with gender). On the one hand, some of the women we interviewed for the soap opera project, employed in minimum wage jobs, took the 'what the heck I have a right to my soap operas' attitude – meaning what do I have to lose? On the other hand, as Charlotte Brunsdon (1990) puts it, 'Watching television *and* reading books about postmodernism is different from watching television and reading tabloid newspapers, even if everybody concerned watched the same television' (p. 69). Everyone involved in television research needs to recognize how romantic fantasies of greater authenticity of experience (be it media use, domestic life, or identity politics) may subtly inform our choices. The pleasures of television viewing come at the cost of a great deal of Lesley's self-esteem – especially in her gendered roles as mother and wife.

I have tried to make explicit the information used to gain impressions, while ultimately relying on a conscientious literary style; to practice self-reflexivity about my own role in shaping the interview; to recognize the absence of rapport in some instances, and focus on where there are tensions along the axes of gender and class. This has been a difficult balancing act and I am unsure of how much longer it could have continued: last year I moved across the country and the group has not met again since my departure.

If I had done this interview as a single encounter with Lesley or with a group of mothers called in for a focus group interview, there is much that I would have missed in the dynamics of the group and the positions and dispositions, as Bourdieu (1984) would say, of the participants in the group. The greatest benefit of this lengthier contact period and greater familiarity with these women's everyday lives is that it allowed me to present a less reified version of television viewing and family life. In particular this type of method helps to identify the changing material conditions of women's lives – to offer a series of snapshots over time of television viewing as embedded in processes of housework and child care which are themselves in flux, a subject of struggle. Finally, such work allows us to connect the ethnomethodological analysis of talk about television with the wider ideological discourses of child-rearing, of marriage, of cultural distinction in which I have found women's conversations are so often saturated. Knowing these women better it is possible to begin to correlate the receptiveness to advice literature with the material circumstances of employment, of child care, of domestic space, of the construction of time.

The glaring limitations of this type of study are those I faced at the onset, especially its homogeneity. While I have noted salient differences among the women in their media consumption and their feelings about this consumption, I must also remind myself that there are other domestic arrangements – especially single parent households or lesbian households – other attitudes (including those uninformed by the dominant themes in advice literature) that I could not capture within this small group. But this type of study may also usefully inform debates about the concept of resistance in cultural studies, and its suitability to the study of the US middle-class mainstream. To what extent can we see media consumption *per se* as a form of resistance to the demands of motherhood, for example? And should the cultural scholar's enthusiasm for uncovering instances of resistance be tempered by the costs exacted from adult women, especially in feelings of guilt or worthlessness? Lesley's comments during this interview suggested a rather pessimistic view of entrapment in feelings of guilt, but my contact with her the following year reminded me of the possibilities for resilience and for change, and the possible benefits of attempting to address directly the issue of guilt over viewing with women.

The last time I saw Lesley was at a going-away party at my house in the summer of 1993 shortly before I moved. Lesley had a lot of news: she explained that she and Wade had finally faced the crisis of the failure of her husband's business, decided to close it, and Wade had returned to the community college to learn nursing. The time of the taped interview was the bleakest point in their marriage and they had contemplated separation and divorce. It is interesting that in the group interview quoted here she attributes the stress on her relationship with Wade to her own pursuit of a little leisure pleasure watching television – not to the economic pressures on the family, which she may have felt embarrassed to discuss. I told Lesley that I had just been to a conference where several academics were talking about *Star Trek*. In the context of that conversation – a private one – Lesley told me brightly that she was still watching *Star Trek: The Next Generation* and especially enjoyed the character Rykker, whom she called a heart-throb.

After that last meeting, I wrote back to all the women after moving. I asked them if they thought their feelings towards television had changed since their children were born, how they had felt about our discussions about television, and whether they had anything to add. Lesley wrote that she had liked our discussions and added something that she never expressed out loud in the group discussions. 'I was surprised to learn most use TV as a babysitter. I don't like doing that. I encourage her to get books or paint (but I don't have two kids).' Lesley takes a little revenge against Karen here, and, contrary to the deprecating tone of the group interview, reveals a quite different strategy for evaluating her television watching as superior to that of mothers who use children's television shows as a babysitter.

In the letter I also asked for an update on what television shows they thought were good for children and 'I find I have become more conservative about TV programmes. I used to sit in front of just about anything but now I don't want to set that example for Morgan. I would rather, now, have our own collection of good movies and limit watching to an occasional movie.' On her list of shows that are okay for Kelly to watch her own favorite programme – *Star Trek: The Next Generation* – slipped in between nature shows and *Sesame Street*.

Bibliography

Acker, J., K. Barry and J. Esseveld (1991), Objectivity and Truth: Problems in Doing Feminist Research, in M. M. Fonow and J. Cook (eds), *Beyond Methodology: Feminist Scholarship as Lived Research*, Bloomington, Indiana University Press.

Bacon-Smith, C. (1992), *Enterprising Women: TV Fandom and the Creation of Popular Myth*, Philadelphia, University of Pennsylvania Press.

Bergstrom, J. and M. A. Doane (eds) (1990), The Female Spectator: Contexts and Directions, in J. Bergstrom and M. A. Doane (eds), *The Spectators*, special issue of *Camera Obscura*, 20–1.

Bourdieu, P. (1984), *Distinction: A Social Critique of the Judgment of Taste*, trans. R. Nice, Cambridge, Mass., Harvard University Press.

Bourdieu, P. and L. J. D. Wacquant (1992), *An Invitation to Reflexive Sociology*, Chicago, University of Chicago Press.

Brunsdon, C. (1990), Television: Aesthetics and Audiences, in P. Mellencamp (ed.), *Logics of Television: Essays in Cultural Criticism*, Bloomington, Indiana University Press.

Cannon, L. W., E. Higginbotham and M. L. A. Leung (1991), Race and Class Bias in Qualitative Research on Women, in M. M. Fonow and J. A. Cook (eds), *Beyond Methodology*, Bloomington and Indianapolis, Indiana University Press.

Gray, A. (1992), *Video Playtime: the Gendering of a Leisure Technology*, London and New York, Routledge.

Jenkins, H. (1992), *Textual Poachers: Television Fans and Participatory Culture*, London and New York, Routledge.

Kreutzner, G. (1990), *Next Time on 'Dynasty*, Trier, Wissenschaftlicher Verlag Trier.

Kreutzner, G. and E. Seiter (1991), Not All 'Soaps' are Created Equal: Towards a Cross Cultural Criticism of Television Serials, *Screen*, 32:2, 154–73.

McRobbie, A. (1991), *Feminism and Youth Culture: from 'Jackie' to 'Just Seventeen'*, Boston, Unwin Hyman.

Morley, D. (1986), *Family Television: Cultural Power and Domestic Leisure*, London, Comedia.

Morley, D. (1992), *Television, Audiences and Cultural Studies*, London, Routledge.

Press, A. (1991), *Women Watching Television*, Philadelphia, University of Pennsylvania.

Seiter, E. (1990), Making Distinctions in Audience Research, *Cultural Studies*, 4:1, 61–84.

Seiter, E. (1993), *Sold Separately: Children and Parents in Consumer Culture*, New Brunswick, New Jersey, Rutgers University Press.

Seiter, E., H. Borchers, G. Kreutzner and E. Warth (1989), *Remote Control: Television, Audiences and Cultural Power*, London, Routledge.

Walkerdine, V. (1986), Video Replay: Families, Films and Fantasy, in V. Burgin *et al.* (eds), *Formations of Fantasy*, London, Methuen.

8

I want to tell you a story: the narratives of *Video Playtime*

ANN GRAY

> There *is* no view from nowhere, indeed the 'view from nowhere' may *itself* be a male construction of the possibilities for knowledge. (Bordo, 1990: 137)

In 1983 I embarked on my doctoral research into women and their use of the domestic video cassette recorder (VCR). Through employing the method of the recorded 'conversational interview' with women in their homes, my research soon expanded into addressing more generally the positioning of women within the domestic and their home-based leisure of which the VCR was but one of a whole range of such practices. The research, therefore, attempted to contextualise women's use of the VCR in the routines of daily life and specific household cultures, focusing on gender, and to a lesser extent class, in the structuring of such practices, social relations and cultures. Whilst my research was concerned to illuminate the complex ways in which new entertainment technologies are used, my educational background – Communication and Cultural Studies, Social History of Art and, finally, in Sociology – plus my feminist politics, resulted in my adopting an interdisciplinary approach to my subject which raised particular and enduring issues around questions of method. Some of these questions were introduced in the published version of my research, *Video Playtime: the Gendering of Leisure Technology* (Gray, 1992) and what follows is a more distanced reflection on these problems.

Some of the most exciting feminist work of recent years has been to propose and investigate 'the politics of knowledge', recognising that the social production of knowledge is cut through with the fault-line of gender and power relations. Thus, from different and distinct positions, Donna Haraway (1991) insists on 'situated knowledges', Liz Stanley and Sue Wise (1990) emphasise the political importance of 'grounded theory' and Patricia Hill Collins (1990) the 'location in experience and shared histories'. These epistemological discussions are an important development in focusing our attention on questions of method and methodology.

Whilst questions of method must be distinguished from those of methodology, I would want to argue that they are, in the research process, intrinsically related. Methodology describes those theoretical and conceptual frameworks which we employ in approaching our particular object of study, whilst method described the particular techniques of research which are selected from a range of possibilities, e.g. structured or semi-structured interviews; questionnaires; content analysis. Thus, any discussion of the more practical elements of the research process can only be usefully investigated and understood in the context of the theoretical underpinning of the project itself. Our rationales for the methods employed in a research project generally assume a selection from a range of possible techniques; however, our adoption of broader theoretical frameworks are also matters of choice made from a range of alternatives, and crucial in understanding the shape and structure of the research. But of course these are not free-floating choices; rather, they are subject to a range of determining factors. Most obviously, there are the dominant paradigms of our disciplinary or interdisciplinary fields and existing related research. But again these paradigms and the specific theoretical developments within them take on palpable form in *institutional practice* and university departments working in broadly similar fields or disciplines will have a range of 'takes' or inflections on these broadly defined approaches. To use an example from my own field, that of Cultural Studies, its manifestation in undergraduate and postgraduate degree programmes in Britain and elsewhere evidences many versions with different foci and emphases. These differences can be understood with reference to institutional histories, but also in relation to the intellectual biographies of academic staff. However, there are many other factors involved in the formation of a research idea and the particular trajectory it takes that go beyond the boundaries of the academy; these are personal and political and can involve emotion, desire and, let's face it, survival and ambition.

My broad aim here is to reveal and interrogate what Liz Stanley (1990) has referred to as 'the conditions of production' of my research into women and their use of the video cassette recorder. I adopt this approach in order to emphasise the importance of material factors in the shaping of intellectual work, but also, I hope, to avoid the danger of reflection on my research becoming too 'self'-oriented. Certainly questions of subjectivity, my own position within the research process, will be quite central to this discussion, I am a key character in the narrative after all, but it is as an agent functioning within a particular historical, social and cultural context that I take my place in the action.

In this complex process there are a number of narratives and what written versions of research tend to produce is a unified narrative, one which carefully smooths out the rough edges of research, suggesting a linear progression through argument and which, above all, renders absent the process itself. Research is a practice which, in most cases, is made up of a number of social interactions and as such is intercut with power relations, poignantly, as has been thoroughly explored within feminist literature, between researcher and 'researched'. However, much less attention has been given to the often very disadvantaged position of postgraduate research students and research assistants within university departments, struggling without funding or on part-time contracts. This engenders feelings of insecurity which constantly threaten to undermine confidence and belief in individual research projects. The raft of belief and self-worth, therefore, must be constructed and reconstructed daily in order that the research can continue and develop, that the next interview be set up or that the word processor be faced. It is often extremely difficult, in these circumstances, to identify with or see ourselves as the 'all powerful researcher' figure posited by critiques of research politics.

My own research was characterised by many such crises, as close friends will testify, but it wasn't until I began to write *Video Playtime* that my research narratives came into sharp focus. Apart from two published articles and two conference papers (Gray, 1986, 1987a, 1987b, 1988), my research took the form of a thesis for Ph.D. examination. Because of the interest shown in my publications, my intention had been to prepare the thesis for publication by way of a re-engagement with the material. This re-engagement would employ and indicate further theoretical developments in theories of language and culture, in feminist theory and in the emerging anthropological critiques which problematised writing and representation. I wrestled with this project in the months that followed, although with a full-time teaching post and a weekly commute between Leeds and Birmingham, time was not in plentiful supply. I began to realise that the whole shape and structure of the project, the way in which my data had been analysed and interpreted and the written form of the thesis itself were recalcitrant to this re-working. The narratives I identified then, and the theories which under-pinned them, were so deeply embedded within the entire enter-prise that it simply had to stand as a specific, small-scale research project whose boundaries had been mapped out by methodological frameworks and methods which were relevant and appropriate in the development of the research itself.

Identifying the narratives

I will structure my discussion by exploring three narrative strands evident in *Video Playtime*: the narrative of experience; the democratic narrative; the feminist narrative. I find the concept of narrative useful in understanding the 'textuality' of the written results of social and cultural research, as employing and drawing on conventions and devices more often associated with literature or rhetoric (Atkinson, 1990). But also in terms of the narratives we live by, the discourses we inhabit and are inhabited by and the personal, political and intellectual investments we make. The notion of narrative enables the exploration of those con-tinuities and dis-continuities between subjectivity and research production/practice *and* biography and history. For narratives are often shared, there are commonalities to be identified within particular formations, just as there are striking differences and distinctions.

The voice of experience and the material world

'Experience' is a concept which has been equally important and significant for cultural studies and feminists. Its limits, and indeed dangers, as evocation of 'authenticity' inherent in those studies which mobilise experience as an unproblematic category have been roundly criticised, if not dismissed, as ludicrously naive. However, in her recent book, *Sexing the Self: Gendered Positions in Cultural Studies*, Elspeth Probyn (1993) suggests that experience can operate in two distinct 'registers', that of ontology which indicates and is testimony to a specific way of being, or location within the social, and that of epistemology, 'here experience is recognised as more obviously *discursive* and can be used overtly to politicize the ontological' (Probyn, 1993: 16). She further argues that 'experience itself speaks of the composition of the social formation' and insists on the placing of experience in the 'terrain of the theoretical' (p. 21) and, quoting Raymond Williams, wishes 'to recall an absolutely founding presumption of materialism; namely that the material world exists whether anyone signifies it or not' (Williams, 1979: 167). Probyn's distinction is timely and insightful and, in articulating my own 'experience', I will try to demonstrate its usefulness in understanding our own positionality and selection of theoretical frameworks.

Like many working- or lower middle-class women of my generation in Britain, born in the immediate post-war period, the opportunity for higher education passed me by and I was schooled into clerical and secretarial work during the 1950s: office and other forms of etiquette shaped my curriculum, along with those other necessary attributes of femininity, being of service, looking good and conforming. Popular culture offered exciting feminine identities and, at the age of 15 with the popular song of the moment, 'Living Doll', running through my head, I began work in a typing pool. This was considered to be a good job for a girl of my background. The work was routinely dull and monotonous, my sister workers shared my class background, all were white and, as far as I know, heterosexual, and our ages ranged from 15 to 60, with the majority being under 25. Most were single or newly married as working mothers were a rarity and our office 'culture' was overdetermined by events in our 'personal' and especially 'romantic' lives. Women's magazines, fashion and cosmetics, popular music and cinema provided us with a currency of expressions of female desire. There were major regular annual events heady with romantic promise and possibility, such as Christmas and holidays, requiring careful saving, extensive planning, preparation and discussion, but every weekend and especially the Saturday night out spent dancing or at the cinema occupied the gossip on Fridays and Mondays. However, each of us had our own particular rites of passage. The first of these was getting engaged, this was usually followed by the 21st birthday which was always celebrated, and then, of course, the Big One: the white wedding. Cash collections and presentations were made for these three events, special outfits were purchased, gifts were displayed and the lucky 'girl' was the centre of attention. The only thing left then was to become pregnant and leave, again in a shower of presents, parties and good wishes.

Here readers will recognise the narrative version of the 'ordinary woman' inhabiting the 'feminine' culture, who has been identified by Charlotte Brunsdon (1991) as the 'other' of feminism produced by audience studies and critically explored by Hallam and Marshment in this volume. There is, however, at least one other possible version of my autobiography which would emphasise my encounters with adult education throughout my working life, significantly, courses taken in Theatre and Film Studies run by The Workers' Educational Association, being inspired by a range of authors, including Schumacer, Illich, Fromm and Pirsig[1] and starting to 'think about thinking'. Then doing two years of an Open University degree which led to leaving the office world and a full-time degree as a mature student, plus engaging with theories and politics of feminism and becoming a postgraduate first as a Masters student at Leeds, then as a doctoral student at York. This narrative is the one I would foreground now, in my identity as a feminist and as an academic, but also an equally strong personal narrative remains in my subjectivity which is to do with that previous life – as one who had been positioned by 'the feminine' in our culture, and had made particular kinds of investments, e.g. low aspirational jobs, conforming to feminine subject positions, marriage, etc. Indeed, I spent the first thirty years of my life assuming that higher education was completely closed to me.

My early experiences have always grounded my feminism, but also my insistence on class as an important social division. The narratives, of course, coexist and my articulated stories, whilst drawing on my subjective experience can best be understood by shifting into the epistemological register. In this move, my 'experience' is the living out of a particular social historical formation, but most significantly it informed my own exploration of theory, just as theories illuminated the structures of my material life. Thus, my various and different encounters with radical, socialist and liberal feminists and my reading were always in some kind of tension with this ontological register; my way of knowing from my being; that is being positioned as 'feminine' and inhabiting that position almost unproblematically.

During my undergraduate studies I had been introduced to the work of the Centre for Contemporary Cultural Studies (CCCS) at Birmingham University, particularly in relation to the gendered and classed aspects of culture and the necessity of understanding culture(s) as ways of life. It was the 'lived' dimension which resonated so strongly with my experience and provided me with a firm theoretically informed, but concrete, base upon which to build my research strategy. My studies at Masters level exposed me to Marxist, structuralist and post-structuralist, psychoanalytic and Foucauldian theories and a critique of the 'sociologism' of the CCCS work.[2] Indeed it became more and more difficult to maintain a materialist position in the face of increasingly sophisticated theories which rendered empirical work, especially that based on more sociological or ethnographically informed modes of enquiry, as essentially empiricist. Add to this dilemma the political and ethical questions of doing research on the constructed other of the academy, the 'ordinary people', and the result was extremely debilitating. I certainly did want to register women's daily lives as an important and neglected area of study and my own experience/knowledge provided, not simply a resource, but undoubtedly shaped the formation of my project. Although my past experience formed a range of 'knowledges' about particular feminine subjectivities, I am not, however, presenting a set of credentials for being *the same* as the women in my study. On the contrary, I cannot now claim that shared identity and whilst I *recognise* it and during the interviews was able to understand and talk about aspects of their experience, their investments, I now know what it is to be positioned very differently.

After much heart-searching and procrastination, I managed to grasp the nettle by convincing myself at least that questions of audience and consumers were empirical questions, i.e. there are things to be known of that audience that we cannot know by sitting at our desks or in our libraries. I found, however, that questions of method were the most pressing and the least satisfactorily answered. The problem was intensified by my wishing to develop the interdisciplinary approach which I felt my topic demanded. Indeed, there seemed to be an implicit assumption in many qualitative studies that we all knew what we were doing and an almost coy unwillingness on the part of many researchers to actually talk about their research methods.

The democratising narrative: method and politics

One area where these issues were being spoken of was within sociology where a number of feminist scholars were already producing interesting, challenging and above all useful work in this area. There are three key works which were important in deciding on my methodology and method; Helen Roberts, *Doing Feminist Research* (1981); Liz Stanley and Sue Wise, *Breaking Out* (1983); and Angela McRobbie, 'The Politics of Feminist Research: Between Talk, Text and Action' (1982). I virtually raided these and other texts, and concluded that, as Liz Stanley (1990) suggests, no one set of methods or techniques was to be seen as distinctly feminist; rather, feminists use every means available to investigate the condition of women in patriarchal society. What I most wanted to do, having worked through this body of material, was to give a voice to women. In 1984 women's voices had not been heard very much in relation to media consumption, but I was also working on a number of hunches, based on what I had observed and experienced. I firmly believed that gender significantly ordered the social relations of consumption and as the home was increasingly becoming the site of leisure and entertainment, the domestic context of such consumption needed to be addressed. Furthermore, women are positioned very differently from men in relation to domestic work and leisure. I wanted to find ways of exploring how women felt about these changes and how these technological and cultural developments were affecting, transforming and changing the routines and practices of daily life.

This (feminist) democratising narrative focused my attention on women themselves; however, this does raise theoretical problems with regard to the category of gender and the consequent danger of essentialising the always and already formed 'woman' as the subjects of my research. This highlights the predicament of the desire to mark out and focus in an intense way on women's lives and experience and the theoretical limitations inherent in such a project. However, questions of strategy and contingency are important here and it is possible for a piece of research to intervene in an existing set of knowledges which are seen to exclude women's experience and to pose new questions for further investigation and theorisation. In addition to thinking strategically, it is clear that we must, as researchers, declare ourselves: not only theoretically and methodologically, but also morally and politically.

Finding the women

It was important, then, to find ways of listening to women and, equally pressingly, to find some women who would be willing to give me their time. I had formulated an 'interview plan' which consisted of a range of topic areas identified to do with the use of the VCR in the household and my supervisor strongly advised me to carry out some 'pilot' interviews. A woman I knew who worked in my local wine bar did not need much persuading to act as my first interviewee and I am eternally grateful to her for being such a co-operative participant in my study. The interview lasted for two hours and, as a television and video enthusiast, she took the conversation in many, quite unforeseen, directions most of which were integrated into my revised interview plan. My second 'pilot' interviewee, a woman introduced to me by a friend and whom I did not know previously, was not so open and forthcoming and, consequently, I had to work much harder to establish a comfortable atmosphere and to keep the interview going. Although very painful at the time, this again proved to be a useful experience in handling difficult interviews. Having carried out my 'pilot' interviews and revised my plan, it was time to find my 'sample' and go into the phase known as 'data collection'. Decisions about the scale of research projects are crucial and it was at this stage that I drew up an 'ideal' sample of women which involved limiting the study to a relatively homogeneous group in order that comparisons could be made and differences explored within such a group. All the women would be white, the majority living with a male partner, with and without children, a range of social class would be attempted, as would age. There are good methodological reasons for selecting this kind of sample which I discuss in the book (Gray, 1992: 29–41), but here I would want to emphasise my moral and political reasons for selecting this sample, particularly in relation to 'race' and ethnicity. I was strongly influenced at the time by the debates within feminism about the power of the researcher, her position in the academy and the implicit exploitation of the subjects of research. In spite of my earlier comments I did recognise that I was in a privileged position compared with the majority, but by no means all, of the women I planned to interview, and I felt unwilling, as a white researcher, to attempt to impose myself and my research on Black and Asian women in a racist society. There is also the issue of certain kinds of 'shared knowledges' which are quite crucial to the kinds of research method I employed and which are part of a cultural 'reservoir' upon which interviewer and interviewee can draw. I realise the implications of this and, indeed, it is still extremely difficult to find British audience studies which are not 'white'[3] which reflect the current 'whiteness' of our academic institutions and the marginalisation of Black experience.

My first group of women contacts came as a result of a small survey I carried out for the owner of a video library. This took about a month of my time and as such was of no use to me, except in enabling me to make contact with some of his members. This produced mainly working-class women. I then made contact with middle-class women through a social encounter and through introductions at my university. All three of my 'sources' were developed through 'snowballing', a system whereby I asked each of my interviewees if they knew of any other women who would be willing to help. Each woman was then approached, usually by telephone, and, if appropriate, a follow-up interview arranged. Paradoxically, my two major interview phases had a sense of 'unreality' about them. During this period of what is called 'data gathering' I was sharply reminded of the fundamentally *constructed* nature of research. This is never quite such an insistent element of, say, doing library research when we are selecting texts to read and analyse, but as you knock on the door of number 15, or engage Mr X in conversation, questions such as 'why not No. 17, or No. 49?' and 'why Ms X and not Ms B?' are constantly worrying away. What I did was construct a 'community' of women who then formed the empirical base for my research, and whilst following certain 'rules' and procedures for selection, it nevertheless could just as easily have been thirty other women.

The subject of women interviewing women has been usefully explored (Oakley, 1981; Finch, 1984) but no one mentions the importance of the researcher's dress codes and presentation of self. This may seem a trivial point, but whole webs of significa-tion are built up around apparently tiny clues when women meet for the first time: rings, ear-rings, clothing, make-up, hairstyle and colour would be scrutinised, assessed and interpreted by the women I interviewed. There would be certain expectations of what a 'researcher' looks like. Should I look like a student? I wasn't a 'traditional' student; being in my late thirties and married, I didn't fit that identity at all. In the end I decided to wear 'working girl' clothes, ironically the kind I would wear in my previous life. I avoided anything which would identify me as a 'feminist' or 'left-wing' – this ludicrously meant parking my Citroen 2CV round the corner as I didn't want to look like 'Heather', a contemporary character in the soap opera, *Brookside*, either. I carried a clip board as well as my tape-recorder as I felt I needed 'props' to establish the nature of the 'event', even if we then went on to 'subvert' the traditional interview structures. Many of the women had taken some care over their appearance, looking smart and wearing make-up, even though at home, and there was a distinct sense of 'occasion' attached to many of my visits. I was invited in as a guest and usually offered cups of tea or coffee before settling down to the business in hand.

Indeed, there was no problem about getting women to talk to me – they tended to talk too much and to range completely off the topics in which I was most interested. This echoes Janet Finch's experience in interviewing women where she interprets it as a sign of loneliness and isolation (Finch, 1984). I would agree to a certain extent, but what Finch overlooks is the *intensity* of the one-to-one conversational interview. The interviewee has the undivided attention of another sympathetic woman who appears fascinated by what she has to say, encouraging her to speak, rarely interrupting, inviting representation of *self* and listening intently. This was a point of concern as I recognised my own power and consequent responsibility during the interviews. Not so much in terms of my position as an academic, or the potential for my career that this research promised, but rather at those points during the interview when I could, and often did, move the conversation in particular ways. There were times when I could see narratives developing which were revealing and sometimes painful in the telling. It was at these very moments of intimate exchange, through that socially and conventionally constructed conversation we call an interview, that my most uneasy and risky moments were experienced. Some of these were around extremely personal information which they revealed and, in some cases, for the first time. Other problems occurred when racist ideas were expressed, or other views with which I did not agree. In these circumstances it is almost impossible to keep nodding encouragements for the speaker to continue, but to contradict and enter into an argument would be equally problematic for the interview. The strategy I adopted was to respond honestly if my views were sought, thereby risking offence or, more commonly, to gently move the conversation on to different areas.

Above all, the women wanted to tell me 'stories', their stories. At first I thought this was going to be of no use, imagining hours of wasted tape, but by re-listening to the tapes, I realised that these stories were an extremely important part of the construction of the interview itself. As female subjects, the women were accounting their experience from particular standpoints; this became very important material in my understanding of their own versions of themselves and their lives.

Finally, an important element in the democratising narrative, and one which has been debated within Cultural Studies is the dissemination of knowledge and the 'results' of our research. Whilst *Video Playtime* is addressed to a broadly academic reader, empirical research of this kind does develop its own impetus and certain kinds of dialogue can open up. In 1986 my research was 'discovered', quite by chance, by a woman journalist on *The Yorkshire Post* who interviewed me and wrote a long article about soap opera, women and popular culture. Such are the workings of media organisations that some of the national newspapers picked up the story and I was rather amused to find myself referred to on page 3 of *The Daily Mirror*. *The Daily Express* described me, quite erroneously as 'Britain's first doctor of soap' and *The Daily Mail* sent a photographer round to my house who wanted to capture me on celluloid wearing a gown and mortar board and leaning over the back of my television! Other forms of local media picked up on my research and I participated in a number of 'phone-in' programmes and day-time chat shows over the period of this phase of my work. I managed to introduce questions about technology in the home, decision making in relation to TV and video use and the issue of women's domestic leisure. This for me was an important channel of dissemination of my interview material, particularly as it was in a form which was accessible to a wide range of women viewers, listeners and readers.

Feminist narrative: reflection

I would identify my work on women's use of VCRs as falling within a 'feminist empirical' epistemology as identified by Sandra Harding. Harding (1987: 181–90) sees this as one of the feminist academic's main responses to biases and absences of traditional disciplines. It challenges the masculine bias and focus of subject areas but also associated research methods. However, my empirical work locates itself within what Harding describes as a feminist standpoint epistemology based on the significance of certain situated knowledges of the women concerned. It was a combination of these epistemological positions which informed my framework and approach to the interviews. When it came to analysis and interpretation of the material, however, I found that the differences between the women in my sample could not be reflected unless I employed concepts which enabled the significance of class to be revealed. It was during the period of interpretation that I found the work of Bourdieu (1980) most useful. Although there are significant problems with his work, especially in relation to gender, his theory of the distinction between the popular aesthetic and the bourgeois aesthetic proved extremely useful in revealing some of the nuances of the cultural competencies which the women brought to their 'reading' of popular and other texts. He uses a spatial metaphor to express the distinction; thus, the closeness and involvement of engagement with popular pleasures compares and contrasts with the critical distance between the informed and discerning reader and the 'culturally valued' text. I find the spatial metaphor is a very powerful way of thinking about cultural distinction and difference, but also about masculine and feminine distinction and difference, as the women expressed their relationships and experience of living with their male partners. Object relations theories of masculine and feminine subjectivity, and in particular the work of Nancy Chodorow (1978) who maintains that 'traditional' family structures of Western cultures produce male children inhabiting masculinity as a 'separate self' and girl children as inhabiting femininity as 'self-in-relation', was also utilising a spatial metaphor. Chodorow and Bourdieu's theories resonated with the women's eloquent accounts of heterosexual relations within the context of domestic and 'family' life, and enabled me to reflect on my interview material.

Many feminists are now extremely critical of the so-called 'gender theorists', referred to by Susan Bordo as those feminists, Chodorow amongst them, who were concerned with 'exposing and articulating the *gendered* nature of history, culture and society' (Bordo, 1990: 137). As I have indicated above, I accept that working with the category of gender alone can be impossibly restricting, and would agree with Susan Bordo in her reflection on 'gender theorists' who, according to her, uncovered patterns that 'resonate experientially and illuminate culturally' (p. 137), describing a new territory which radically altered the male-normative terms of discussion about reality and experience. They forced recognition of the difference gender makes. We must beware of dismissing work that uncovered patterns which still 'resonate experientially and illuminate culturally'.

Whilst there are obvious problems in using any category which glosses over other dimensions of identity and location, those of 'race' ethnicity and class, for example, I feel equally concerned about those approaches which see gender as only one axis of a multiple range of identities. Whilst this is an arguable position, I feel it cannot be declared at the level of theory. Gender rarely expresses itself in pure form, but within a complex set of social contexts and relations. Theoretically sophisticated empirical work enables the exploration of these concrete contexts and settings and I optimistically believe that there are many feminist researchers and scholars pursuing such work.

Where do we write from?

To return to my own narrative, I must confess that one of the main factors in deciding about how to do the book and who it should be for, was my new institutional location as a full-time permanent lecturer in a busy and demanding teaching and research department, where the pressure is on to maintain a high research profile, as well as teach increasing numbers of students. It is bound to compromise our work. Feminism has entered the academy and in some areas transformed it, but how much is the academy shaping feminism and how much the other way around in these beleaguered times?

The implication might be that we turn our attention from more complex and practically difficult, time-consuming, empirical work to equally complex, but perhaps more manageable, theoretical work which becomes the only site for exploration of gender relations, of identity and subjectivity. Whilst I would agree, in terms of gender theories, that the duality of male/female is a discursive formation, a social construction, nevertheless, this duality has had and continues to have profound consequences for the construction of experience of those (and that includes us) who live by them. Also, these divisions are resilient and persistent, produced and reproduced within social and cultural contexts. Future work into consumption will, I hope, continue the ethnographic turn of television audience work by addressing actual contexts and the exploration of the complexity of gender relations without allowing them to become, before we start, only one aspect of a whole 'matrix of subjectivity'. Let us look, not everywhere and from nowhere, but from our specific locations and reflect constantly on the politics of our research.

Notes

1 Just *how* people with the minimum of formal education find and read books which extend their thinking or begin to explain some of their questions is an area which would bear investigation. In my case these books were recommended by a (male) colleague who had a degree in architecture.

2 This can be characterised as the difference between the 'culturalism' of CCCS work in the 1970s and the 'structuralism' of film theory, exemplified by *Screen*. For me this solidified around the voluntarism and humanism of CCCS, to which I obviously leaned, and the determinism and anti-humanism put forward by 'structuralist' and 'post-structuralist' theories. This debate also raged within the Open University Popular Culture Course, where I worked as a tutor.

3 One notable exception to this is Marie Gillespie's study of Asian families in Southall (Gillespie, 1989 and 1993).

Bibliography

Atkinson, P. (1990), *The Ethnographic Imagination*, London, Routledge.

Bordo, S. (1990), Feminism, Postmodernism, and Gender-scepticism, in L. J. Nicholson (ed.), *Feminism and Postmodernism*, London, Routledge.

Bourdieu, P. (1980), The Aristocracy of Culture, *Media Culture & Society*, 2:3, 224–54.

Brunsdon, C. (1991), Pedagogies of the Feminine: Feminist Teaching and Women's Genres, *Screen*, 32:4, 364–81.

Chodorow, N. (1978), *The Reproduction of Mothering: Psychoanalysis and the Sociology of Gender*, Berkeley, University of California Press.

Finch, J. (1984), It's Great To Have Someone To Talk To: The Ethics and Politics of Interviewing Women, in C. Bell and H. Roberts (eds), *Social Researching: Politics, Problems, Practice*, London, Routledge & Kegan Paul.

Gillespie, M. (1989), Technology and Tradition – Audio-Visual Culture Among South Asian Families in West London, *Cultural Studies*, 3:2, reprinted in A. Gray and J. McGuigan (eds (1993), *Studying Culture: An Introductory Reader*, London, Edward Arnold.

Gillespie, M. (1993), *The Mahabharata*: From Sanskrit to Sacred Soap. A Case Study of the Reception of Two Contemporary Televisual Versions, in D. Buckingham (ed.), *Reading Audiences: Young People and the Media*, Manchester, Manchester University Press.

Gray, A. (1986), Women's Work and Boys' Toys – Video Recorders in the Home, Paper presented to the International Television Conference, London.

Gray, A. (1987a), Reading the Audience, *Screen*, 28:3, 24–35.

Gray, A. (1987b), Behind Closed Doors: Women and Video, in H. Baehr and G. Dyer (eds), *Boxed In: Women on and in Television*, London, Routledge.

Gray, A. (1988), Reading the Readings, Paper presented to the International Television Conference, London.

Gray, A. (1992), *Video Playtime: The Gendering of a Leisure Technology*, London, Routledge.

Haraway, D. (1991), *Simians, Cyborgs, and Women*, New York, Routledge.

Harding, S. (ed.) (1987), *Feminism and Methodology*, Milton Keynes, Open University Press.

Hill Collins, P. (1990), *Black Feminist Thought: Knowledge, Consciousness, and the Politics of Empowerment*, Boston, Unwin Hyman.

McRobbie, A. (1982), The Politics of Feminist Research: Between Talk, Text and Action, *Feminist Review*, 12, 46–59.

Oakley, A. (1981), Interviewing Women, A Contradiction in Terms, in H. Roberts (ed.), *Doing Feminist Research*, London, Routledge & Kegan Paul.

Probyn, E. (1993), *Sexing the Self: Gendered Positions in Cultural Studies*, New York, Routledge.

Roberts, H. (1981), *Doing Feminist Research*, London, Routledge & Kegan Paul.

Stanley, L. (ed.) (1990), *Feminist Praxis: Research, Theory and Epistemology in Feminist Sociology*, London, Routledge.

Stanley, L. and S. Wise (1983), *Breaking Out: Feminist Consciousness and Feminist Research*, London, Routledge & Kegan Paul (new edition: Stanley, L. and S. Wise (1993), *Breaking Out Again: Feminist Ontology and Epistomology*, London, Routledge).

Stanley, L. and S. Wise (1990), Method, Methodology and Epistemology in Feminist Research, in L. Stanley (ed.), *Feminist Praxis: Research, Theory and Epistemology in Feminist Sociology*, London, Routledge.

Williams, R. (1979), *Politics and Letters*, London, Verso.

9

Questioning the 'ordinary' woman: *Oranges are not the Only Fruit*, text and viewer

JULIA HALLAM and MARGARET MARSHMENT

> I knew that real changes had to be made to my experimental ... novel to render it the kind of television that would bring viewers in off the streets.
>
> I know that *Oranges* challenges the virtues of the home, the power of the church and the supposed normality of heterosexuality.
>
> Jeanette Winterson on the television adaptation of *Oranges are not the Only Fruit*.[1]

Setting out to offend viewers' cherished values might not seem the most obvious way to bring them in off the streets, but there is little doubt that Winterson succeeded in doing exactly that. In an earlier article, we analysed the television version of *Oranges are not the Only Fruit* with a view to accounting for this success: what mechanisms of closure had the text employed in order to secure a reading of its lesbian heroine that sympathised with her in her conflict with home and church? We concluded that the familiar pleasures of 'quality' realist drama, together with a casting of religious fundamentalism as the villain, were central, not only in persuading viewers to identify with the lesbian character, but also in 'naturalising' her sexuality.[2] Testing these findings against the responses to the text of a small number of 'ordinary' women viewers suggested that our analysis had been broadly correct. But there was another, equally important, factor which we had not anticipated. The experiences and values which these viewers brought to the text were not as ordinary or conventional as academic constructions of 'the ordinary viewer' tend to imply. Despite its extraordinary characters and events, *Oranges* offered the pleasure of recognition; and the pieties of home, church and heterosexuality proved a less stable trinity than we, or Winterson herself it seems, had imagined. We were led by this to question the concept of the 'ordinary woman viewer'.[3]

Our sample of eight women was clearly too tiny to generalise from. But we did wonder if our way of proceeding through textual analysis to in-depth viewings of a single text had yielded results that might be of interest to other feminists working in the field of popular culture. When Beverley Skeggs asked us to be interviewed as a contribution to this volume, we therefore welcomed the opportunity to reflect upon this and other aspects of our methodology.

BS Start from the background of how you developed the project: why you decided to do it the way you did, who you decided to interview and why, and why you decided to do questionnaires.

JH It was actually a longer process than that.

MM It started because I was asked to write something for a collection on popular culture and lesbianism. I was very busy at the time, so I suggested Julia might be interested, but she hadn't much time either, so after talking about it we decided we could probably manage it timewise if we did something together.

BS Why did you choose to work on *Oranges are not the Only Fruit*?

JH At the time I was teaching it as part of a television drama course. I felt it was important to include work by women cultural producers in what is traditionally a very male-dominated field. So I'd already done some research on who had written about it, and found very little; the only articles I found at that stage were Hilary Hinds' (1992) piece on the press reception of *Oranges*, and Rebecca O'Rourke's (1988) account of teaching the novel: nothing on the television drama itself, even though it was such a controversial production.

MM I was primarily interested in it as a feminist intervention in popular culture. I was interested in what the transformation of a cult novel by a feminist writer into a piece of popular television might mean in terms of the sexual politics involved.

JH The first piece we wrote was an analysis of the television text in terms of its sexual politics. As we were writing, we became increasingly convinced that the text had been quite deliberately constructed in order to make the audience respond in a certain way in relation to these sexual politics – in short, that it was designed to ensure a sympathetic response to its lesbian protagonist and to lesbianism in general.

Textual analysis

MM We saw it therefore as a text that uses the popular medium of television to intervene in the politics of heterosexuality. In a sense, it wouldn't matter if this is what the makers had intended or not: it was useful to us to analyse it on the assumption that it had been produced with this political purpose. It allowed us to identify the strategies employed in adapting the novel for television; not so much in terms of the difference in genre, but in terms of the difference in audiences. The novel doesn't have a popular format. It wasn't sold, say, at stations or airports for people to pick up as an easy read on a journey. Winterson's fiction appeals to those who enjoy more experimental work; and *Oranges* had a kind of cult readership among women-identified women. We were interested in how the production team had taken that text and made it into a piece of popular television without compromising what it had to say about lesbianism. Because of this, the textual analysis we did had an unusually clear aim. We were looking for the mechanisms of closure in the drama that produced the meanings they wanted. We assumed that they were actually seeking to close down the possible polysemy of the text so that the audience could not read the lesbianism as negative or in some way explain it as deviant.

BS How did you identify mechanisms of closure?

MM We used a very broad definition, that ranged across a whole range of features of the text.

JH We thought pleasure, for instance, was a very important mechanism of closure. Whether people had enjoyed the text or not would obviously affect their response to it. Viewers would be unlikely to respond positively to its subject matter if, for example, they had been bored, or bewildered, or, as Winterson was aware, if they were left with a sense that they had been manipulated. So we concluded that aiming to make *Oranges* pleasurable and memorable could be defined as a mechanism of closure. This meant producing a work that involved a mix of the familiar and the distinctive.

BS Can you explain that?

JH Take the narrative structure, for example. The novel is not at all linear, whereas the television version has a very clear chronology, so it is more conventional, and easier to grasp, as a narrative. But it isn't entirely conventional: it is put together rather like a triptych, with a central section in which the principal dramatic conflict takes place, and wings on either side (i.e. the before and after) that support this key narrative action. More conventional texts tend to work towards a grand climax at the end of the story, through which the conflict is resolved. The climax in *Oranges* occurs in the middle episode. The series starts with a detailed portrait of a few months in the life of a small seven-year-old girl who is very appealing, very attractive; she hooks you into watching the next episode because you want to know what becomes of her. In the second episode, Jess, now an adolescent, meets Melanie and falls in love with her. The love scene between the two young women and the climactic exorcism that follows partially resolve Jess's conflict between her feelings for Melanie and commitment to her religion, but it is left to the third episode for Jess to confirm her lesbian identity through another relationship and find a way to live that allows her to be herself. The third episode in fact takes you forward to see how she resolves what's happened in her life. Episodes one and three are the before and after to the life-changing events of episode two, but narratively there is much less action in them.

MM Or take the issue of realism. Whether realism can be used effectively to challenge dominant ideological positions has been a matter of debate among film and television theorists for some twenty years now. I would want to argue that you can use popular forms to convey unpopular messages, so I was interested in *Oranges* as a text that tried to do just that. The novel wasn't realist, but the television adaptation clearly was, which would make it accessible to a larger audience. And yet it wasn't quite the kind of realism that aims simply for verisimilitude – such as you find in British 'soaps' like *EastEnders* or *Brookside*. The surrealism of the credit sequences or the hospital scene, the tableau-like quality of some scenes, the use of extreme close-up and wide-angle lens, of occasional non-diegetic music, the almost Dickensian elements of caricature in characterisation and performance: these are all non-realist techniques which give *Oranges* a very distinctive feel to it, and help make it more memorable.

JH 'High production values' are something else we defined as a mechanism of closure. *Oranges* is clearly an expensive production, with attention given to the precise detail of *mise-en-scène*, accomplished performances from the cast, a clear sense of pace and direction and an innovative visual style. It belongs in what is defined as the 'quality' television drama slot, and is the first piece written, directed and produced by women to occupy that particular institutional space. 'Quality' demands to be taken seriously, so for *Oranges* to be broadcast in that slot in itself constituted a statement that lesbianism was a subject worthy of serious attention, of respect.

MM We could sum up these mechanisms of closure as clustering around issues of pleasure and accessibility. The other important cluster concerns what we might call the ideological: how the narrative and characterisation embody ideological positions and conflicts. The most important of these is the ideological positioning of religious fundamentalism against lesbianism, which we summarise as setting up one unpopular minority against another unpopular minority. The evangelical church is easy to present as a villain in the context of British culture and very difficult within the text to identify with, given the extremely negative portrayal, especially of the pastor. So when this church attacks the heroine for her lesbianism, it is impossible not to empathise with her position, and by extension her sexuality. It is obviously not 'normal' in our culture to see lesbianism as caused by devils and attempt to cure it by tying the victim up and praying over her. This inevitably normalises the lesbian character by comparison, and in fact her relationship is the only truly loving couple-relationship represented in the text, which naturalises lesbianism in comparison with the rather negative representations of heterosexual relationships.

All these are strategies which are commonly used in texts which serve to support the ideological *status quo*. So what we are saying is that the production team are using more or less the same techniques as mainstream cultural producers – but in order to get over a counter-ideological message.

BS So your method was to analyse the text in a relatively traditional way and then bring in lots of different ways of seeing the text in terms of realism, structure, comedy, etc. And then you think: is this working in a traditional way in terms of how these elements are put together? Is that ...?

MM In some ways I don't think it is a very traditional way of analysing a text. It has been a bit old-fashioned to talk about authorial intention. Cultural analysis that identifies ideological meanings at work in texts usually sees these as being produced through the routine workings of institutions and discourses rather than as the outcome of a deliberate authorial intention to be sexist, racist or right-wing, for example. Common-sense ideas about what is normal or natural, about what makes a good story, what constitutes humour, and so on, themselves embody ideology, so the analyst's job is to identify how ideology gets reproduced without any individual setting out consciously to reproduce it. It's a different matter when what you are analysing can be seen as a conscious attempt to challenge the ideology of common sense. We are really evaluating it as a feminist strategy; not to leave the text open to multiple readings but to close it down to produce a specifically counter-ideological reading.

JH   We wanted to think about that as a strategy for women working in mainstream film and television production. Women writers and directors have often commented on the degree to which they have to compromise their messages because they are working in a popular commercial mass medium.

BS   But how popular was it, given that it was shown on BBC2?

MM   It was first shown during peak viewing hours, in the winter schedules, and had an audience of about six million. That's a pretty sizeable audience. And it's been repeated twice since, most recently on BBC1.[4]

Ordinary viewer

BS   I was really interested in your critique of 'the ordinary viewer', because it is a very strong critique in the sense that you are arguing for a quite profound paradigm shift in audience studies. How did you get to that?

MM   Well, to answer that we have to go on to the next stage of the research. Having argued that the producers of *Oranges* had a feminist aim in making it and that this aim had succeeded, we wondered if our responses would be typical of viewers as a whole.

JH   At the time I was doing interviews for my doctoral research. I was trying to find ways of analysing the relationship between texts and subjectivity using in-depth interviewing methods, so I was already thinking about what you could learn about texts and readers from talking to people.

MM   So we thought we should talk to some other people who had watched *Oranges* to compare our responses with theirs.

JH   We wanted to ask women who we thought of as 'ordinary' women – on the assumption that, as feminist academics, we couldn't be defined as 'ordinary viewers'.

MM   And we decided initially to exclude not only colleagues, but friends, on the assumption that as feminist academics we wouldn't have 'ordinary' women as friends. What we obviously had in mind was a notion of how audience research defines 'ordinary viewers'. So we went to look for some. We began with women who were acquaintances, whom we knew in roles outside our academic ones. It started with the mother of my adolescent daughter's best friend – we'd have a coffee and a chat together, nothing more, but we got on well enough for me to feel able to ask her.

JH She was quite enthusiastic, and brought along her best friend. So we did those sessions with both of us present.

MM Then I asked a neighbour with whom I had a fairly traditional neighbourly relationship – watering each other's plants when we were on holiday, that sort of thing. And Julia asked a friend of a friend.

JH Then I asked someone I'd known from where I used to work, and someone else I knew who worked as a secretary. Again, not people I knew *very* well, but I knew them well enough to ask. So they were those sorts of relationships, and I suppose we had to feel we liked them enough to spend whole evenings together. And in the end we did include a couple of friends who happened to be visiting Liverpool. This did extend the geographical spread a bit.

BS How did you decide how many?

MM We carried on until we ran out of time. It was a fairly time-consuming process. We watched the whole of *Oranges*, all three episodes, and talked about it at length. This took between two and four evenings per viewing. We did it either in my front room or Julia's over several months.

JH I also went to a couple of people's houses and did it there.

MM The sessions were pretty relaxed. We'd have a cup of tea, or a bottle of wine, some snacks, and lots and lots of talk. A lot more talk than we expected.

BS So it was pleasurable?

JH Oh yes, very. For us, and for the women who agreed to watch it with us. They all said how much they enjoyed it – and the talk. And how interesting it all was. A few people said to me it really opened their eyes, they didn't realise how much they knew about television.

BS And did it challenge what you thought about *Oranges*?

JH Well, I can't say it did really. We found that these viewers certainly read the text in the way we assumed the authors had intended, and picked up a great deal of its finer points. Most of them expressed awareness of how it was constructed to portray lesbianism sympathetically, and were quite comfortable with this. We had wanted to find this out, whether people would feel they had been manipulated by the text and feel resentful about it, which Winterson herself had thought they might.

MM One great surprise was the viewer who turned out to be an evengelical christian – which we had not known. She had resisted the text when it was first shown, and in fact hadn't watched all of it, because she didn't want to watch propaganda that told her that homosexuality was all right, and that her church was hypocritical. She was the viewer who was most accomplished in how she analysed the way the text was doing precisely that. But she wasn't angry. There was so much about the text that she found pleasurable. The realism, the humour, how much she liked young Jess in the first episode. She really enjoyed it and said repeatedly, 'I'm so glad you asked me to watch this, I really enjoyed this, I'd really like to see it again'.

BS How did you get her to agree in the first place?

MM I just asked her.

JH Because we didn't have any constraints on who we should ask based on sociological categories, we didn't have to ask people anything about themselves before we asked them. We told them we had written something on *Oranges* and wanted to compare our response to it with their response as someone who would have watched it purely for pleasure.

MM Had we said to ourselves, we must get a statistically valid sample of ordinary women – with respect to say, class, age, ethnic origin, sexuality, etc. – it would have been impossible for us to do the project. We hadn't got the resources for that kind of research. Since we couldn't do it on that scale, we decided just to ask people more or less at random; as long as we avoided an obviously homogeneous group, we assumed this would be as representative as any sample that small could be. In any case, our interest was in how they responded to the text, not in the viewers themselves. So what surprised us when we reflected on the viewings was just how much we had found out about them as people. What we found out, like who was and wasn't heterosexual and the fact that someone was an evangelical christian, what kind of a religious background people had had as children – those things were all revealed to us during the viewings.

JH What people's childhoods' had been like turned out to be an extremely influential factor in their response. Of course we didn't know that initially, and sociological trawling wouldn't find that out. How could we have constructed a sample based on whether people had had happy childhoods or not, or whether they were adopted? Jess is adopted. One of our viewers was adopted. That made the text important for her in ways in which it wasn't perhaps quite so important for other people because it had a particular kind of resonance for her. And that was also true of people I had taken to be completely heterosexual, who in certain ways revealed some ambiguity around their positions, which if you attempted to construct a sociological profile of ordinary women, would never be revealed. Somebody who seems to be happily married, in a typical ordinary woman's situation with two kids, husband at work, working a bit of part-time herself, that sort of person, would be unlikely to reveal that she has homosexual feelings and talk about that experience, other than in an exceptional situation. So it brought up all sorts of things for people because of the way we did the interviews; and because we vaguely knew people, they felt relaxed enough to talk about quite a lot of those things.

BS Did you discuss beforehand how you were going to do it, how you were going to interview, who was going to do it?

MM We didn't interview really. That's not the right word. We said we are doing a piece of research on this text and we want to test out how people who are not professionals in writing about this sort of thing respond to the text, how women respond to the text, would you be willing to watch it? And all we are going to do is to sit and watch it with you. And make some notes on your responses. If you wish to comment as we go through please do, we can stop the tape. And in fact we would sometimes ourselves stop it in order to ask a question – how did you respond to that? what do you think is going on? etc. So there wasn't a structured interview at any point. And it would quite often end with long discussions, or sometimes in the middle, about particular points – around the relationship between the mother and the daughter, about what people's own childhoods had been like, about the question of sexuality, around issues of religion. Those things became conversations. We tried not to participate too much or lead the conversation. In fact, they were conversations rather than formal interviews. There were points where people said things like 'oh, what will you do with this information ...?' so they were aware that they were revealing things about themselves that were very personal. I mean very personal, and in many cases very painful. It is amazing how many people's memories of childhood are of pain. It was quite clear that some people's memories of childhood, which for them meant the family, and which for some meant religion, were actually extremely negative. Watching something about a child who is brought up in a very dogmatic, religious environment, they recognised parts of their own childhood, what they clearly now see as a painful experience of oppression by adults and by religion. The family did not mean to them a kind of utopia that they didn't want to see attacked. And this was all the more surprising because they didn't seem to regard Jess's situation as particularly extraordinary. In fact, Jess is brought up in what in realist terms would be described as an extraordinary, extreme, caricatured environment. Yet these viewers didn't feel that. They didn't just say 'How extraordinary! Poor kid! Isn't that an amazing way to bring up a child?' Rather, they would say, 'I can remember feeling that', or 'How many times I was told that', or 'I have even said it myself'.

BS It's making me think that if you wanted to do a straight socio-logical survey and asked how do you feel about your marriage, or how do you feel about lesbianism, you would get very, very different responses.

JH Yes, because *Oranges* stimulates the memory, doesn't it? It stimulates a response based on recognising experience and because it is a strong piece, because it is a piece of quality work, it does what all good art can do. It creates a strong response, which here stems from empathy based on recognition. It arouses strong emotions. Even though people's situations are not the exact situation being described, they can none the less see how, even within their, perhaps less restricted, lives, they could create a similarly unjust situation.

BS So recognition strategies are being used for methodological pur-poses to get people to talk about things that you can never access very easily?

MM I don't think you could access them – certainly not through a questionnaire. We did a questionnaire study and in that respect it wasn't really very useful. Except for two people whose own experiences were very close to Jess's experience, in a quite literal sense, who had sought me out to talk about this, they didn't give those details on the questionnaire. One of the viewers had also had an experience as a teenager which was very similar to Jess's. The notion, therefore, that what was going on in the text was quite improbable was denied by people's experience. That's how we arrived at the position of questioning the notion of 'ordinary' women. If these women didn't respond as 'ordinary' women might have been expected to, then did that mean they weren't ordinary women? But then where were these ordinary women, who are solely heterosexual, living in a world that worships god and the family, who are all white, married with two kids?

BS It's interesting, isn't it, when you think of the kind of research done by people like Paul Willis (1977) and all the lad culture stuff, which has been criticised for concentrating on extraordinary cultures and ignoring the culture of most people – ordinary people, you might say. You are saying that neither of these positions would represent the complexity of the audiences you are trying to talk about.

JH It's not a question of whether people are simple or complex. There is a whole literature, a discourse, about the masses, about the ordinary, that presents a very particular view of what ordinary people are like. That their sensibilities are different, that they live very dull, very boring lives.

MM What we are saying is that all our assumptions about ordinary people and ordinary life need to be re-thought. They are too narrow, they exclude too many people, too much of most people's experience. Most people don't fit the definitions. And ordinary people experience things, and do things, that are thought of as extraordinary. One of the reasons to question the concept of the ordinary is that when people have even a single traumatic experience it lives with them all their lives, and informs their ordinariness, or perhaps we should say, it redefines it. In the same way, the viewers of *Oranges* we talked to were living with memories of traumatic experiences from when they were children or teenagers.

BS How did you come to do the questionnaire? How did it fit into the project as a whole?

JH We were curious as to what you might get from a questionnaire looking at the same kind of issues. The questionnaire asked the same kind of questions that we'd asked the viewers: 'what did you like about it?' and so on, but phrased in terms of 'what do you remember about it?' By then it was over two years since *Oranges* had been broadcast, so we decided to ask a group we thought would probably have seen and remembered it. Margaret was teaching a Women's Studies summer school, so that provided us with a convenient opportunity.

MM What I remember as most significant from the questionnaires was how vivid people's memories were, how well they could remember particular scenes and images after two and a half years – that's a long time to have those kind of memories. So it seemed that it had had quite an impact.

JH That came through very strongly – the sense that *Oranges* was a piece that people remembered for its high production values, for its aesthetic qualities. They remembered scenes, the colour of people's hair, characters; they remembered very specific details. And they remembered the issues, what it was about. But they didn't remember the story. This interested us, because one of the characteristics of women's memory, as it has been constructed by academic research, is that it is a narrative memory, based on women's association with story telling and oral history. Women are rarely associated with visual culture – the visual field and its discourses are still very much, I feel, left to the boys. There is very little work done on women and visuality other than in specific contexts like fine art. In terms of television studies, in particular, there is very little attention given to the visual, full stop, because traditionally television has not been seen, in comparison to film for example, as a visual medium. So I found these visual memories of *Oranges* very interesting, because my own memory tends to be more visual than narrative. People were remembering things like they might remember a photo, which, of course, might relate to Beeban Kidron's direction, with her history as a stills photographer, working with Eve Arnold. She has a particular way of framing movement, very much a snapshot sense that depends on capturing a moment. Her shooting is very still, very composed. All the close viewers commented on aesthetic issues: how well acted it was, how beautiful to watch, how they remembered particular scenes and images. This is an area that we feel audience studies, especially feminist audience studies, has neglected. Perhaps because of the kind of texts they have focused on (like soaps and sitcoms), it's been assumed that aesthetics are not an important factor in women's viewing pleasures. Whereas both the questionnaires and the in-depth viewings clearly demonstrated that it is an extremely important aspect of the pleasure women get from watching television. People were very, very aware of what they themselves called 'high-production values': the concern with scripting, *mise-en-scène*, performance and visual style is clearly not just an academic concern.

MM There were comments about the surrealist scenes, for instance.

Although one of the viewers didn't like them, others made the kind of observations you hope your students would make about what they were doing in a basically realist text; like, 'this is creating meaning visually in a way that can't be done verbally'. What we felt was important was that the awareness of the text's aesthetic qualities, the appreciation of it dealing with themes and issues, the sensitivity to nuance and detail, all this contradicted the apparent assumption that ordinary viewers are only really grabbed by content and narrative. And especially in relation to women, it challenges the construction in academia of the woman viewer as constantly distracted because she is always doing the ironing or something when she watches television.

JH I remember Margaret saying to me one evening, 'what do you really want to say about all this'? And I said, 'I want to say more than anything, how fed up I am with the way women always seem to get categorised as only viewers of soap when it comes to television drama, as if they never watch anything else. Women have always formed the majority audience for single plays and serial drama of all kinds as well as soaps. They watch a whole range of programmes, so why are we only regarding them as viewers of soap? That in itself seems to be becoming a bit of an orthodoxy. When we started researching work on women viewers we found the odd piece on women watching football and sport, but the vast majority of the literature on women viewers seemed to be on them as viewers of soap.

MM And readers of romance. These are two popular women's genres that feminist academics are often suspicious of, so that their interest in women who enjoy them is probably a kind of puzzlement ...

BS Which means they want to justify why women enjoy them?

MM Yes, the redemptive reading that Charlotte Brunsdon (1993) talks about. It often seems that feminist academics are wanting to say that women are not cultural dupes, that there must be some good reason why they like the things they do. We don't want to say that work wasn't valuable; on the contrary, we think it has been very valuable, and very interesting. But one spin-off seems to be that women continue to be seen as viewers of soap and readers of romance. But even if women do watch soap and read romance, that isn't all they do. And it isn't necessarily the cultural experience that gives them the most pleasure, or has most impact. The experience of watching a drama like *Oranges* is clearly a very different experience. We're not claiming that one kind of viewing experience is better, or more important, than another; but we would want to open up the notion of what women's relationship to popular culture actually is.

BS Do things like class or race or religion or region have an effect or is it just so much more complex than reducing it to those variables?

JH We've certainly thought that, in terms of the people we talked to, possibly there was a regional effect. Jess is from the north-west, of course. But the important factor was rather that a high proportion of the viewers had a Catholic background, which may be because several of them were from Liverpool. The interesting thing about the religion was not really what religion it was, that didn't seem to be the important point, but the intensity with which a religious ethos permeated childhood life. That seemed to be quite important, and those with Catholic backgrounds seemed to draw more parallels between their own experiences and Jess's evangelical one than did viewers from Protestant backgrounds. (None of them had any other religious background.) I would say that was probably the most important distinguishing factor amongst the women we talked to, in terms of affecting their responses to the text. Certainly more important than race or class.

BS Ellen Seiter (1989) comments on how difficult it is to ask people about class. When you're doing audience research and you start asking people what their income is, or where they go shopping, or whatever signifier of class we use, they get embarrassed. Maybe that's one reason we avoid it? Did you make any analysis in relation to class?

MM We weren't doing sociological research, so we didn't ask anyone anything about themselves. Almost everything we know about the in-depth viewers came out of the conversations.

JH Apart from the obvious, such as whether they were Black or white.

MM But we didn't ask them whether they defined themselves as Black or white. Nor, for instance, whether they defined themselves as feminists. That was quite interesting, because when we thought of sketching out a profile of the in-depth viewers in relation to categories like that, we decided they could probably all be described as feminist in one way or another. Not formally, not because they had read feminist theory or belonged to a women's group, but because feminist issues are issues that women think about. So instead of dividing women into feminists and non-feminists, what you have to say is that ordinary women

turn out to be influenced by feminism and feminist ideas quite
a lot. Which meant we abandoned any attempt to profile them
on the basis of such categories, because it simply wouldn't have
been faithful to what we knew about them.

BS How can we retain a sense of class or race or feminist politics,
if we keep collapsing the categories into these sorts of levels of
complexity?

MM Because concepts like class and feminism are theoretical tools,
they are things to think with. They are ways of thinking about
the complexities of hierarchies and difference in society. It
doesn't mean that people stack neatly into these pigeon-holes.
We could have divided our group into Black and white, straights
and gays, mothers and not mothers, graduates and non-graduates,
northerners and southerners, etc. Class would have been more
complicated: in one way or another they could all be defined as
coming from working-class or lower middle-class families, but
they had all experienced changes in terms of class definitions,
because of education, for instance, or marriage or divorce. But
these kinds of definitions would only have been interesting to
us if they had correlated with readings of the text. And, in fact,
we didn't find that there was, for instance, a lesbian reading of
it, or a Black reading. People understood the text in the same
way, they didn't think it was doing something different because
they were Black or because they were lesbian. There were differences of emotional response to particular moments but they
weren't necessarily tied up with those sociological categories
in any neat way. It wasn't necessarily the case, for instance, that
the Black viewers felt very differently about this text because
the lead character was white, even though one of Jess's relationships is with a Black girl. In fact, it was a white viewer who
thought this was a token casting. Other factors seemed to be more
important, like age or sexuality, but again, not in a neat way.
I would still hold to class politics and feminist politics and Black
politics. I think that those are areas of activity that are areas
of resistance to what are dominant structures of power in our
society. It doesn't mean that because we join together in a party
or a movement or a demonstration, we necessarily relate to
something like a television text in a preordained way. In any
case, it's important to distinguish between how people understand something and how they evaluate it or respond to it emotionally. Although there weren't huge differences in how the
viewers responded to *Oranges* emotionally, there were more

differences in that respect than in actual interpretations of the text.

JH   And we must stress that our focus was the text and how people had responded to it. The text was what mattered and we went with that. We weren't looking for people to represent specific groups or identities. Later on we realised that we had actually covered quite a wide spectrum of people, in terms of categorisable identities, but that wasn't due to planning, that was how it happened. And some of the more significant differences weren't necessarily ones we would have planned for anyway. For instance, we noticed more differences between mothers and non-mothers than we did on the basis of differences in class or race. People who were mothers responded differently to the relationship between Jess and her mother from those who hadn't had children. The latter tended to identify much more strongly with Jess against her mother. This came through quite strongly both from the questionnaires and from the in-depth studies, and was a more significant factor in terms of responses to the text than anything else. Apart from religion, as I mentioned earlier. Religion was much stronger as a factor than class, race ...

MM   Or sexuality, which isn't what you might expect. It is important to emphasise that we weren't doing an audience study. We weren't studying the audience. And it is not an ethnography.

BS   Would you argue then against the idea of a generalised gendered reading of anything?

MM   No, not in principle I wouldn't. Categories and generalisations are essential for any kind of research. But it's also important to keep questioning them.

JH   And I don't think we would argue against the concept of a gendered reading. After all, that's what we did. We didn't watch *Oranges* with any male viewers. We did talk about whether we should, but in the event we didn't. We thought that there would probably be a much more significant difference between male and female viewers than any of the other differences we've mentioned, but we can't say because we didn't watch it with any men. So we don't really know.

BS   You seem to be saying very strongly that this is not an audience study, this is very much about responses to a text, but because of the nature of these responses you found that you had to mount a critique of audience research too? You got to that from a very textual study?

JH   Yes. Because we wanted to think about our own work in relation to existing discourses about women as viewers. So we read what we could find on women watching television. And we were surprised at how out of sync the results of our study seemed to be with quite a lot of the other findings. We weren't sure why this was. Perhaps it was because of the way research funding tends to shape the patterns of audience study work. Because we weren't funded we weren't tied to a particular research programme.

MM Or perhaps it was because we were studying a single text, and one that straddled the divide between 'high' and popular culture. Or perhaps because our methodology was different.

BS Did you both know each other's feminist positions before you started working together?

MM I don't think I knew in any detail what Julia's position was. I suppose Julia might have known more about mine because *The Female Gaze* (1988) argues for intervention into popular culture as a feminist strategy.

JH I came relatively late in my life to academia, but I've always considered myself a feminist activist in the other areas that I've worked in. I worked in community arts for a long time, where trying to make productions with feminist intentions was something that I was involved in on a day-to-day level. So whenever I'm analysing a text I'm always conscious of the production process, and the formal strategies that went into making it.

BS Were you working together at the time that you began this?

MM We were working in the same department, yes.

JH I was very new in the department at that point. I knew Margaret had edited *The Female Gaze*, so I certainly had an idea of the kind of scholarship I was interested in, which was a scholarship that was accessible to the broader audience of women that are outside academia, because that was where I had come from. That book had made sense to me as an undergraduate at a point when some feminist film theory seemed to obscure the political issues. I wanted to write things myself that dealt with feminist ideas in a way that made them more accessible.

BS How have you worked as a team on this?

JH We had a lot of regular meetings, didn't we?

MM We began by watching it through together. We taped our first discussions about the text, and made notes of our responses. And we talked through and talked through and talked through. The actual writing was very much like that. It was very co-operative and I would think by now, while there are occasional sentences that I know come from Julia, the rest of it feels like ours.

JH I can see bits that come from Margaret, but it's hard to separate it all out now. One of us would draft some material and the other would look at it and re-write it, using the draft as a base. And one of us would say, 'yes, that's a good bit, yes, you can develop something from that', or, 'maybe that bit is irrelevant and not quite the way we want to go', but it was that sort of process.

BS Was that smooth or was it quite painful?

MM I found it very enjoyable for the most part.

JH Yes, I did too. I hadn't worked in that way academically before, but because I come from a background of making things with people, it seemed to me to be a very natural way to work.

MM I think it gave me confidence, for instance, in those areas where I felt that perhaps I would not have the time to research facts and figures, dates, references, and so on. That's one area where Julia's strengths really complemented mine. She also knows more about the production side of film and TV; and she's more alert to the visual aspects than I am. If I'd written it on my own I might have been in danger of writing about the text as if it were a novel, with too much emphasis on narrative and ideology, and too little on aesthetics. I think our respective strengths really proved to be creatively complementary. I was really happy to say 'oh good, you've done that, so I'll do this', or 'I've got that right? Great, so can you do that bit?' And I don't think I felt any sort of sense of ego. When Julia said, 'that doesn't seem to make sense', 'that isn't very clear', 'can't we do something else with this?', or 'this is a bit woolly', I found it useful rather than painful.

JH So did I. I certainly felt it was very illuminating to work with somebody who had such a wide theoretical base, with Margaret's experience behind her. I have not had the time yet to build up that solid base in theory that Margaret has. So I found it very useful.

BS How did you feel that worked?

MM I don't think I'm conscious of using theory, I'm just thinking.

JH I wouldn't say that I was particularly conscious of Margaret pushing theoretical paradigms at me or anything like that. But certainly some of the techniques she was using for analysis did seem to fit better with some areas of the field than others.

BS Continuing on the process: you read, you collected all this information. Did you tape the conversations with the viewers? Did you transcribe them?

JH We taped some, and some Margaret took down in shorthand. And we transcribed them all.

BS Did you both sit down together and go through them? What was the process by which you came to construct the final analysis?

MM Yes, we went through them together, and we talked through what we found, what struck us as interesting, what our worries were and what ...

JH Lots of conversation. And I seem to remember I changed jobs and suddenly I had a bit more time and I started writing. That was literally how it happened.

MM When you're working full-time you need deadlines – even self-imposed ones – to find time for research. That's another thing about working together, you give each other more short-term deadlines.

Conclusion

BS Do you feel that there is anything I should have asked you that I haven't?

JH No. In terms of thinking about methodology, for textual critics to talk about their methodology in this way is perhaps a new development, because there's been a taken for granted assumption that you develop a skill as a textual critic but it's not a group skill. It's something you learn by doing textual analysis in a university context, but there are no clear guidelines that define what a textual critic does. I think there is much less written about the process in that area than there is about sociological methods. One of the disciplinary bridges that still has not been crossed satisfactorily is between the different methods used in textual studies and the social sciences, which perhaps is partly due to the fact that textual critics do not often look at their methods. Until we examine our methods, how can we relate textual analysis to sociological analysis in any kind of concrete way, because it is only when you start to look at those processes that you can really begin to unpick some of those principal areas of difference between the two disciplines and decide which ones are useful to feminism which is by nature multifaceted and interdisciplinary.

MM You can trace the development of feminist approaches to texts, based around images of women, issues of identification, psychoanalysis and polysemy, semiotics and regimes of representation.

JH But that's more a description of the discourse.

MM Yes, but when you are confronted with the prospect of writing about a text, you do have to ask yourself what you want to say about it. What questions are you going to ask about it? Are you going to use it to test some hypothesis? I mean when we accepted the commission to write about *Oranges*, the fact that it was for a collection on lesbianism and popular culture meant we would obviously focus on the issue of lesbianism in some way – but how? Traditional literary criticism tended to focus on what the text meant, and supply evidence to support that interpretation, with a strong assumption that it was a worthwhile, life-enhancing text. We could have done something like that, I suppose, but it isn't the way most discussions of popular culture or issues like lesbianism in texts are conducted these days. We could have asked whether it was a positive representation of lesbianism, and then said it does do this, and it doesn't do that, and should do this and should do that, and come to some conclusion in relation to the politics of representation and feminism and lesbianism. A lot of feminist textual work is done in that way. I suppose that's more or less what we were doing in *The Female Gaze*. I was interested in trying a different approach to *Oranges*. One of several approaches we began with was asking what changes had been made to the novel in adapting it for television. We weren't really interested in questions of form as such, but that led us to ask what the production team were aiming for in doing the adaptation, which led us to questions of politics and realism and so on. Why had they made it more chronological as a narrative? Why had they made the exorcism more violent, or the love scene more explicit? These were aesthetic choices that we chose to assume had a purpose in relation to the sexual politics of the piece. We didn't begin with a hypothesis about realism; we got to that through exploring various questions that we asked ourselves about the text. I think it was a useful strategy to have adopted.

BS Would you do the project any differently, if you did it now?

JH Yes. Definitely. I don't think I'd do the same thing again in quite that sort of way: if only because having done it has made me want to ask different sorts of questions. But, we were quite happy with the way we did it really. The method we chose raised some interesting questions, and went some way to answering them. I think it has been very interesting, very satisfying.

MM But it actually raised a whole lot more questions.

JH Perhaps any methodology does that.

Notes

With thanks to Pennie Drinkall for the transcription.

1 Winterson, J. (1990), *Oranges are not the Only Fruit: The Script*, London, Pandora.

2 Marshment, M. and J. Hallam (1994), *Oranges are not the Only Fruit*: String of Knots to Orange Box, *Jump Cut 39* (Spring), 40–50. A version of this article can also be found in B. Budge and D. Hamer (eds) (1994), *The Good, the Bad and the Gorgeous: Popular Culture's Romance with Lesbianism*, London and New York, Pandora.

3 Hallam and Marshment, Framing Experience: Case Studies in Reception of *Oranges are not the Only Fruit*, *Screen*, forthcoming, Spring 1995.

4 *Oranges* has been screened three times: January 1990 (BBC2), repeated on BBC2 the following summer, repeated on BBC1 Spring 1994.

Bibliography

Brunsdon, C. (1993), Identity in Feminist Television Criticism, *Media, Culture and Society*, 15:2, 309–20.

Gamman, L. and M. Marshment (1988), *The Female Gaze: Women as Viewers of Popular Culture*, London, The Women's Press.

Hinds, H. (1992), *Oranges are not the Only Fruit*: Reaching Audiences Other Lesbian Texts Cannot Reach, in S. Munt (ed.), *New Lesbian Criticism: Literary and Cultural Readings*, New York and London, Harvester Wheatsheaf.

O'Rourke, R. (1988), Fingers in the Fruit Basket, A Feminist Reading of Jeanette Winterson's *Oranges are not the Only Fruit*, in S. Sellers (ed.), *Feminist Criticism: Theory and Practice*, London, Harvester.

Seiter, E. *et al.* (1989), *Remote Control: Television Audiences and Cultural Power*, London and New York, Routledge.

Willis, P. (1977), *Learning to Labour: How Working-Class Kids Get Working-Class Jobs*, Farnborough, Saxon House.

10

Theorising, ethics and representation in feminist ethnography

BEVERLEY SKEGGS

I had always been good at femininity, my mother taught me well. I was also good at fighting. When I arrived at university, something not even thought of as a possibility until a year prior to entry, I realised I'd got it all wrong. The things at which I had culturally excelled were completely undervalued and many of the things that were valued I had not even known about. It was my stark awareness of the limits of my cultural capital and my fierce belief in the wrongs of inequality that motivated my post-graduate research which will finally be published as *Becoming Respectable: An Ethnography* and has been published in journal articles (Skeggs, 1989, 1991a, 1991b).

This chapter will provide a background to the research and then focus on three issues: how we use theories when doing research; the ethical dilemmas of ethnography and how we represent the researched. Elsewhere I have written about the epistemological and ontological dimensions of feminist ethnography (Skeggs, 1994).

I began the research as a Ph.D. student with eleven young white working-class women I was teaching on a Community Care course at a local further education college to supplement my grant. I had signed up for a similar course when I left school. I found their responses to femininity to be fascinating. Although they were enrolled on a course closely associated with femininity, which enabled them to convert their already acquired feminine cultural capital into an educational resource, their behaviour was far from the ideals of femininity. I was interested in this incongruity. In the following year I was given access to more students and the number for the research rose to eighty-three.

For three years full-time I became involved in their lives in and outside of the college. I also spent time working on details of the national and local economy, housing, poverty and education statistics. I used such information to map out the general economic and cultural framework in which the young women were located. I used cultural information to build up a picture of what Berger and Luckmann (1971) describe as plausibility structures, i.e. what they see to be possible and plausible. To understand their movement through this mapping I traced the trajectories of the young women through the education system and asked them for biographical details[1] constructing a 'case-study' file of each student. I also conducted formal and informal interviews and meetings with family members, friends, partners and college teachers.

My research was put on hold when I took a job as a full-time research fellow on a completely different type of research which involved quantitative analysis and completely new skills. I had collected too much information and the prospect of sorting it all into a coherent 100,000 words, whilst learning computing and statistical analysis seemed impossible. With my new-found computing skills I decided to do a follow-up analysis. In retrospect I'm not sure if this was to put off the final write-up, which became more and more daunting the longer I left it.

Eighteen months after the end of the research and my grant I managed to complete by working mainly for fifteen hour days over a three month period.[2] My central problem was that I had too much data. I still have tapes which have not been transcribed and transcripts which have not been used. I loved doing the research: I was so completely absorbed in every little detail I didn't stop to think how it would all fit together. I just collected and collected. My absorption was linked to being able to study what could have been my life with critical distance and under-standing. I only managed to finish by being completely ruthless and abandoning whole areas of interest by making arbitrary decisions about what to include. To keep up to date with the women this meant I did two more sets of follow-up work, the last being in 1992. So I now have ten years' worth of contact to use and understand.

I also think that part of the problem with completion began right at the start. I didn't really know how to do research with real people. I was quite happy with the neat and tidy world of theory but the messy world of real lives was something for which I was totally unprepared. I was a student in a period where methodology courses were not available. I did not know, for instance, that feminist ethnography has a long tradition, emerging from the travel literature of the radical feminists of the nineteenth century (see Reinharz, 1992). I learnt by trial and error and sheer nosiness. Sometimes it felt like detective work: trying to put lots of different information together to make a coherent picture. Other times it just felt like an impossible mess. The interesting theoretical debates about ethnography and method emerged after the bulk of the research was completed.[3]

Theoretical constructions and motivations

What I did learn as a result of doing ethnography was that ethnography is not itself a method, rather it is a combination of different methods; hence it is a theory of the research process – an idea about how we should do research. It usually combines certain features in specific ways: some account of context; of fieldwork that will be conducted over a *prolonged period of time*; conducted *within the settings* of the participants; *involving the researcher in participation* and observation; involving an account of the development of relationships between the researcher and the researched; involving study of the 'other'; focusing on experience and practice; having culture frequently as the central focus; treating participants as microcosms of wider structural processes. Methods such as questionnaires; historical documentation; statistical analysis can also be used – they often provide a wider socio-economic context.

Whilst ethnography is a theory of the research process, ethnography itself is defined by its relationship to theoretical positions. These theoretical positions are not clear cut and it is often easier to understand the differences by examining the assumptions which underpin how they approach: reality, their participants, their analysis and writing. For instance: *naturalist ethnographers* are usually associated with anthropology and their research is underpinned by the ontological assumption that you can only know about people through their 'natural' settings. Marcus (1992) distinguishes between *modernist* and *realist* ethnography. Realist ethnographers believe in coherence, community, historical determination and structure. They also believe that there is a reality 'out there' which can be discovered. Modernist ethnographers do not concentrate on communities but on the complex formation of identity across a range of sites in relation to wider global issues. They emphasise the role of re-presenting when discussing reality. *Social constructionist* ethnographers believe in the power of their questions and the use of representation to construct the lives of the people they are studying (see Steier, 1991) and *post-modern* ethnographers privilege discourse over text, foregrounding dialogue, fragmentation, bricolage and emphasise the collaborative nature of the ethnographic exchange (Tyler, 1987). However, it is hard to make these definitions work in practice because they overlap so much. Many of the concerns of the post-modern ethnographers were already in existence in much feminist work. (The re-naming of feminist work as post-modern is a huge trend which extends further than just ethnography (Morris, 1988; Skeggs, 1992).) My own ethnography combines aspects of many of these different theoretical positions.

All ethnography involves a close relationship to theory. It is always informed by theory even if it is not acknowledged. For instance, theory informs crucial methodological decisions: why choose ethnography in the first place? Which methods are combined? Who are the participants? What is your relationship to them? Where to do the research? How to make sense of what is happening? How do you represent the researched? What writing strategies do you use?

Theoretical decisions inform how the research is used. It can be used as grounded theory by developing theories from empirical experience (Glaser and Strauss, 1967, 1971). It can be used with the specific intention to improve pre-existent theories (Burawoy *et al.*, 1991) or for theoretical modification, so that existing theories can account for the specificities and the context of the group being studied (Griffin, 1980[4]). It can be used in a manner which proves or disproves theories through empirical evidence (Hammersley and Atkinson, 1983). It has also been used to challenge the concept of reality by contesting the idea that ethnography can be a conduit to a real world and showing that all knowledge is textually produced and cannot exist outside of social constructions (Clifford, 1986).

By the time I was a postgraduate student, I had already come into contact with, resisting and embracing, particular theories. I readily welcomed the many different variants of Marxist and feminist theory. When I read certain theorists I would go through a process of overwhelming enthusiasm, believing they had the answer to the problems of capitalism and patriarchy, only to be disappointed when I read critiques. I soon learned to anticipate the critiques. It was Gramsci's (1971) claim for pessimism of the intellect and optimism of the will, that enabled me to approach theorists with healthy scepticism whilst still believing in the necessity for political change. The theorists which I used to generate the questions for my research were those whose ideas resonated with my past and current experiences. This process is described by Liz Stanley (1990) as an 'intellectual biography', i.e. our trajectory through the theorists we use is closely tied into our autobiographies. I was always searching for theorists who could understand class and gender together.[5] Books such as Heidi Hartmann's (1981) *The Unhappy Marriage of Marxism and Feminism* and Annette Kuhn and Ann-Marie Wolpe's (1978) *Feminism and Materialism* embroiled me in detailed analysis and understandings of the workings of different systems, institutions and experiences. I used to wait with excitement for the arrival of the journal *Feminist Review* to see how the debates were forming. I had no idea how much pleasure can be gained from theories until I applied them to try to explain my life and the lives of others. I believed I was engaged in trying to work out how to change the world and this inspired me to do research. I really wanted to know answers. My enthusiasm and incredible naiveté are conveyed in my 1981 research diary account:

> I believe in my research because of the political motive. I want to change things and I believe we have to be able to identify the processes involved before we can actually change them, so I can in fact, to some extent, come to terms with being an academic and a feminist. This research is my life, it is not a job, it is not an academic means to an end, it is something I believe in emotionally and politically. I can't be objective, I'm part of what I'm studying: a female on the end of class and gender power games.

My research was and still is a highly emotive affair. Ideas are emotional: they can be inspiring, satisfying, rage and guilt inducing, terrifying, etc. They involve you.

I also wanted to use my research as a corrective to previous research. When I began I was working in a historical period in Sociology in which the French Marxist, Louis Althusser, was influential. His work circumscribed the questions asked and the answers made. One of his main arguments and strongest legacies was the assertion that people are interpellated by ideology (Althusser, 1971), i.e. it is ideology that places them in relation to the world; people are empty vessels waiting to be filled by ideology. My experience of how I had taken on and off femininity made me circumspect of this precept. So my research question developed (from a critique of Althusser through Gramsci (1971)) into 'why do young women, who are clearly not just passive victims of some ideological conspiracy, consent to a system of class and gender oppression which appears to offer few rewards and little benefit'. It wasn't long before I asked myself: what alternatives do they have? As the research became more complex my focus changed to a more general exploration of how gendered (and classed) subjectivities are constructed through discourse, institutions and structures.

The research was also corrective in that I did not consider many of the available representations of the working class to be plausible. There were classic studies of heroic male labourers and skilled workers who struggled with dignity, of sensitive working-class boys who became academics and of oppressed working-class women. I could not find any contemporary sociological accounts of working-class women who were not ground down and who did not take on ideology intact. The autobiographies of Black women and the downright anger of Angela Davis spoke loudest to me.[6] I thus wanted to do research which both filled the gap in existing knowledge about working-class women and which challenged many of the dominant ideas of the time. To do this I felt I had to speak to real working-class women rather than relying on the representations available. This combined with the fact that I was learning to speak out from a limited and marginalised position as a working-class woman in academia, having spent my first six months as an undergraduate totally intimidated and silenced by the articulate middle-class students. I was thus arguing for and from a stand-point theory, although I did not know this at the time.[7] I believed that the working class had a greater knowledge of the working of oppression because they had experienced it. As the final section will show I have now problematised the concept of experience, so I no longer hold the certainty expressed in this position.

I chart this partial history to show that the period in which research takes place, the social location of the researcher and access to theories is central to the motivations and framing of the research. In writing this history I'm aware that I'm re-constructing and re-presenting a messy process as a coherent narrative, highlighting certain features and in the process obscuring others (although unintentionally, but it would be impossible to provide a complete account of ten years of research, theoretical development and eighteen years of studying).

— If I began the research now after the emergence of post-structuralism I would be asking different questions. The theoretical movements which have occurred have shifted from concerns with institutional organisation to identity politics; from economy to subjectivity, etc. I wonder what would happen to the anger and rage which was so easily channelled into Marxist feminist theories. As an insecure graduate student would I be seduced by post-modernism? Would I talk about difference instead of inequality? How would I understand structures? My concerns have changed as I have come into contact with many more theories and politics. Time has allowed me to re-work some of the initial research findings in the light of my access to new theories. We are thus being continually positioned by and positioning ourselves in relation to theory. This is not just a case of what we read but who we talk to, our institutional location, what our colleagues read, which conferences we go to and sometimes how we feel at the time.

There is an in-built theoretical insecurity to ethnography which makes it very different from textual research. Primarily because it is not fixed. If you leave a text when you return to it it will not have altered significantly – although you may have. Lynne Pearce (Chapter Four) disagrees: the text, she argues, is not fixed. However, this does not detract from the fact that when you return to a group of people they may have completely changed: their minds, opinions and behaviour. Texts, at least, do not change their minds. The theories I used to explain people or events had to be continually re-evaluated. This volatility made me very conscious of the temporality of theories. They may work to explain things one day, they may not the next day. Validity becomes a matter of the most plausible theory which explains some phenomena over a period of time. This does generate enormous insecurities for the ethnographer who constantly experiences the anxiety not only of just not getting it right but knowing that it is impossible. This is why standard textbook representations of research as a neat and rational process are so dangerous and deceiving. The value of ethnography is that the researcher is continually exposed to these changes, so that *processes* rather than 'facts' have to be explained.

I also used theories which should have been fundamentally incompatible. For example: when examining how the women, when older, used their heterosexuality, I drew upon psycho-analytic theories. From my reading of Joan Riviere's (1929/1986) psychoanalytic account of masquerade (i.e. the placing of a gendered mask to make a performance), I developed a sociological version. This appropriation of theories from epistemologically incompatible areas may disturb other theorists but I was not going to let notions of epistemological purity deter me from exploring concepts. I found the psychoanalytic concept of masquerade useful for thinking through the ways in which femininity is deployed to normalise heterosexuality. Through my analysis of one woman's comments I was able to show how women used masquerade not as a desire to be male, as Riviere would suggest, but as a cultural resource in situations of uncertainty or where evaluations of women were made. Masquerade was used tem-porarily to resist the imposition of power. It was used as a defen-sive strategy rather than as ironic mimicry. By working through the uses made of the masquerade I was able to develop and challenge the previous use of the term. I was able to transfer it from the unconscious to the conscious.

Ethics

Feminist ethnographers enter into a culture of indebtedness always grateful that people will actually speak and spend time with you. Ethnography is very different from other forms of research because of the intensity of the experience. This, Judith Stacey (1988) argues, means that it is often the most exploitative form of research because ethnographers subject the researched to greater risk of exploitation, betrayal and abandonment. I began the research with some knowledge of feminist research ethics: I wanted to reciprocate, not exploit, not abuse power, to care, to empower and to be honest. Putting these principles into practice was often difficult. During three years of full-time contact many close friendships were formed but I found it very difficult to sustain the level of commitment that any friend-ship requires. Juggling old friends, new friends and writing is a constant problem. Reciprocity and friendships increase the demands on the researcher in a way in which a text is unlikely to do.

The demands were also increased by the intimacy of exchange which is enabled by ethnographic relationships. I began with limited awareness of the level and number of social/personal problems likely to be experienced by the young women. Those who had shared, often for the first time, awful histories and experiences needed proper counselling, but they were unwilling for a variety of reasons to use it and I became their sole source of support. This was not only traumatic for them but I was hopelessly unaware of how to deal with the issues of abuse they were raising. It moved the research on to a different terrain, for which few researchers are equipped. I was completely unprepared for the emotional intensity of these ethnographic relationships. The principle of empowerment seemed miles away from the research I was doing. As Liz Kelly, Sheila Burton and Linda Regan (1994) have noted:

> Some of the glib ways in which 'empowerment' is used in discussions of feminist research concern us greatly. They reflect either an arrogance of viewpoint or a failure to think through what 'power' consists of (p. 37)

I was often overwhelmed by their and my powerlessness to do anything at all about the situations they experienced. Similar situations have led some feminist researchers such as Kirkwood (1993) to seek counselling for themselves. The feminist methodology texts which suggest that research should be used for consciousness raising seemed particularly inappropriate. On some issues the young women had highly raised consciousness; what they did not have were the right economic conditions to put them into effect. Homelessness was a problem for some of the young women. Under the feminist rules of reciprocity it is only fair that the ethnographer should provide a home if necessary, but you can imagine how this impinges on your life. Texts, fortunately, may desire shelves but they do not demand beds, food and money.

As a result of regularly having to handle this sort of information and relationship, if there was ever a chance of being able to do anything to improve a situation I would throw myself into it wholeheartedly and discard the research. I nearly jeopardised the whole project when I organised a sexual harassment case for one of the young women. Even though I am now better equipped to handle these situations the despair unleashed on my recent visits to their homes was overwhelming. It is very difficult to drive away in a nice car to a warm house to write when the person you have known for the last ten years is about to have the last of her furniture removed by bailiffs for unpaid bills. It is this sort of research experience which stops me from ever becoming completely absorbed in abstract theorising which does not have any political imperative. It also stops me from indulging in work which has no understanding of economic constraints. I now believe it is only the privileged who are able to avoid these issues.

There is also the ethical dilemma of how to use the information you have collected which will be discussed in the next section.

Representing experience

How we understand the experience of the research, the researched and our own had always presented specific dilemmas for feminist theorists and ethnographers. Ethnographers and feminists often give overwhelming authorial weight to the concept of experience. Because you spend so much time as an ethnographer with people, or because you have had a particular experience doing the research you may believe that this gives you access to a particular form of knowledge to which others may not know about; that it is authentic and privileged. Yet, experience is always being interpreted by those who are experiencing it, so the researcher *always* enters the second stage of the interpretative process (Grant, 1993). (See detailed discussion and references on experience in the introduction to this book.)

Scott (1992) argues that it is not individuals who have experience but subjects who are constituted through experience. Hence gender (class and race, etc.) must be represented as processes that proceed through experience (Probyn, 1993). It is this imperative which has led to considerable differences within both feminist theory and ethnography. My ethnography focused on the *processes* by which women were gendered and classed through their experiences. Conversely, some feminist theory and ethnography represents people as vessels of their experience without any emphasis on process, on the production of them as subjects.

All research involves the researcher in the process of representation which itself is historically situated within theoretical debates and frameworks. Initially it was the perceived disjunction between women's experiences and the few representations of women's lives offered by traditional disciplines that provided the spark for the unearthing and elaboration of their omissions and biases in feminist research (Spender, 1981). By filling in the gaps and revealing the biases, different representations, constructed by women for women, are offered; but they are still representations.

This is why understanding representations, how they work, what they are and the processes by which they come into existence, are crucial to understanding the production of ethnographic research. However, any focus on representation must be careful not to collapse the cultural into the social (see Lury, Chapter One, this volume). Avoiding issues such as which groups have access to the forms and means of representation has led to an ignorance of social processes.

Thinking through issues of ethnographic representation raises many more ethical issues and confronts the power relations involved in research. When writing about the thoughts and actions of others you have to think about what you are doing with their words and how you are using your descriptions of their actions. The status and knowledge value of words becomes an issue: do words produced in different contexts such as intimate conversations, overheard snippets, questionnaire responses, formal interviews all have the same status? No, argues Pearce (1994).

Ethnographers are then forced to confront the conditions of their productions. What do you do when faced with numerous contradictory responses? How do you decide which comments or descriptions to include and which to cut? What do you do if your analysis of a situation is directly challenged by the researched who were involved in it? These questions are formed through assumptions that the ethnographic researcher makes about what is 'writeable' and what is 'readable' (Atkinson, 1992).

One of the most interesting and difficult dilemmas I continually have to face is how to describe the women. Remember, I began the research by wanting to correct what I saw as previous absences and mis-representations of working-class women. So I chose a group of working-class women and wanted to represent them as such. To me, a feminist sociologist, they were clearly working class. Practically everything about them signalled working class from their education, housing, cultural practices, choices, etc. They, however, with only a few exceptions, did not want to be defined as working class. It was something that most were expending great amounts of energy and money trying not to be.

They thought my original title for the book 'An Ethnography of Working-Class Women' was offensive. What was I to do? I had to change the title because I did not want to offend the women who had been so generous and gracious with their time and their lives, but I wanted to explore why the label 'working-class' was so problematic for them.

They rarely spoke of class, although it was articulated through discourses of economic limitation and cultural choice. If I had listened for directly articulated class comments I would not have heard them; I had to use *my* frameworks to understand *their* comments. Some theorists have dealt with this differently: Angela McRobbie (1991) notes the disparity between her 'wheeling in' class in her research and its almost complete absence from the girls' talk and general discourse, leading her to suggest that being working class meant little or nothing to the girls she researched. This is, however, problematic. If the researched do not speak concepts does it mean that the researcher cannot use them? As Barker and Beezer (1992) ask: is it possible for the theorist to have any critical position independent of the people she or he is studying? If the theorist cannot theorise, why bother doing research? Theory is a different language which draws on concepts which are not used on a daily basis (if they were, why bother with higher education?), so it automatically positions the theorist/writer differently to the speaker/researched. Ethnography makes these differences very explicit. This is why Harding (1991) points out that women's experiences in themselves or the things that women say *cannot* provide reliable grounds for knowledge claims about nature and social relations because experience itself is shaped by social relations. It may be more useful to think about knowledge being produced through different discursive sites in which the researcher and the researched have different access to discursive resources. I had access through higher education to feminist and sociological explanations which led to my understandings.

In ethnography academic styles of writing are juxtaposed with everyday speech, part of what Lury (1991) describes as the aesthetics of authenticity. This can make the researched sound inarticulate and the researcher as the font of knowledge. This need not always be the case.[8] The use of everyday oral articulations is central to the authority which ethnography claims. Their inclusion is one of the stylistic conventions that define ethnography as a distinctive genre, as a distinctive textual production, as a realist text (see Atkinson, 1990). Oral commentary from the researched provides a form of plausibility constructed from vicarious access into a world which the majority of readers are unlikely to inhabit or know about but which may have enough similarity to other contexts to elicit momentary recognition. In this sense ethnographic texts may work on the reader in similar ways to visual media products: they may elicit similar structures of feelings such as recognition and empathy.[9] Ethnography, because it is not just purely theoretical, and because it relies on narratives and/or accounts as 'dramatic indicators' (Collins, 1983) may engender similar responses.

The division between academic theoretical writing and everyday talk is a structural product of the difference between the researcher's position in the academic mode of production and the researched within the unemployed/unskilled secondary labour market which creates problems for accountability. As well as my autobiographical reasons for wanting to re-present working-class women I was also doing the research for an entry ticket into academic employment. To achieve this I had to submit to the system that would assess me. I had to learn to write in a way that would impress Ph.D. examiners and this does not square with accountability to the researched. I have not abandoned my responsibility for accountability but I see it as an ideal. I carry images of the young women in my consciousness; I continue to meet and try out ideas with them. They keep me grounded in the same way as my mother has always done. My theorising must be able to speak to them and women like them. This makes me continually reflect on my positioning in power relations. I hope it also counteracts any tendency to produce obscure, irrelevant and pretentious feminist theories.

The ethnography and desires for providing particular representations can conflict. I wanted to find dignity, resistance and strength. I had earlier been influenced by and impressed with Paul Willis's (1977) *Learning to Labour*, a study of 'how working class kids (read males) get working class jobs' which gave humour and power (although with disastrous consequences) to young working-class men (Skeggs, 1992). I wanted to find similar tenacity and belligerence. I often found the opposite. I found fatalism, acquiescence, passivity *as well as* anger, determination and insolence. It was emotionally and politically far easier to write about challenges than to write about despair and powerlessness.

Representations can play a key role in shifting the limits of our understandings so it is crucial that we understand their political implications. I became completely blocked when asked during a conference presentation, which illustrated the coping strategies of women to withstand desultory welfare provision, if I wasn't exposing the women to surveillance by agencies of state control such as the DHSS (The Department of Health and Social Security, as it was then known). Such exposition could, it was argued, enable more effective exploitation of these women. This stopped me from writing for a long time and made me less naive and far more careful about the sort of information I released.

Conclusions

To focus on the process of producing I chose to emphasise theorising, ethics and representation. I could have chosen other features. I could have stressed the 'in the field' problems more. In fact the whole process of ethnography is riddled with methodological and ethical issues at every point, with few straightforward prescriptions for how to deal with them. Sensitivity to, and responsibility for, power relations, representation, dissemination are, I would argue, far more important than issues of which method to use. And attention to the processes by which we produce our research and theories is far more important than the concern with 'getting it right'. To do feminist ethnography you have to be prepared to live in conditions of emotional, political, economic and theoretical insecurity.

Yet I wouldn't swap my research experience for anything. It was brilliant, it made me engage in issues, taught me to think in different ways, stopped me being reliant on badly thought through theories and forced me to engage in political practicalities. It stopped me remaining in an ivory tower and it made me wary of seductive pretentious theory. I made excellent friends and had some great times. It was a rich and rewarding, if also traumatic and painful, experience.

Notes

1 It was important to keep details of these biographical responses, because they changed often in the process of the research. This led me to analyse the importance of memory and how we construct narratives of our own lives (see Stacey, 1994).

2 Thanks are always due to Tony Kidd, Erica Stratta, Kate Berry, Alan How and Catherine Neal at Worcester College of Higher Education who covered my work to make this possible.

3 See Atkinson (1990); Bell, Caplan and Karim (1993); Burawoy *et al.* (1991); Clifford (1983, 1986); Clough (1992); Marcus (1992); Reissman (1987); Reissman-Kohler (1993); Stacey (1988); Warren (1988); Wolf (1990).

4 Chris Griffin was struggling with the problems of doing feminist ethnography at the Centre for Cultural Studies, Birmingham University in 1980. The reference here is drawn from a working group paper presented in June 1980. I am greatly indebted to Chris for her insights and support. Her ethnography was written up as *Typical Girls* (1985).

5 I was so normalised that it wasn't until later that I became sensitised to issues of 'race' and heterosexuality.

6 Angela Davis's autobiography was re-published by The Women's Press, London, in 1990.

7 See Harstock (1983); Smith (1988); Hill Collins (1990); Harding (1991) and Bar-On (1993) for debates about standpoint theory in feminist research.

8 Mac an Ghaill's (1994) ethnography does exactly the opposite. The clear understanding and exposition of power offered by young, gay, Asian males in his study exposes the lack of understandings of some theorists of sexual politics.

9 Leibes and Katz (1986) found audiences from very different ethnic backgrounds, countries and regions were able to negotiate the meaning of 'Dallas' by confronting it with their own traditions and experience.

Bibliography

Atkinson, P. (1990), *The Ethnography Imagination: Textual Constructions of Reality*, London, Routledge.

Atkinson, P. (1992), *Understanding Ethnographic Texts*, London, Sage.

Althusser, L. (1971), *Lenin and Philosophy and Other Essays*, London, New Left Books.

Barker, M. and A. Beezer (1992), Introduction in *Reading Into Cultural Studies*, London, Routledge.

Bar On, B.-A. (1993), Marginality and Epistemic Privilege, in L. Alcoff and E. Potter (eds), *Feminist Epistemologies*, London, Routledge.

Bell, D., C. Caplan and W. J. Karim (1993), *Gendered Field: Women, Men & Ethnography*, London, Routledge.

Berger, J. and T. Luckmann (1971), *The Social Construction of Reality*, Harmondsworth, Penguin.

Burawoy, M. *et al.* (1991), *Ethnography Unbound: Power & Resistance in the Modern Metropolis*, Oxford, University of California Press.

Clifford, J. (1983), On Ethnographic Authority, *Representations*, 1:2, 118–46.

Clifford, J. (1986), Introduction: Partial Truths, in J. Clifford and G. Marcus (eds), *Writing Culture: the Poetics and Politics of Ethnography*, Berkeley, University of California Press.

Clough, P. (1992), *The End(s) of Ethnography: From Social Realism to Social Criticism*, London, Sage.

Collins, H. M. (1983), The Meaning of Lies: Accounts of Action and Participatory Research, in G. Nigel Gilbert and P. Abel (eds), *Accounts and Action*, Aldershot, Gower.

Glaser, B. and A. Strauss (1967), *The Discovery of Grounded Theory*, Aldine, Chicago.

Glaser, B. and A. Strauss (1971), Discovery of Substantive Theory, in W. Filstead (ed.), *Qualitative Methodology*, Markham, Chicago.

Gramsci, A. (1971), *Selections from the Prison Notebooks of Antonio Gramsci*, ed. Q. Hoare and G. Nowell-Smith, London, Lawrence and Wishart.

Grant, J. (1993), *Fundamental Feminism: Contesting the Core Concepts of Feminist Theory*, London, Routledge.

Griffin, C. (1985), *Typical Girls*, London, Routledge.

Hammersley, M. and P. Atkinson (1983), *Ethnography: Principles and Practice*, London, Tavistock.

Harding, S. (1991), *Whose Science, Whose Knowledge? Thinking from Women's Lives*, Milton Keynes, Open University Press.

Harstock, N. (1983), The Feminist Standpoint: Developing the Ground for a Specifically Feminist Historical Materialism, in S. Harding and M. B. Hintikka (eds), *Discovering Reality: Feminist Perspectives on Epistemology, Metaphysics, Methodology and Philosophy of Science*, Dordrecht, Reidel.

Hartmann, H. (1981), *The Unhappy Marriage of Marxism and Feminism: A Debate on Class and Patriarchy*, ed. L. Sergeant, London, Pluto.

Hill Collins, P. (1990), *Black Feminist Thought*, London, Routledge.

Kelly, L., S. Burton and L. Regan (1994), Researching Women's Lives or Studying Women's Oppression? Reflections on What Constitutes Feminist Research, in M. Maynard and J. Purvis (eds), *Researching Women's Lives from a Feminist Perspective*, London, Taylor and Francis.

Kirkwood, C. (1993), Investing Ourselves: Use of Researcher Personal Response in Feminist Methodology, in J. De Groot and M. Maynard (eds), *Perspectives on Women's Studies for the 1990s: Doing Things Differently?*, London, Macmillan.

Kuhn, A. and A.-M. Wolpe (1978), *Feminism and Materialism: Women and Modes of Production*, London, Routledge and Kegan Paul.

Leibes, T. and E. Katz (1986), Patterns of Involvement in Television Fiction: A Comparative Analysis, *European Journal of Communication*, 1:2, 151–71.

Lury, C. (1991), Reading the Self: Autobiography, Gender and the Institution of the Literary, in S. Franklin *et al.* (eds), *Off-Centre: Feminism and Cultural Studies*, London, Hutchinson.

Mac an Ghaill, M. (1994), *The Making of Men: Masculinities, Sexualities and Schooling*, Buckingham, Open University Press.

Marcus, G. E. (1992), Past, Present and Emergent Identities: Requirements for Ethnographies of Late Twentieth-Century Modernity World-Wide, in S. Lash and J. Friedman (eds), *Modernity and Identity*, Oxford, Blackwell.

McRobbie, A. (1991), *Feminism and Youth Culture*, London, Macmillan.

Morris, M. (1988), Introduction: Feminism, Reading, Postmodernism, in M. Morris (ed.), *The Pirate's Fiancee: Feminism, Reading, Postmodernism*, London, Verso.

Pearce, L. (1994), *Reading Dialogics*, London, Edward Arnold.

Probyn, E. (1993), *Sexing the Self: Gendered Positions in Cultural Studies*, London, Routledge.

Reinharz, S. (1992), *Feminist Methods in Social Research*, Oxford, Oxford University Press.

Reissman, C. (1987), When Gender is Not Enough: Women Interviewing Women, *Gender and Society*, 1, 172–207.

Reissman-Kohler, C. (1993), *Narrative Analysis*, London, Sage.

Riviere, J. (1929/1986), Womanliness as a Masquerade, in V. Burgin *et al.* (eds), *Formations of Fantasy*, London, Methuen.

Roberts, H. (ed.) (1981), *Doing Feminist Research*, London, Routledge and Kegan Paul.

Scott, J. W. (1992), Experience, in J. Butler and J. W. Scott (eds), *Feminists Theorise the Political*, London, Routledge.

Skeggs, B. (1989), Gender Reproduction and Further Education: Domestic Apprenticeships, *British Journal of Sociology of Education*, 10:4, 131–51.

Skeggs, B. (1990), Gender Reproduction in Education and its Alternatives, in D. Gleeson (ed.) (1990), *Training and its Alternatives*, London, Routledge.

Skeggs, B. (1991a), Challenging Masculinity and Using Sexuality, *British Journal of Sociology of Education*, 12:2, 127–39.

Skeggs, B. (1991b), Postmodernism: What is all the Fuss About?, *British Journal of Sociology of Education*, 12:2, 255–79.

Skeggs, B. (1992), Paul Willis 'Learning to Labour', in M. Barker and A. Beezer (eds), *Reading into Cultural Studies*, London, Routledge.

Skeggs, B. (1994), Situating the Production of Feminist Ethnography, in M. Maynard and J. Purvis (eds), *Researching Women's Lives from a Feminist Perspective*, London, Taylor and Francis.

Smith, D. (1988), *The Everyday World as Problematic: A Feminist Sociology*, Milton Keynes, Open University Press.

Spender, D. (ed. (1981), *Men's Studies Modified*, London, Pergamon Press.

Stacey, J. (1988), Can there be a Feminist Ethnography, *Women's Studies International Forum*, 11:1, 21–7.

Stacey, J. (1994), *Star Gazing: Hollywood Cinema and Female Spectatorship*, London, Routledge.

Stanley, L. (1990), Feminist Praxis and the Academic Mode of Production: an Editorial Introduction, in L. Stanley (ed.), *Feminist Praxis: Research, Theory and Epistemology in Feminist Sociology*, London, Routledge.

Steier, F. (ed.) (1991), *Research and Reflexivity*, London, Sage.

Tyler, S. A. (1987), *The Unspeakable: Discourse, Dialogue and Rhetoric in the Postmodern World*, Madison, University of Wisconsin Press.

Warren, C. A. B. (1988), *Gender Issues in Field Research*, London, Sage.

Willis, P. (1977), *Learning to Labour: Why Working-Class Kids get Working Class Jobs*, London, Saxon House.

Wolf, M. (1990), *A Thrice Told Tale*, Stanford, Stanford University Press.

11

The personal, the professional and the partner(ship): the husband/wife collaboration of Charles and Ray Eames

PAT KIRKHAM

This essay considers issues related to my book, *Charles and Ray Eames: Designers of the Century* (1995) which I began researching in 1983. They married in 1941, he an architect/designer and she an abstract artist, just as *he* was establishing an international reputation. For the next thirty-seven years they jointly ran the most exciting design office of the mid-twentieth century, designing 'classics' of modernist machine mass-produced furniture, buildings, exhibitions, multi-media presentations and over eighty short films. I set out to contextualise and analyse all the areas of their work and to re-evaluate the contribution of Ray. Charles is regarded as one of, if not *the*, most influential designer of this century but she is generally regarded as a less than equal partner and blamed for their 'pretty' deviations from spartan modernism. Despite his higher public profile and acclaim, however, the work was the product of their *joint* endeavours – and therein lay the kernel of my feminist project. The first section of this essay situates the project within my own trajectory through and across academic disciplines and feminism and is more autobiographical. The second addresses some of the problems encountered during researching and writing the book.

I still fear accusations of self-indulgence when centrally positioning myself in academic writing. Yet, despite my training in 'scientific method' and historical materialism, I have always felt comfortable with the under-rated and under-explored areas of the autobiographical, the self-reflexive and the affective. The shift in my own work over the last decade towards more directly dealing with the autobiographical is part of a more general turn by feminist academics, one which picks up on the early women's movement's emphasis on understanding one's subject positions.

At that time I restricted my expositions on such matters to activities within the women's movement; my academic research did not fit easily into such considerations and one of the pleasures of more 'personal' work for me today is the *direct* engagement missing in earlier years when I was struggling to find my way in terms of both subject matter and methodologies. However, such work also relates to certain modes of address of the working-class culture in which I grew up, including what I would now label 'women's culture'. My debts, in this, and in the choice of certain subject matters, are due as much to that collective culture and to my parents, particularly my perceptive, articulate and feminist mother,[1] as to my academic and Marxist mentors.

Situating the project

Hidden from history

My re-evaluation of Ray Eames is rooted in the feminist project of rescuing women formerly marginalised and 'hidden from history', to which Sheila Rowbotham's writings, particularly *Hidden From History* (1973) were seminal. Linda Nochlin's (1971) posing of the question of why were there no 'great' women artists forced me to think in similar terms about designers. Nochlin emphasised the need to look at institutional, intellectual and educational practices in order to understand the ways in which women's art was and is produced, as did Rozsika Parker and Griselda Pollock's (1981) *Old Mistresses: Women, Art and Ideology*. Both influenced the ways in which I thought about the different experiences, education and training of Charles and Ray Eames, particularly in the areas of mathematics, science, technology and practical skills. One of the first 'academic' feminist articles to focus on designed objects and their production, reception and criticism was Patricia Mainardi's (1973) study of quilting in the USA. Her insistence on the importance of a highly marginalised domestic craft (needlework) to women's cultural heritage and her consideration of issues of anonymity, authorship, 'high' and 'low' culture and the prejudices of modernism and gallery culture in relation to women, decoration, the crafts and the 'decorative arts' were to inform my study of the Eameses.

My background and interests

It seemed a simple enough task to outline how my research interests were shaped, from undergraduate studies to the new academic discipline of design history and to note my commitment to popular history, cultural studies and feminism as well as my more recent work in film studies and dress history. But life and history are complex and I am conscious that how I came to be researching, teaching and writing what and how I do now involves odd and accidental conjunctures as much as any coherent academic plan. Indeed, my lack of the latter is a factor in the combination of interests and bodies of knowledge which brought me to the Eameses. I make the points about not quite knowing what I was doing and the importance of chance and unlikely conjunctures to cut against certain conventions of scholarly presentation and the tendency of historians, myself included, when tracing influences to produce neat accounts brimming over with coherence, cause and effect.

I regard myself as a historian with wide interests. My undergraduate studies (1963–66) were in history, with some sociology and politics. I became interested in art and design through a sculptor boyfriend but did not even bother to attend the 'sales' talk for the only undergraduate history course taught in Britain to deal with it. I had decided to specialise in American history (an enthusiasm which later steered me towards American design and the Eameses). I changed track, I'm afraid to say, only when my then current boyfriend, who had attended the talk, encouraged me to enrol on 'Patrons, architects and craftsmen, 1660–1840', the title of which appealed to my crude but rapidly developing interest in historical materialism and Marxist interpretations of 'art'. I knew next to nothing about furniture, which was eventually to bring me to the Eameses, when I began postgraduate research (1966–69). I had vaguely thought of further exploring notions of patronage but my supervisor steered me to furniture history[2] and I ended up with a ludicrously broad study of furniture making in London *c.* 1700–1870.

I identified with the 'History Workshop' approach to 'people's history'[3] but, with the exception of Raphael Samuel, my topic remained as marginal to 'History Workshop' enthusiasts as it did to 'mainstream' history. I found marginalisation within the radical fringe of which I became part more difficult than within the academy (to which I, as a female working-class student, did not feel particularly close), but both spelled academic isolation.

Retrospectively, I can see that my research interest in the sexual division of labour was quite radical for the time and my research on workshop organisation and the division of labour within business, craft and design partnerships not only original but pertinent to my later Eames study. At the time, I mainly felt frustrated. My interests were too cultural and artistic for labour historians and too sociological, radical and feminist for orthodox historians like my supervisor; they were too social, economic and design oriented for art historians and regarded as esoteric in the extreme by the 'decorative arts' specialists who wrote about furniture.

To make matters worse, I was studying objects with which I then had little aesthetic engagement. I could admire but was not excited by the products of the trade I was studying. I sat on 'Pop Art' yellow plastic coated paper chairs as I wrote about marquetry furniture made for the Duke of Bedford or George IV. Part of me wanted to be learning and writing about those yellow chairs but it was not until I began teaching design students from 1970 that I began to do so. It was then that I discovered Eames' chairs.

I wished I was researching 'the woman question' or something related to my background (my mother was a factory worker, my father a miner), my International Socialist politics or something that engaged me aesthetically. Teaching design history, its development as an academic subject and feminism saved the day. From the early 1970s my academic work found a new and more welcoming home and flourished in a congenial atmosphere of common enthusiasms. Drawing on emphases on the commonplace, the popular, gender and the contemporary in historical and cultural studies, design history legitimated, and provided space for me to bring together, my varied interests.[4] The Eames project, for example, brought together feminist issues, fine art, design, architecture, historical contextualisation, modernism and post-modernism as well as film and media and propelled me into new areas of study such as exhibitions, animation, multimedia presentations, the popularisation of science and technology in the post-war years and Indian history and design policies.

Issues in methodology

The main issues to exercise me when researching the partnership of Charles and Ray Eames related to historiography (particularly pro-male and pro-modernist biases within historical and critical

writings), the modernist/post-modernist debates, the marginalisation and trivialisation of 'women's work', the assessment of
decorative projects within a body of work considered well within
the canons of minimalist modernism and the evaluation of the
interplay of the personal with the professional. I drew on many
ideas from feminist scholarship including those mentioned in the
preceding section, gender stereotyping, patriarchy, sexism, male
'genius', autonomy, woman as victim or active agent, mutual
support and respect, women's marginalisation within certain
professional spheres as well as within critical and historical
writing and a number of binary oppositions supposedly related
to male/female, some of which are discussed below.

Bias and marginalisation

I examined contemporary commentaries on the Eameses in order
to establish which aspects of their work were privileged and
which marginalised and to ascertain if this related either to a
male/female bias or a pro-modernist/anti-decoration one. I also
studied their lives and work *before* they worked together (including Charles's previous professional partnerships – all with
men, one of whom, like Ray, was a sculptor) in order to ascertain
what each brought and gained from the partnership. This established Ray's interests and capabilities independent from those
of Charles and helped me better to assess her initial contribution
to the partnership. I was taken aback by the discrepancy between
the myth of Charles the purist functionalist and Ray the supplier
of artistic 'touches' and the findings of my research which
revealed Ray as part of the New York avant-garde in the 1930s
and Charles designing some interesting but fairly traditional
buildings. In order to estimate the aesthetic input of Ray in the
early years I considered each project in relation to previous work
done by both her and Charles, finally attributing much of the
originality of form of one of their famous 1946 moulded plywood
chairs to her. I had not set out to 'turn the tables' (or even to
establish 50–50 input into projects), but my findings clearly
counteracted claims about her marginality.

Modernism, post-modernism, 'functioning decoration' and the trivial

No one had problems with giving Ray credit for the decorative
side of their work – largely because it was considered of little
significance. The problem for me was classifying and analysing it.

Trying to understand those aspects of their work which favoured an additive, fragmented, excessive and decorative aesthetic of inter- and intra-cultural reference, particularly their 'functioning decoration' (the decorative arrangements of objects which first featured in their own home), eventually led me to a re-evaluation of what constituted modernism in the post-war years. This was both prompted and informed by the debates of the 1980s and 1990s about 'post-modernism', modernism and the relationship between them.[5] The new debates made me return to a special issue of *Architectural Design* (1966) dedicated to the Eameses, most of which I had previously found rather esoteric. Written by people associated with The Independent Group,[6] they addressed (albeit sometimes tangentially) issues of addition, fragmentation, juxtaposition and popular and cross-cultural imagery. In other words, it took the debates of the 1980s and 1990s for me to re-examine and better understand discussions of twenty years earlier.

My research into their interior design had alerted me to the fact that Robert Venturi, the high priest of post-modernism, had also praised it at about the same time for qualities antithetical to modernism.[7] His likening of the Eameses' 'functioning decoration' to Victorian 'clutter' was too near the knuckle for most Eames admirers; such things were deemed the antithesis of modernism and too trivial for consideration. My interest in things too trivial for academic consideration relates to a some-times perverse anti-high culturalism, pleasure in and love of the popular and the 'ordinary' (including the culture of my childhood, particularly china cabinets) and a fascination with how people (mostly women) decorate their homes. Cultural studies and design history gave respectability and focus to my closeted interests in the decorative, but ornaments and knick-knacks remain marginalised within academia, including Women's Studies. It seemed important therefore to de-trivialise this aspect of material culture as part of a broader feminist agenda by treating it as seriously as the other design historical material.

I made a link between Melissa Meyer and Miriam Schapiro's (1978) idea of 'femmage', with its parallels between modernist art practices (collage) and 'traditional' women's decorative work and Ray's collage-ist art which led me to analyse her and Charles's 'functioning decoration' as three-dimensional 'collages' of objects. Thinking of it as both collages (fine art) and groupings of ornaments made me realise just how far the modernist myth was tied up with avant-gardism and a hostility towards the decorative. Ray's two-dimensional 'fine art' collages were hailed as modernist abstract art, whereas those she made with small objects for decorative purposes in the home were not. Thinking of 'functioning decoration' as groupings of *domestic* objects led me to use the idea of living space as a 'memory palace' and the objects therein as examples of cultural capital and display which I found discussed in an article about the Victorian parlour (Grier, 1992). A chance meeting with Jennifer González at the University of California, Santa Cruz, introduced me to her then unpublished work[8] which made reference to both memory and 'femmage' and led me to consider parallels with the domestic shrines made by Mexican women, which invoke memories through the use of found and personal objects, and the assemblages of the Eameses.

Living history

When I first lectured on the Eameses in the late 1970s, I remarked, with methodological naiveté, that it should be relatively straightforward to investigate their collaboration because, even though Charles had just died, Ray was still alive as were many of their employees. As it turned out, my meetings with Ray were less productive than I had hoped in terms of new information or insights into the collaboration, although those I conducted with others were amongst the most informative and fascinating I have ever done. I should point out that not all interviews were conducted face to face. This was new for me. Without thinking about it, I had accepted that information obtained over the telephone was somehow less 'authentic'. However, because of costs and time involved in travelling to and within the USA (I made four visits) as well as the demands of time upon some of the interviewees, several were conducted by telephone. They were a revelation to me in terms of methodology; they were as productive as the face to face ones, partly because the United States has a well-established 'telephone culture' and people are generally easy and relaxed about using telephones. I realised that some people are more open about sensitive issues over the telephone than face to face, or more openly critical, and the fact that 'distance' between the two speakers can facilitate as well as detract from openness should not be forgotten when proclaiming the virtues of 'live' interviews.

This project involved interviewing certain people with higher public profiles than my own and, in particular cases, I was conscious of feeling that it was a privilege to be so doing. I felt a little diffident about 'chasing up' people like Paul Schrader and Billy Wilder, let alone interviewing them, but need not have worried because, so great was the respect for Charles and Ray, that people were glad to make time for anyone with a serious interest in them. Once the interviews began I realised that I had something to offer above and beyond space to pay tribute to two remarkable talents. The longer the exchanges, the more the balance of relations evened out. What I had was ten years of studying all aspects of the Eameses' work, some of which were not known to those whom I was interviewing. I sent draft chapters to the interviewees if requested and received a comment from Deborah Sussman, a close friend of the Eameses and something of a surrogate daughter, to the effect that she had learned a tremendous amount from reading my manuscript, even about the years in which she had worked in the firm. This gave me much more confidence in approaching other people.

The balance of relations in interviews, as well as their general tenor, was also affected by the extent to which particular individuals had thought through some of the issues. I was impressed by the way that many of the women whom I spoke to about Charles and Ray had already analysed their relationship and collaboration from a feminist viewpoint. It was not just a case of them being passively interviewed; they had their own agenda and very definite opinions. Some spoke of Ray as victim not only of Charles's charisma, self-focus and desire to control but also of his love affairs. I took their points of view into consideration but it seemed that this view of woman as victim was prevalent in the 1970s when this subject most engaged them. Ray was dead by the time I was discussing it but I am sure I would not have dared to ask her about Charles's affairs – no one did. When I met Ray I was not aware of the assertions of certain design historians to the effect that she could not have been central to the partnership because Charles had affairs with other women. The *non sequitur* irritated me and I decided I needed to address the topic. This was helped by the fact that once Ray was dead people talked more openly about the relationship between the Eameses' personal and professional lives. I also became more open to considerations of Ray as agent and/or victim within a triangular relationship when, in 1989 and for the first time, I found myself in one. I believe it is possible to write sensitively about many things without having experienced them but in this

Ray Eames, 1983: photograph taken by Pat Kirkham the first time she interviewed Ray Eames.

Pat Kirkham discussing Charles and Ray Eames with Billy Wilder. (Photo: Andy Hoogenboom)

case my preconceptions were such that I had apprehended few of the nuances between the positions of victim and agent that I experienced. I was aware when writing that the less I thought of myself as victim the less easy it was to assume Ray was one.

Closeness and critical compromise

Ray's tenacious attachment to a sanitised view of Charles and a refusal to consider important his non-modernist work before 1938 proved a problem for me and all other Eames commentators. I did not know when I formulated my project that the only other serious scholar writing on the Eameses, apart from Marilyn and John Neuhart (co-editor with Ray of a *catalogue raissonné* of the work of the Eames Office), had given up trying to work through her and was waiting for the office archive to be transferred to the Library of Congress.[9] Ray simply could not let the catalogue go; it was her link with Charles as well as a tribute to him (and herself).

I had been warned that she could be a prima donna and I now know from interviews with employees that, at times, she could be difficult to work for and with. But I was not an employee and Ray continued the tradition she and Charles had established of generosity towards interested visitors. In terms of power relations she was impressed that I was lecturing at the Getty Museum, but we 'hit it off' for other reasons. I arrived bearing a bunch of large white daisies and luck had it that she had announced only minutes before that what the office needed was a bowl of daisies. She kept joking that I must be psychic and a friend of hers later told me that had I taken chrysanthemums I would never have reached first base. Closer moments came when she wanted to know about my arthritis treatment (she suspected she had it). This is an example of reciprocity; she also wanted me to obtain a particular type of ribbon for her. Our closest moments came when I told her that the two feminist academics with whom I was staying had remarked on Charles's 'film star' good looks. I still remember acknowledging disavowal as they said it; it had not seemed appropriate to a serious study of extremely serious designers. Yet it was a factor and I was wrong to try and ignore it. It cropped up frequently as people tried to account for Charles's charisma; Schrader, for example, described him as one of the most dynamic and sexually attractive people he had ever met. Had I deliberately thought of methods to shift the interview to more intimate matters, I could not have done better. The mention of Charles's looks led to an 'off the record' account of how wonderful he was, how supportive he had been of her talents and how much she missed him. She asked about my family and suddenly it was not an interview but a conversation between two women about loved ones, memories, intimacy and loss. It was not 'usable' to publish but it gave me valuable insights into her relationship with Charles – or at least her version of it.

It shifted our relationship, but I cannot say that thereafter she spoke very differently about the collaboration. She did not find such discussions easy and it was difficult to get beyond general-isations about all the work being a joint effort. She stressed the importance of structure to her as well as to Charles, as he had in public and private statements, but I was not hearing anything new. There I was with Ray intensely engaged with me, but reiterating what she and Charles (mainly Charles) had said many times before. I wanted more details to flesh out her particular contributions. Ray was correct to repeat that it was joint work and, as the husband/wife design team of Alison and Peter Smithson emphasised when I interviewed them, 'no-one ever nit-picks over the issues of who did what or who thought of what' (see below).[10] But my problem was that joint male/female authorship is open to claims that all the important ideas and designs flow from the man, as Alison Smithson bitterly con-firmed. Anger at the ill-founded assumptions of the secondary importance of Ray and the power of the combination of pro-modernist and sexist biases gave me a new momentum and I decided to take a different tack by talking about specific projects. By that method I obtained, in passing, some very useful details as to who thought of and did what.

I cannot say how my relationship with her would have developed. Had I had more time to devote to the project and/or been on the spot in Los Angeles, I could have obtained more information and insights. I could have been more pushy from the other side of the Atlantic but that is not my style – although I am more confident now. As it was, I was busy with other projects, my job and three children. Although we kept in touch and I met her once again before she died, my first response to her death was regret that I had only just finished the first draft of the book and she had not been able to check it. I felt sad at the loss of a remarkable person (who had made me feel 'special'), touched by her dedication to Charles and impressed by her sense of style to the last – she died exactly a decade after him, to the very day.

That coincidence, that serendipity, moved me; my research (including readings of photographs of them as a couple, some of which included them wearing matching or complementary clothing – a very new and immensely rewarding method of working for me) had built up a picture of an intense closeness between them. It began to weigh on me, its affect acting as a new piece of evidence and I found myself in a strange methodological dilemma. When I confessed to colleagues that I was resisting reading it as confirmation of that closeness, one told me to get a grip on myself, the other simply asked 'why resist?'.

I am acutely aware of the subtle binds of the bonds forged with people whom one admires and comes to know through research. Critical comment can sometimes be seen as betraying kindnesses, generosity and hospitality and part of me felt relieved that I would never have to risk upsetting Ray. There is no doubt that had she been alive when the catalogue the Neuharts edited with her was finally published, the introduction would not have included 'Charles was one of the most *self*-centered persons we have known'.[11] But the problem did not stop with Ray. I am also aware of not wanting to upset one of Charles's lovers who has been helpful to me. I respect her and her work. Some of what she told me was in confidence, but I have wondered if that gave me something to hide behind, if it enabled me to not debate in print a point she made about Charles's collaboration with Ray.

Comparative collaborations

In order to investigate the Eames collaboration I searched out other husband and wife collaborations and read and/or listened to Charles's statements about Ray. Once I realised that Charles was constantly claiming Ray to be as crucial to the partnership as he and as talented as he, I had to reassess my notions of how and why she (and other women) are marginalised, and I found a somewhat similar situation with the Margaret Macdonald–Charles Rennie Mackintosh collaboration.[12] I found no detailed studies of husband/wife architectural partnerships but Lynne Walker's (1984) book on women architects proved useful as did the interview with the Smithsons. It seemed that it was probably no coincidence that another woman in a similar collaborative arrangement was amongst the first, if not *the* first, to fully appreciate Ray's centrality to the joint work. Alison Smithson's testimony, which referred to her own experience and to her options of the Eameses who she knew, confirmed what Lynne

Eames House, Pacific Palisades, Los Angeles, California; designed by
Charles and Ray Eames. (Photo: Pat Kirkham)

Walker and I already thought rather than suggesting new approaches. But the fact that it came from a female professional designer younger than, but contemporary with, Ray, meant that it added the weight of direct and contemporary experience to our positions and enhanced their academic validity. It gave me confidence to push an approach which I felt important – and to push it in the face of those, mainly male, contemporaries of the Eameses who reiterated the orthodoxy that everything flowed from Charles – despite his own constant refutations. The confirmation of my findings of the Eameses by the Macdonald–Mackintosh and Smithsons' case studies enabled me to focus more clearly on Ray as a person *overshadowed* rather than *unacknowledged* by Charles. That led me to the question of Charles as an overshadowing person and also to him as 'genius'.

The talented, the exceptional and the genius

Although I am in favour of contextualisation and de-emphasising the roles of 'great men', in design history it has resulted in a tendency to so contextualise that the designer(s) is forgotten and/or to overemphasise the role of employees. I am not against de-mythologising Charles Eames but it seemed necessary to address assertions that key products, particularly furniture, sprang not from him, or indeed from him *and* Ray, but from certain key workers. One method I used was to examine individual commissions and also whole areas of work such as furniture in order to assess developments before and after those particular persons worked in the firm. I also considered the projects in areas where those people were not concerned and used the consistent high quality across *all* the areas over nearly forty years, as well as the Eameses' propensity to keep tight control over projects while expecting innovative and quality work from employees, to argue the centrality of the Eameses to the output of their office. Questions to former employees about working practices, particularly about who had the original design ideas, final say over what was or was not approved and made and about the contributions of Charles and Ray as well as the testimony of others about their talents, were also central to that part of the study. At the end of the day, whilst giving some very talented workers their dues, the exercise revealed to me that, if anything, I was in danger of underplaying the immense creativity of Ray and Charles' partnership. I had never dealt with such dazzling talents before and my fear of eulogising was leading me to underplay their achievements.

Moulded plywood and metal DCM chairs; designed by Charles and Ray Eames and the Eames Office, 1946. (Photo: Herman Miller)

Similarly with my re-evaluation of Ray, although I admired her fine art and graphics, my awareness that much of what I was arguing about her contribution cut against the grain, together with my own lack of confidence in pronouncing about artistic (as opposed to design) matters, acted as a brake on expressing that admiration. It was only when a sculptor colleague waxed lyrical about Ray's sculptures that I stopped worrying, only to wonder if I had done her the justice she deserves. My reticence was, again, rooted in a fear of being seen to be arguing a case from an aesthetic, and apparently less 'objective', position. Methodologically that reticence was a luxury I should not have afforded myself.

My first method of dealing with recurrent references to Charles as a genius was to ignore it because genius was something of a dirty word in the circles within which I moved. I had difficulty uttering the word, let alone deciding how to deal with it methodologically. In the 1960s I dismissed the concept as elitist: used in studies which wrenched individuals out of their social context. In the 1970s feminist scholarship proclaimed it, together with 'great art', as a male-defined concept and it seemed best ignored.

Christine Battersby's (1989) explorations of the intertwinings of gender and genius has now re-placed the concept on the feminist agenda and encouraged me to reassess my material and explore the hypothesis that the concept of the (male) genius worked to the detriment of women. In the Eames case, however, other factors, such as Ray's extreme reluctance to take part in the public face of the partnership, needed to be borne in mind. It also seemed necessary to differentiate between the prioritising of the male within a partnership and the prioritising of a (male) genius. Assumptions about genius are accompanied by assumptions that everyone working with that person was/is less than them, but the same applies to the male partner within design partnerships. What, then, was I to do with people labelling Charles as genius? Did I define genius and try to prove Ray one? Did I speculate on the effects of being the partner of someone regarded as a genius by certain eminent peers? I decided on the latter, but also to go back to what was actually said about Charles.

Comparisons with Leonardo da Vinci forced me to address more directly that here was an exceptional man. In studies such as mine it is always easier to state that one will not highlight the contributions of the woman at the expense of the man than it is to carry it out. The exercise helped me resist any temptation to avoid giving Charles his full credit. It also helped differentiate between the particular contributions of Charles and Ray. But finally, because the term was generally used to describe Charles as an exceptional man, rather than someone who conformed to 'classic' expressions of the state of being a genius, I decided to use the fact that Charles was considered exceptional as a framework within which to examine how Ray was overshadowed.

Binary oppositions

I drew on the structuralist tradition of binaries and used a series of oppositions to locate some of the likely differences between Charles and Ray within the collaboration. Associating them with, at times, oversimplistic and essentialist polarities, I was wary of using them, yet the propositions they suggested fascinated me. Those related to design which proved most useful in relation to female/male included: traditionalism/modernism, existing technologies/new technologies, hand/machine, crafts/industrial design, one-off/mass production, decoration/functionalism, innovation/custom and practice and whimsy or fantasy/reason while others more relevant to the couple's collaboration included public/private, professional/amateur and male genius/female talent. I used them as starting-points rather than frameworks for proving oppositions; indeed, they often threw up unexpected continuums or contradictions. For example, the modernist love affair with functionalism and disapproval for decoration has general and important links with the latter being more associated with women and the former with machines and the male world. However, both Charles and Ray were avowed functionalists and, although she was the more creative decorator, he was by no means opposed to decoration. Furthermore, any understanding of Ray's decoration involves not only traditional 'women's' work but also modernist fine art practices.

Similarly, the oppositions of male/female, public/private, around which so much feminist analysis has centred in the last twenty years needs qualification in the Eames case. She did not remain at home while he was in the office. In terms of dominant codes of masculinity and femininity, neither Charles nor Ray made any radical breaks, but her choice (for whatever reason) to work full-time and not have children was not the typical one for a middle-class woman in the USA in the years after the Second World War. She relinquished any (private/domestic) autonomy she might have had as a housewife for the shared (public/non-domestic) life of a thriving design firm with her creative and sexual partner. But, when I investigated the activities within the latter space, it was apparent that, to the extent the Eames Office became their 'second home' (they employed a cook and worked there at least twelve hours a day, often seven days a week), they shared a space that was part domestic, part work; part private, part public. Another example of how I used an opposition to think around an issue is the professional/amateur divide. This neglected aspect of design history relates to gender, paid work, anonymity, quality, respect and status. In the case of the Eameses, however, both Charles and Ray were professionals and, at first, there seemed little else to say. It was not until I was considering the implications of Ray playing a greater part in 'functioning decoration' than Charles that it occurred to me that this work was more domestic in nature than their other work, having evolved in relation to their own home. The fact that 'functioning decoration' was not originally part of a paid commission, i.e. 'amateur', confirmed the marginalisation of an activity already denigrated because it was thought to demand no special training, was traditionally women's work and also decorative (even though the Eameses added the (male?) term 'functioning' to decoration to make it more acceptable within orthodox modernism). Once again, however, Charles was not absent from this aspect of the work and crude male/female oppositions needed qualification.

Conclusion

I am painfully aware that my Eames study, together with Janice Helland's[13] work on Mackintosh and Macdonald, are, as yet, the only substantial pieces on design collaborations between partners – and two is not a satisfactory sample. More empirical research, informed but not restricted by theory, is needed to tease out particular and historical specificities in order to better analyse the different ways in which women's collaborations with creative and/or famous partners are experienced and have been perceived. The recent feminist anthology of case studies of visual artist couples (Chadwick and de Courtivron, 1993) confirms my own findings; the collaborations were more rich, complex, mutually respectful and supportive than any of the authors or editors initially suspected.

In terms of the wider project of the feminist production of knowledge, it seems that, although I have veered between the personal and the 'academic', I may still have produced an overly neat account of both my development and the ways in which I approached researching the Eameses. Looking back over the route from china cabinets in a pit village to a major study of two designers of world stature, one of whom deserves greater recognition than she has been given, I see a great deal of both coherence and chance in the interlockings of my varied interests. That one of my current projects is the film title sequences designed by Elaine and Saul Bass, another United States husband/wife collaboration, indicates a logical progression from the Eames project.[14] But other projects include women's dress in the Second World War, gendered objects, an exploration of reception and female spectatorship in cinema through a study of my readings of a silent movie star who reminds me of my brother, and affectivity in design and film. To understand these as either logical progressions from earlier work or coincidental conglomerations of my varied interests, or both, requires another, possibly different, story.

Notes

1 See Kirkham, P. (1981), Salt of the Earth/Remembering My Mother, *Spare Rib*, 102, 26–7.

2 The Furniture History Society was founded in 1963.

3 *History Workshop Journal* was first published in 1976.

4 The Design History Society was founded in 1977.

5 Jameson, F. (1984), Postmodernism, or the Cultural Logic of Late Capitalism, *New Left Review*, 146, and Harvey, D. (1989), *The Condition of Post-modernity*, Oxford, Blackwells.

6 Robbins, D. (ed.) (1990), *The Independent Group: Postwar Britain and the Aesthetics of Plenty*, Cambridge, Mass., MIT Press.

7 McCoy, E. (1973), An Affection for Objects, *Progressive Architecture*, 67, 64–7.

8 González, J. (1993), Rhetoric of the Object: Material Memory and the Artwork of Amelia Mesa-Bains, *Visual Anthropology Review*, 9:1, 82–92, and Autotopographies in G. Brahm and M. Driscoll (1994), *Prosthetic Territories*, Boulder, Colorado University of Colorado Press.

9 That scholar was Christopher Wilk, now Keeper of Furniture, Victoria and Albert Museum, London. I am grateful to him for many discussions about the Eameses.

10 Interview (1991), Alison and Peter Smithson with Pat Kirkham.

11 Neuhart, J., M. Neuhart and R. Eames (1989), *Eames Design. The Work of the Office of Charles and Ray Eames*, London, Thames and Hudson.

12 Helland, J. (1994), The Critics and the Arts and Crafts: The Instance of Margaret Macdonald and Charles Rennie Mackintosh, *Art History*, 17:2, 205–23. See also Burkhauser, J. (1990), *'Glasgow Girls'. Women in Art and Design 1880–1920*, Edinburgh, Canongate.

13 See Helland (1994).

14 Kirkham, P. (1994), Looking For The Simple Idea, Sight and Sound, 4:2, 16–20.

Bibliography

Battersby, C. (1989), *Gender and Genius. Towards a Feminist Aesthetics*, London, The Woman's Press.

Broude, N. (1982), Miriam Schapiro and 'Femmage': Reflections on the conflict between Decoration and Abstraction in Twentieth-Century Art, in N. Broude and M. D. Garrard (eds), *Feminism and Art History. Questioning The Litany*, New York, Harper & Row, 315–29.

Chadwick, W. and I. de Courtivron (eds) (1993), *Significant Others. Creativity and Intimate Partnership*, London, Thames & Hudson.

Eames Celebration (1966), *Architectural Design*, special issue.

Grier, K. C. (1992), The Decline of the Memory Palace: The Parlor after 1890, in J. Foy and T. J. Schlereth (eds), *American Home Life, 1880–1930*, Knoxville, The University of Tennessee Press.

Kirkham, P. (1995), *Charles and Ray Eames: Designers of the Century*, Cambridge, Mass., MIT Press.

Mainardi, P. (1973), Quilts: The Great American Art, in (1982), in N. Broude and M. D. Garrard, *Feminism and Art History. Questioning The Litany*, New York, Harper & Row, 331–46.

Meyer, M. and M. Schapiro (1978), Waste Not/Want Not: Femmage, *Heresies: A Feminist Publication on Art and Politics*, 4, 66–9.

Nochlin, L. (1971), Why Have There Been No Great Women Artists?, *Art News*, 69:9, 22–39, 67–71.

Parker, R. and G. Pollock (1981), *Old Mistresses: Women, Art and Ideology*, London, Pandora.

Rowbotham, S. (1973), *Hidden From History*, London, Pluto Press.

Walker, L. (1984), *Women Architects. Their Work* (RIBA catalogue), London, Sorella Press.

Index

Note: 'n.__' after a page reference indicates the number of a note on that page.

accessibility, *Oranges are not the Only Fruit*, 173
access to cultural forms, 6
accountability of researcher, 202
additive feminism, 35–6
admiration of films, 73
aestheticism in *Oranges are not the Only Fruit*, 180, 181, 188
All in the Family, 46
Althusser, Louis, 10, 94n.1, 194–5
American cinema, 102
anger, Roseanne, 53
Arliss, Leslie, 79n.14
Arnold, Eve, 180
Arnold, Roseanne, *see* Roseanne
Arnold, Tom, 57, 59n.2
Asian women, exclusion from research, 161
aspirations, and television viewing, 143
audience research
  aesthetic issues, 180
  children's television viewing habits, 138, 140
  films, 97, 98–116
  Oranges are not the Only Fruit, 174, 175, 185
  and self-reflexivity, 141
audience response, 103
authorial privilege, 24n.5

author intentionality, 94n.3, 173
author–text–reader relationship, 82, 83, 84

babysitter, television as, 151
Bakhtin, Mikhail, 10, 51–2, 90, 94n.4, 121
  authoritative word, 130
Barker, M., 201
Barr, Roseanne, *see* Roseanne
Barthes, Roland, 76, 94n.1
Bass, Elaine, 224
Bass, Saul, 224
Battersby, Christine, 222
Belsey, Catherine, 85, 88, 94n.7
Benjamin, Walter, 10
Black women
  enunciation, politics of, 8
  exclusion from research, reasons for, 161
  and Hollywood stars, 108
  and responses to *Oranges are not the Only Fruit*, 183
  and the social, 34
  social service agencies, resentment incurred by, 141
Blanchot, M., 122
Bordo, Susan, 165
Bourdieu, P., 10, 141–2, 143
  aesthetic, popular and bourgeois, 165

British cinema, 102
broadcasting, as domestic medium, 38
Brontë, Charlotte, 86
Brunsdon, Charlotte, 149, 158, 181
Burton, Sheila, 198
Butler, Judith, 41

carnivalesque, Bakhtin's theories of, 51, 52
childhood, experiences of, 177–8
Chodorow, Nancy, 165
cinema, *see* films
Cixous, Hélène, 121, 122
Clare, John, 84, 85, 86, 91
class
  ascertaining women's, 107, 141–2
  complexity, 183
  deconstruction of term, 13
  neglect in psychoanalytically informed feminist cultural studies, 37
  and responses to *Oranges are not the Only Fruit*, 182
  video cassette recorder, use of, 165
closure, mechanisms in *Oranges are not the Only Fruit*, 171–3
Code, Lorraine, 76
comedy
  conventions, 52
  feminist scholars' interest in, 59 n.6
  neglect in feminist media theory, 48
  romantic films, 54–5
  Roseanne, 50, 53, 54
common knowledge, 62–4, 73, 77
commonplace, 129–30
consciousness raising, research for, 198
constructivism, 44 n.4
controversies in discussion of cultural products, 63, 73

Cosby Show, The, 46
Coward, Rosalind, 76
criminology, dominant concerns, 129
critics
  and audiences, 97
  dominant discourse, satisfaction of requirements of, 78 n.3
  positioning, 81–93
  power, 127–8
'cultural', use of, 4
cultural reproduction, 35, 39
Cultural Studies, differences in degree programmes, 154

Dam Busters, The, 71
Davis, Angela, 195
Davis, Bette, 110
Davis, Natalie Zemon, 51, 52
Day, Doris, 105
Dean, James, 79 n.13
deconstruction
  of feminist concepts, 13
  within post-structuralism, 127
de Coutivron, I., 123
definition of character, 72
democratising narrative, 160–4
denigration of films, 73
Derrida, Jacques, 10, 121, 122
dialogics, Bahtkin's theories of, 10, 94 n.4
diasporic theory, 8
disc jockeys, 91
discourse analysis, 42, 121, 122
discourses, wider, 5
(dis)simulation, 39
Doctor at Sea, 71
domesticity, work of, 39
domestic sphere
  devaluation of, 64
  re-placement of women in, 64
Douglas, Mary, 53
Durbin, Deanne, 110
Dyer, Richard, 75, 106

Eagleton, Terry, 85, 88, 94 n.7

Eames, Charles, 207, 210–12, 214, 216–24
Eames, Ray, 207, 208, 210–24
Eames House, 219
East of Eden, 71, 79n.13
Ellis, John, 74
empirical description versus psychoanalysis, 113
empiricist feminists, 16
empowerment in feminist research, 198
Empson, William, 93n.1
enunciation, politics of, 8
epistemology, 2
  experience, 157
  feminist, 24n.1
    empirical, 164
    meaning of, 14
    ontology, links with, 14–15, 20
    standpoint, 165
essentialism, 87
  cultural, 41–2, 43
  social, 43
ethical issues, feminist ethnography, 197–9
ethnography, 190–2
  and audiences, 112–13, 115
  ethics, 197–9
  experience, representing, 199–203
  self-reflexive, 137, 141
  theoretical constructions and motivations, 192–7
evaluations, 19–20
experience
  narrative, 156–9
  of oppression, 16, 195
  positioning, 15–18
  and representational construct of 'woman', 40
  representing, 199–203
  and theory, relationship between, 33–4

fan mail, 105
fatness, female, 53

female-embodied social subject, position of, 7
feminine, construction of, 66
femininity
  definitions of, 99
  discourse of, 5
  as (dis)simulation, 39–40
  ethnography, 190, 197
  experience of, 17
  representations of in conventional narrative forms, 54
feminist concepts, deconstruction, 12–13
feminist empirical epistemology, 164
feminist epistemology, 24n.1
  meaning of, 14
  ontology, links with, 14–15, 20
feminist standpoint epistemology, 165
feminist research, 11–12, 23–4
  and experience, 15
femmage, 212
Ferguson, Kathy, 87–8
fiction, romantic, 38, 181
films
  audiences, 97, 98–116
  feminist theory, 47–8
  historical evidence, 'nature' of, 65–75
  psychoanalytic perspective, 47, 112, 115
  significance to women in 1940s, 102
  targeting of women for specific genres of, 38, 39
Finch, Janet, 163
Fish, Stanley, 94n.6
Fleet, Jo Van, 79n.13
formalist criticism, 93n.1
Foucault, Michel, 10, 77, 94n.1
fragmentation of contemporary culture, 52
Frankfurt School, 51–2
Freud, Sigmund, 10, 53, 75

Frye, Northrop, 50, 52
functioning decoration, Charles
    and Ray Eames, 212–13,
    223–4

gendered reading, 184
gender inversion
    Davis's observations, 51
    romantic comedy, 54, 55
gender theorists, 165–6
Gledhill, Christine, 76
González, Jennifer, 213
Goodrich, P., 121
Gorris, Marleen, 59 n.3
Gramsci, A., 10, 194
Greenham Common women,
    119, 120–1, 122–7, 131–3
Greer, Germaine, 85, 94 n.7
grotesque
    Bakhtin's observations, 51,
    53
    Roseanne, 51, 53
    Russo's observations, 50
grounded theory, 193
    political importance of, 154
guilt in TV viewing, 144, 145,
    150
gynocentric textual analysis,
    25 n.17

Hall, Stuart, 91
Handel, Leo, 106
Haraway, Donna, 153
Harding, Sandra, 164–5, 201
Hartmann, Heidi, 194
Hedren, Tipi, 79 n.14
hegemony and ideology, 74, 75,
    77, 78 n.1
Heidegger, M., 128
Heidensohn, F., 131
Helland, Janice, 224
Henley, Nancy, 53
Hepburn, Katharine, 75
Hertmann, Anne, 95 n.16
heterosexuality
    discourse of, 5
    universalisation of, 41

high production values, *Oranges
    are not the Only Fruit*,
    172–3, 180
Hill Collins, Patricia, 154
Hinds, Hilary, 170
historical evidence, 62–3, 64
    and memory, 108–9
Hitchcock, Alfred, 79 n.14
homelessness, and feminist
    ethnography, 198
humanism, liberal, 82, 94 n.3

identity
    concept of, 13
    and identification, effect of
    representation, 40
    and performance, 41
    politics of, 16
    of Roseanne, 49
ideology
    Althusser's observations,
    194–5
    and hegemony, 74, 75, 77,
    78 n.1
    Oranges are not the Only Fruit,
    173–4
'images of women', 36–7
    significance during 1950s
    consumer boom, 99
imitation process amongst
    audience, 39
independently produced feminist
    film and video, 55
individualistion thesis and
    cultural essentialism, 42
inequality, theories of, 9
institutional positions of
    researchers, 7–8, 158
intellectual biography, 194
intentionality, author, 94 n.3,
    173
interpretation
    and experience, 16, 17
    of spectators' recollections of
    stars, 111–12
Irigiray, L., 10, 121, 122, 131
irony, 88

Joyce, James, 83–4

Kaplan, Cora, 85, 94 n.7
Kazan, Elia, 79 n.13
Kelly, Liz, 198
Kidron, Beeban, 180
Kristeva, Julia, 121, 122
Kuhn, Annette, 194

Lacan, Jacques, 94 n.1
language
  Bakhtin's theories of, 51
law, 121
legal theory, 121
Leonard, Diane, 11
lesbianism, *Oranges are not the Only Fruit*, 169, 170, 188
  'ordinary' viewer, 176
  textual analysis, 81–97, 171, 172, 173
letters
  to magazines
    authenticity, 103
    about stars, 102–5
  to stars, 105
Levi-Strauss, C., 76
liberal humanism, 82, 94 n.3
liminality, 52
locations for production of research(er), 6–12
Lockwood, Margaret, 79 n.14
Lury, C., 201
Lyotard, Jean-François, 121

Mac an Ghaill, M., 204 n.8
Macdonald, Margaret, 218, 220
Mackerey, Pierre, 94 n.5, 95 n.13
Mackintosh, Charles Rennie, 218, 220
magazines, women's, 38
Mainardi, Patricia, 208
marginalisation, Charles and Ray Eames, 211, 218, 223
Marks, E., 123
Marnie, 79, 14
Marx, Karl, 78 n.1
masquerade, 197

Mattelart, Michele, 75
McRobbie, Angela, 11, 160, 201
melodrama, 48
memory
  of childhood, 177–8
  of locations, 9
  in oral history, 66
  of *Oranges are not the Only Fruit*, 179–80
  of stars, 106–7, 108–14
methodology
  definition, 2
  ethnography, 193
  and method, relation between, 154
Meyer, Melissa, 212
Millett, Kate, 85, 94 n.7
Millman, Marcia, 53
Milton, John, 88
Miss Piggy, 52
Mitchell, Juliet, 11
modernism, Charles and Ray Eames, 212–13
modernist ethnography, 192–3
Moi, Toril, 76
Monroe, Marilyn, 110
Montgomery, Martin, 91
morality in television use, 5
Morrison, Toni, 93
motherhood, experience of, 17
motivations for research, 11–12, 15
Mulvey, Laura, 50–1
myths, 76

narratives
  democratising, 160–4
  experiential, 156–9
  feminist, 164–6
  liberating potential of, 50
  memory, women's, 180
  Oranges are not the Only Fruit, 171–2
  popular films, 72
  of research, 155
  Roseanne, 54–6
nationalism, discourse of, 5

naturalist ethnography, 192
Neuhart, John, 216, 218
Neuhart, Marilyn, 216, 218
New Criticism, 93 n.1
Nochlin, Linda, 208

objectification of women, 38
object relations theories, 165
ontogenic question, 44 n.4
ontology
  and experience, 156–7
  links with feminist
    epistemology, 14–15, 20
  meaning of, 25 n.13
oppression
  experience of, 16, 195
  in popular culture, Frankfurt
    School, 52
  women's struggle against,
    Roseanne, 52
  Oranges are not the Only Fruit,
    169–70
  'ordinary' viewer, 170,
    174–85, 186–7
  textual analysis, 171–4,
    187–8
Orbach, Susie, 53
'ordinary', use of, 4
'ordinary' viewer, *Oranges are
  not the Only Fruit*, 170,
  174–85, 186–7
'ordinary' woman, 158
O'Rourke, Rebecca, 170

Parker, Patricia, 53
Parker, Rozsila, 208
passivity in television viewing,
  146
Pecheux, M., 121
performance and personal
  identity, 41
phylogenic question, 44 n.4
Pine Gap, 120
plausibility structures, 191
pleasure, as mechanism of
  closure, 171
polemic, 88

political activity, deconstruction
  of, 75
Pollock, Griselda, 36–7, 208
polyphony, 84, 91, 94 n.4
popular culture, discourse of, 5
popular films, defining 65, 66,
  67, 68–70
pornography and representation,
  82
positionality, politics of, 18
positionings, 6–7
post-feminism, 59 n.7
post-modernism, 121, 122, 196,
  212
  ethnography, 193
post-structuralism, 93–4 n.1,
  121, 122
  deconstruction within, 127
Pre-Raphaelite painting, 86, 87,
  89
presentation
  of character, 72
  of researcher, 162–3
press reports, Greenham
  Common women, 122–4,
  126–7, 129–31, 132–3
Probyn, Elspeth, 156–7
professors, numbers of women,
  7
psyche, centrality in research
  and communication, 9
psychoanalysis, 10–11
  the cultural, explicit gendering
    of, 37–8
  film and TV theory, 47–8, 140
  female spectatorship, 75–6,
    99, 112–13, 114–15
  Roseanne, 53
  masquerade, 197
publications, productivity
  measured through, 7

quality drama, *Oranges are not
  the Only Fruit*, 172–3
Question of Silence, A, 55,
  59 n.3

race
  deconstruction of term, 13
  neglect in psychoanalytically
    informed feminist cultural
    studies, 37
  neglect in research, 36, 161
  and responses to *Oranges are
    not the Only Fruit*, 182, 183
  and self-selection in
    qualitative research, 141
  see also Asian women; Black
    women
radio D-Js, 91
Radway, Janice, 76
Ransome, John Crowe, 93n.1
Reach for the Sky, 71
reader-jealousy, 91
reader-power, 82–3
reader-response theory, 93n.1
realism
  challenges to, 193
  and *Oranges are not the Only
    Fruit*, 172, 188
realist ethnography, 192
Rebel Without a Cause, 71
'Reclaim the Night' marches,
    25n.11
recognition, empathy based on,
    178
redemptive reading, 181
Regan, Linda, 198
regional effects on responses to
    *Oranges are not the Only
    Fruit*, 182
religion, and responses to
    *Oranges are not the Only
    Fruit*, 182, 184
representation
  cultural, 34–5, 43
  of experience, 199–203
  of Greenham women in press,
    124, 125
  letters to magazines, 104
  masculine, blind spots of, 131
  memories of stars, 113
  and pornography, 82
  and subject, relationship

between, 40
researchers
  accountability, 202
  institutional positions of, 7–8
  and power, 155, 161, 163, 200
  presentation of, 162–3
resolution, character, 72
rhetoric, 87, 88
Richards, I.A., 93n.1
Richardson, Samuel, 88
Ricoeur, Paul, 122
Riviere, Joan, 197
Roberts, Helen, 11, 160
romantic comedy, 54–5
romantic fiction, 38, 181
Roseanne, 46–7, 48, 50, 51,
    52–3
  audience, 56
  defining, 49
  interview, 56–8
  narrative, 54
  Star Spangled Banner
    controversy, 59–60n.12
Roseanne, 46
Rosie the Riveter, 64
Rossetti, Dante Gabriel, 86, 89
Rowbotham, Sheila, 11, 208
Russo, Mary, 50

Samuel, Raphael, 209
Saussure, Ferdinand de, 93n.1
scale of research, 161, 175
Schapiro, Miriam, 212
Schrader, Paul, 214, 216
Scott, Ridley, 83
Scraton, P., 119
Searchers, The, 71
Sedgwick, Eve, 43, 44n.4
self-selection in qualitative
    studies, 141
self-worth, 5, 6
semiotics, 51
Seneca Falls, 120
Sesame Street, 151
sexuality, social organisation
    and cultural reproduction,
    39

shared knowledges, 161–2
signification, Bakhtin's theory of, 51
situated knowledge, 87, 95 n.10, 153
Smithson, Alison, 217, 218, 220
Smithson, Peter, 217, 218, 220
snowballing, 162
soap operas, and literature on women viewers, 181
social
  and cultural, relationship between, 40, 43
  use of, 4, 38
  and 'women' category, 34, 43
social constructionist ethnography, 193
social ensemble, 39
sociologism, 159, 167 n.2
Spivak, Gaytri Chakravorty, 42
Stacey, Judith, 197
Staiger, Janet, 100–1, 103, 104
standpoint epistemologies, 34, 195
  meaning of, 25 n.18
  and oppression, 16
Stanley, Liz, 11, 153–4, 160, 194
Stanwyck, Barbara, 110
stardom, discourse of, 5
stars
  and female spectators
    fan mail, 105
    letters to magazines, 102–5
    memories of, 106–7, 108–14
  ideological contradictions, 49
  in popular films, 69, 74–5
Star Trek, 144, 145, 146–7, 148, 150
Star Trek: The Next Generation, 150, 151
structuralist criticism, 93 n.1
Sun, The, 123–4
surrealism, Oranges are not the Only Fruit, 172, 180–1
Sussman, Deborah, 214

symptomatic reading, 94 n.5, 95 n.13

targeting of women as market for cultural production, 38–9
Taylor, Helen, 106
telephone interviews, 213
television
  children's viewing patterns, 137–41
  feminist theory, 47
  psychoanalytic perspective, 47
texts as object of theoretical conceptualisations, 4–5
textual analysis, Oranges are not the Only Fruit, 171–4, 187–8
Thelma and Louise, 83
time resources, 20
Tonight, 147
transparency metaphor as description of experience, 16
Turner, Victor, 52

unconscious, 10
  and female spectatorship, 99, 112–13, 114–15
unruly woman, figure of, 54
use-value, 62–3, 76

validation of women's experiences, 16
Van Fleet, Jo, 79 n.13
Venturi, Robert, 212
video cassette recorder (VCR), women's use of, 153, 161, 164
visual culture, 37
Voloshinov, V.N., 94 n.4
vulgarity, discourse of, 5

Walker, Alice, 91–2
Walker, Lynne, 218–20
Wicked Lady, The, 79 n.14
Wilder, Billy, 214, 215
Wilk, Christopher, 225 n.9

Williams, Raymond, 10
  hegemony, 75, 78 n.1
  materialism, 157
Willis, Paul, 179, 202
Winterson, Jeanette, 169, 171,
  176
Wise, Sue, 11, 153–4, 160
Wolf, Christa, 95 n.16
Wolpe, Ann-Marie, 194
'woman' term
  and the cultural, 35, 43
  deconstruction of, 13
  and the social, 34, 43
  universalisation of, 38
women's magazines, 38
Women's Studies courses, 11
Woolf, Virginia, 95 n.16
working-class women
  gap in knowledge about, 195
  representation of, 200–1
Wright, Will, 76